Pandora's Daughters

Pandora's Daughters

Kalyani Shankar

BLOOMSBURY
LONDON • NEW DELHI • NEW YORK • SYDNEY

Copyright © 2013 *Kalyani Shankar*

All rights reserved. No part of this publication may be reproduced or transmitted in any form or by any means, electronic or mechanical, including photocopying, recording, or any information storage or retrieval system, without prior permission in writing from the publishers.

No responsibility for loss caused to any individual or organization acting on or refraining from action as a result of the material in this publication can be accepted by Bloomsbury India or the authors/editor.

BLOOMSBURY PUBLISHING INDIA PVT. LTD.
www.bloomsbury.com

ISBN: 978-93-82951-04-9
10 9 8 7 6 5 4 3 2 1

Published by Bloomsbury Publishing India Pvt Ltd
Vishrut Building, DDA Complex, Building No. 3,
Pocket C-6 & 7, Vasant Kunj
New Delhi 110 070

Typeset by Eleven Arts
Keshav Puram, Delhi 110035

Printed and bound by Replika Press Pvt Ltd, India

The content of this book is the sole expression and opinion of its author, and not of the publisher. The publisher in no manner is liable for any opinion or views expressed by the author. While best efforts have been used in preparing this book, the publisher makes no representations or warranties of any kind and assumes no liabilities of any kind with respect to the accuracy or completeness of the content and specifically disclaims any implied warranties of merchant ability or fitness of use for a particular purpose.

The publisher believes that the content of this book does not violate any existing copyright/intellectual property of others in any manner whatsoever. however, in case any source has not been duly attributed, the Publisher may be notified in writing for necessary action.

For

Annika

Contents

Preface	ix
Introduction	1
Sonia Gandhi	28
Mayawati	88
Mamata Banerjee	124
Jayalalithaa	152
Sheila Dixit	184
Pratibha Patil	205
Sushma Swaraj	222
Mehbooba Mufti	240

Preface

PANDORA'S DAUGHTERS AIMS TO illuminate and interpret the strengths and weaknesses of eight prominent, contemporary women leaders of India. The book is not a biography but a political profile of Sonia Gandhi, Mayawati, Mamata Banerjee, Jayalalithaa, Sheila Dikshit, Pratibha Patil, Sushma Swaraj and Mehbooba Mufti. They have all set a record in their own way.

The Italian-born Sonia Gandhi is the chairperson of the UPA and the president of the Congress party. She has created many records by uniting and leading the party, restoring dynastic politics, becoming the first woman Leader of the Opposition, bringing the UPA to power twice and declining to become the prime minister not once but thrice. She has also experimented with a dual power centre where she has retained all powers without accountability while making her nominee the prime minister, who was accountable but with no power.

Mayawati symbolizes rising Dalit strength as she has been the chief minister of Uttar Pradesh four times—a breathtaking feat for a woman from a poor, oppressed Scheduled Caste family. She has not only co-founded the Bahujan Samaj Party (BSP) but also expanded it and has become a force to reckon with.

Mamata Banerjee has created history by winning against the communists who were in power for 34 years to become the first woman chief minister of West Bengal. Hailing from a middle class family, she has reached the top by sheer hard work and determination.

Film star-turned politician Jayalalithaa was appointed the chief minister of Tamil Nadu for the third time and believes in her own personality cult. After losing power in 1996 due to several corruption charges many thought she would fade away, but she fought and came back to power in 1998, joined the NDA government and also contributed to its collapse in 1999. She came back to power in 2001 and again in 2011 with a massive majority.

Sheila Dikshit, a Congress chief minister, has achieved a hat trick by winning Delhi three times in a row and is poised to win it for the fourth time. She has built up an image of the "granny next door".

President Pratibha Patil, who retired in 2012, became the symbol of women power as the first woman president of India. She has proved that a low-profile leader can reach the top of the ladder with the patronage of the Gandhi family.

Sushma Swaraj is the Leader of the Opposition in the Lok Sabha and a shadow prime minister-in-waiting. She is one of the few women who have reached the top in a male-dominated BJP and the only woman member of its Parliamentary Board.

Mehbooba Mufti is the Leader of the Opposition in Jammu and Kashmir. She has become a leader in her own right in the last decade, although she was initially promoted by her father, former chief minister of Jammu and Kashmir Mufti Mohammad Sayeed.

There are some commonalities and dissimilarities among these women leaders. They fall under three categories. The first ascended to power because of their family background (Sonia Gandhi, Sheila Dikshit, Mehbooba Mufti), the second through the patronage of a mentor (Mayawati and Jayalalithaa) and the third on their own (Mamata Banerjee). Politics infuses every moment of these leaders' lives.

But one commonality is that they are all undisputed leaders of their parties and rule with an iron hand. Secondly, they have all risen to power in the past two decades, although India has had some prominent women leaders in the past like Indira Gandhi, the first woman prime minister; Sucheta Kripalani, the first woman chief minister of UP; and Nandini Satpathy, the first woman chief minister of Orissa.

These are not the only women leaders in India; there are many more but I have chosen only those who are or have been presidents, prominent leaders of their parties or chief ministers.

The strength of this book is that I have personally known all these leaders and interacted with them over the years and had access to their friends and detractors. Most of the analysis is based on primary sources and my own understanding of the ups and downs in their political careers, which I have followed carefully as a journalist. Those interviewed for this book have been quite forthcoming and frank in their assessment of these leaders whom they know well.

This book would not have been possible without the support of the Woodrow Wilson International Center for Scholars, Washington, D.C., which gave me a fellowship to work on my project. The director of the Asia Program Robert Hathaway and Ambassador Dennis Kux were extremely helpful while I was at the center. My sincere thanks also goes to Cyana Shilton, who researched for me, and Prof Ralph Buultjens of the New York University, who encouraged me throughout. Premila and her husband John Mussells made my stay in Washington very pleasant by their constant care and I am grateful for that. I would like to thank veteran journalist Inder Malhotra for his valuable suggestions. My son Dilip, my daughter-in-law Rebecca and particularly my daughter Shylashri have been fully supportive of the project and helped me in every possible way. A word of thanks is also due to my copy editor Mona Joshi.

We are thankful to Outlook India for providing images for the cover of the book.

Above all, I am grateful to my publisher Mr. Rajiv Beri, CEO of the Bloomsbury India, and his team who have been kind enough to publish this book and give me all the support.

Introduction

THE UNITED NATIONS GENERAL Assembly adopted the Convention on the Political Rights of Women in 1952, seven years after it was founded. This landmark agreement codified women's rights to vote and hold political office without discrimination on the basis of gender. In 1979, the General Assembly adopted the Convention on the Elimination of All Forms of Discrimination against Women (CEDAW), which requires ratifying states to include measures promoting gender equality in their national laws.[1] Despite these measures of progress, global politics remains remarkably stratified on the basis of gender.

Even decades later, only 7% of the serving heads of government in the world are female and only 6% of elected heads of state are women.[2] The 2008 U.S. Presidential Election proved that Americans are still hesitant to choose a woman as their head of state when Hillary Clinton lost the presidency at the nomination stage itself. Women make up less than 20% of upper and lower legislative bodies worldwide. Regional differences are notable, to be sure; on average, in Arab states women constitute 10.6% of the legislative bodies, while the number stands at 42% in Nordic countries.[3] In Rwanda, women make up 53% of the bicameral parliament—the most in the world.[4] Arguably, progress has been made. The incoming Socialist government in France under Francois Hollande has fulfilled its campaign pledge of equal Cabinet participation by women, something former President Nicolas Sarkozy never accomplished.[5] But in other areas, stagnation and regression are the pattern. In the 2010 U.S. elections, the number of women in Congress dropped for the first time since 1979 and men regained leadership positions in that body.[6] Globally, women are increasing their legislative participation by 0.5% per year, which means gender equity will not be achieved until 2068.[7]

A GLOBAL OVERVIEW OF WOMEN IN POLITICS

The explanations for these phenomena are, of course, country dependent, though some conclusions can be drawn from a global overview. Many countries have policies that limit the participation of women in any public arena, whether codified laws or cultural practices. Several governments mirror the patriarchal societies from which they spring—though this generalisation should not be understood strictly on a regional basis, given the struggles of Western countries to normalise female political participation. A feminist interpretation of the seminal Western philosopher Immanuel Kant argues that he portrays women as "being simply incapable of the kind of mental activity required of reasoning subjects, thus justifying their exclusion from self-governance and participation in the public sphere."[8] The strict delineation between public and private activity in many societies means that women rarely accede to public office. When they do, as pioneers for gender equality they are often subjected to intense double standards. For example, in the 2008 U.S. Presidential Election, Hillary Clinton was criticised both for not being feminine enough—news anchor Katie Couric asked her to verify that her nickname was "Miss Frigidaire"[9]—and for being too feminine, after she cried during a campaign speech.[10] But the cause of gender bias in politics lies not just with men and the institutions they dominate. As Claire Rasmussen wrote, "women themselves often accept the social construction of their roles and thus are unwilling or unable to move away from these constraints because of the forces of socialisation, peer and family pressure, and a lack of role models,"[11] suggesting that the solution to the problem can be approached by both men and women.

Beyond the cultural exclusion of women from politics, there are also institutional barriers to their participation. Women are generally more successful in parliamentary political systems, where their ability to hold a leadership position is often based on their work or leverage within a political party, as opposed to their ability to win the popular vote. As of 2009, only 12 of the 52 female heads of state had been empowered initially by popular vote.[12] Prime ministers also share a more diffused version of executive power, as they work with their Cabinet and can be removed from office through a no-confidence vote. This version of power, if wielded by a female, is arguably less threatening than the concentration of power in a presidency. Incumbency is also an advantage for many politicians, depending on the country; while Indian incumbents tend to be voted out of power, 95.3% of incumbents in America win re-election, meaning that women will find it hard to break into politics.

The effects of electing or appointing women to power are difficult to measure, given the small sample size. But in one indicative study in 2001, economists Esther Duflo of the Massachusetts Institute of Technology (MIT) and Raghabendra Chattopadhyay of the Indian Institute of Management Calcutta (IIMC) found that women leaders elected to village councils in West Bengal were more likely to allocate funding for public goods, e.g., water, fuel, and roads, whereas their male peers were more likely to invest in education. Under women leadership, more women participated in the policy-making process.[13] This study suggests concrete policy and social implications of more equitable political participation.

WOMEN'S PARTICIPATION IN POLITICS

In many countries where women do not run for or win political office, activists and politicians often discuss how to encourage their participation and representation. Some suggest that increased female political participation can be achieved through a quota system in which some governmental seats are expressly reserved for women. This solution has had mixed success, but in Pakistan, women's representation increased dramatically after a quota law was passed in 2002. The Indian model has reservation for Scheduled Castes (SCs) and Scheduled Tribes (STs) but no quota for women. Indian women are agitating for a 33% reservation in Parliament and state legislatures, but the men are wary of it. The bill is in cold storage. Others propose increased education and employment opportunities for women, given that many do not have the background to make them compelling political candidates.

Another way of analysing female politicians is by analogy: attempting to replicate domestic or international women's ascension to power. In Asia and Latin America, many powerful women have come from political dynasties: Benazir Bhutto in Pakistan, Sheikh Hasina in Bangladesh, Argentina's Isabel Perón and Cristina Fernandez de Kirchner, and India's

Sonia Gandhi, for example. Typically, women come to power during periods of transition.[14]

If one looks at South Asia specifically, there are many examples of female political leaders. The late Benazir Bhutto is one of the most globally renowned. The daughter of Zulfikar Ali Bhutto—former prime minister of Pakistan and founder of the Pakistan People's Party (PPP)—she was educated at Harvard and Oxford universities, where she became the first Asian woman to lead the Oxford Union, a prestigious debating society. She became the chairwoman of the PPP in 1982 at the age of 29. Six years later, she was elected prime minister, the first and youngest woman to lead a Muslim country. She would serve two non-consecutive terms. Nicknamed the "Iron Lady", Bhutto withstood an attempted coup d'état in 1995 and cracked down on labour unions and domestic opponents while also deregulating and denationalising business. After charges of corruption were levelled against her government in 1996, she was forced to withdraw and went into self-imposed exile. She returned to Pakistan in 2007 under a supposed agreement with President Pervez Musharraf by which the corruption charges were withdrawn. She was the leading opposition candidate in the 2008 elections, but was tragically assassinated two weeks before the vote. Her widower, Asif Ali Zardari, is Pakistan's current president, and her son, Bilawal Bhutto Zardari, is the head of the PPP, forming a formidable political dynasty.

More recently in Pakistan, Hina Rabbani Khar was appointed Minister of Foreign Affairs in July 2011 after the resignation of Shah Mehmood Qureshi. Hina is the daughter of politician Ghulam Noor Rabbani Khar and the niece of Ghulam Mustafa Khar, a former governor of Punjab. She is a member of one of the richest landed elite families in Pakistan. Khar was elected to Parliament in 2002 and 2008, became Minister of State for Foreign Affairs in 2004 and Minister of State for Finance and Economic Affairs in 2008. She broke the glass ceiling by getting these two hefty portfolios. Khar first ran for Parliament from her district in the Punjab when a new campaign law requiring candidates to possess a bachelor's degree disqualified her father from contesting the election. During the election, Khar did not attend rallies or post pictures of herself in her district; her father made the speeches and appearances on her behalf.

Elsewhere in South Asia, other examples include Sri Lanka's Sirimavo Bandaranaike, the first female head of state in the world. Bandaranaike was the wife of assassinated Prime Minister Solomon Bandaranaike; their daughter Chandrika rose to become president of the country while their son Anura was a former Cabinet member. Sirimavo served three terms as prime minister, during which time she nationalised businesses and notably used emotion to garner support—she often started crying while discussing policies. She also decreed that all business be conducted in Sinhala, the language of the majority Sinhalese people—a policy the Tamil minority argued was discriminatory. After being charged with delaying elections from 1975 to 1977, Bandaranaike was expelled from office and banned from seeking office for a decade. She maintained control of her party in the meantime, though by the time she returned to power the Constitution had limited the scope of the prime minister's position and she died only a few months after regaining office.

India in itself is a case study of women rising to political power. The participation of women in politics is not a new concept in the country. Though recent international news has fluctuated between heralding India as the world's largest democracy, an up-and-comer on the global market and the good guy to Pakistan's villain, recent articles have detailed horrifying attacks on women in various Indian states, the prevalence of foeticide in some parts of the country and dowry deaths. The gang rape of a 23-year-old college student on December 16, 2012, in Delhi has shocked the country to such an extent that there is demand for change of laws to punish the guilty. The whole country has woken up to the raw deal given to women.

This apparent contradiction is also present in women's general participation in Indian politics. Politics was regarded as a public activity dominated by men, while women were relegated to positions of home keepers. But this changed in the 20th century with more women coming out to participate in the country's freedom struggle and making a foray into politics, thus changing the perspective of women's role in politics. Access to higher education also expanded their scope and interest in the political scene. Women have collectively struggled against the direct and indirect barriers to their development in terms of social, political and economic participation.

CONSTITUTIONAL AMENDMENT TO THE PANCHAYATI RAJ ACT

The first step towards political empowerment of women was initiated with the 73rd Constitutional Amendment Act in 1992. As per this act, Indian women got an equal share in political administration. They were not only part of local and state administration, but came forward to participate in national politics as well. Since then, they have also achieved a significant role in the Parliament. Already more than a million women are functioning as elected members of Panchayati Raj institutions and municipal bodies, and the number is only growing.

WOMEN'S REPRESENTATION IN LEGISLATURES

India is in the lowest quartile as far as the number of women in Parliament is concerned. According to comparative data by an international organisation—the Inter-Parliamentary Union—India ranks 99 in the world for women's representation in Parliament. It lags behind other Asian countries such as Pakistan, China and Bangladesh. Even African countries such as Rwanda and Mozambique have more representation with 56.7% and 34.8% respectively.

Representation of women in the Lok Sabha, the Lower House of Parliament, has basically remained stagnant. The First Lok Sabha in 1952 had just 23 women members across 474 seats, making up 4.9% of the total. In the next elections in 1957 the number rose to 5%. In the Third Lok Sabha, of the 500 seats, only 37 were held by women, accounting for 7.4%. The Fourth Lok Sabha had women in only 31 out of 505 seats, constituting a mere 6.3%. In the Fifth Lok Sabha, it further declined to a negligible 5%. The Sixth Lok Sabha saw 3.3%—the lowest ever. The next Lok Sabha saw an increase up to 5.8%. It reached a high of 8.1% in 1984, then increased to 9.0% in 1999 and declined to 8.2% in 2004. The year 2009 witnessed an increase to 10.8%. This is despite the fact that in their manifestoes, most political parties have declared their support for a one third reservation for women in legislatures.

PATH TO POWER

Though largely a patriarchal society, women in India have been playing some kind of a leading role for forty years since Indira Gandhi became the prime minister in 1966. Naturally, as heirs to the Nehru-Gandhi dynasty, Indira Gandhi and now her daughter-in-law Sonia Gandhi had somewhat of a head start. There are other political families who follow this dynastic tradition. Former Defence Minister Babu Jagjivan Ram's daughter, Meira Kumar, is currently the Speaker of the Lok Sabha. Former External Affairs Minister Dinesh Singh's daughter, Ratna Singh, is a Member of Parliament (MP) and heads the Committee on Empowerment of Women. Former Chief Minister of Andhra Pradesh N.T. Rama Rao's daughter, Purandeswari, is a minister in the Manmohan Singh government. Delhi Chief Minister Sheila Dikshit is the daughter-in-law of the veteran Congress leader, the late Uma Shankar Dikshit. There are several others who are carrying on the dynasty by becoming Members of Parliament or legislators.

Indira Gandhi, who was prime minister from 1966 to 1977, and 1980 to 1984, was the daughter of India's first Prime Minister Jawaharlal Nehru. After her father's death, Lal Bahadur Shastri became the prime minister for a brief period and Indira became a minister in his Cabinet. After Shastri's untimely death, Gandhi was elected as prime minister in 1966. Fighting her way up against the old guard of the Congress party, she implemented socialist policies, including nationalising businesses and investing in rural agricultural programmes. She ushered in the Green Revolution, much needed in the agricultural sector, and the White Revolution in the dairy sector. She won the Bangladesh War and brought in populist schemes like the 20-Point Programme for the poor. She boldly went in for the Pokhran nuclear tests in 1974. Perhaps the most notorious period of Gandhi's regime was the Emergency from 1975 to 1977. Accused of using government funds to contest elections, Gandhi imposed Emergency to silence her political opponents. She packed the Supreme Court with judges of her choice, imposed press censorship and gagged the media. This period was marked by highly controversial policies. These included beautification during which slums were razed to the ground to make way for modernised construction; forced sterilisation that led to workers rushing to meet quotas, especially of vasectomies to prevent overpopulation; and the imprisonment of various labour leaders who participated in mass strikes. Gandhi then called for elections in 1977, and she lost. In 1978 the Congress split again and she led the Indira Congress, which became the real Congress. In 1980, the Congress party returned to power. She faced the Assam agitation, Punjab militancy and the Khalistan Movement, Mizo rebels and the Naga Movement bravely. Operation Blue Star against Sikh militants proved to be a major challenge; as a result she was assassinated by her own Sikh security guards on October 31, 1984. Her death led to mass violence against India's Sikh population.

Upon her death, Indira's son Rajiv assumed the prime minister's position at the age of 40. He was the youngest prime minister India ever had. He won a landslide victory, winning 405 out of the 543 seats in the Lok Sabha, on account of sympathy votes. He brought a modern outlook to Indian politics and thought ahead; envisioning India's role in the 21st Century, he introduced computers and information technology in the government. He also brought in several legislative measures to improve the condition of women, but he lost the goodwill of the people within five years when he got caught up in the Bofors gun purchase controversy and lost the 1989 elections. Two years later, Rajiv was tragically assassinated on May 21, 1991, while he was campaigning in Tamil Nadu. When the Congress wanted his Italian-born wife Sonia Gandhi to take over, she politely declined. The Congress party led by P.V. Narasimha Rao formed a minority government, which lasted a full five-year term. Sonia Gandhi, who kept a low profile for nearly seven years after Rajiv's death, agreed to lead the Congress party in 1998 to check the deteriorating political situation. In 1999, after Gandhi decided to run for the Lok Sabha, London's *The Independent* wrote, "Of all South and South-East Asia's dynastic widows and daughters—from Benazir Bhutto in Pakistan to Megawati Sukarnoputri in Indonesia, by way of Chandrika Kumaratunga in Sri Lanka and Aung San Suu Kyi of Myanmar—Sonia Gandhi now seems without rival as the most ill-qualified, by temperament and intelligence, to carry the flame."[15] Proving *The Independent* wrong, somewhat surprisingly, a decade later, Gandhi is recognised as a highly powerful and inscrutable politician, twice named one of the most powerful women in the world by *TIME* magazine. She also brought the Congress party to power in 2004 and 2009.

POLITICAL FIRSTS

Interestingly, women in politics do not confine themselves to women's issues only. The legislators feel they represent both men and women. Like men, they are also drawn into the world of power with all its ruthlessness, although they may adopt their own individualistic style. Several states had and continue to have women chief ministers, including Delhi, Rajasthan, Madhya Pradesh, Orissa, Tamil Nadu, Goa, West Bengal, Madhya Pradesh and Uttar Pradesh. In 1963, Sucheta Kripalani became the chief minister of Uttar Pradesh (UP), the first woman to hold that position in any Indian state. Nandini Satpathy of Orissa became a chief minister in 1971. Vasundhara Raje Scindia was elected as the first woman chief minister in Rajasthan, as was Uma Bharti in Madhya Pradesh. Jayalalithaa became the Tamil Nadu chief minister thrice and Mayawati four times in UP. The current political landscape is filled with powerful women in power and in the opposition who are fully integrated into national politics at both the centre and state level.

The Janata Party President Dr. Subramanian Swamy does not see anything strange that these women hold control over their parties. 'The question of being a woman when they are in power never comes up. It is not as if you are dealing with a woman leader and you have to deal with her differently. You find this in Indian-influenced cultures like Burma and Indonesia. In the Hindu tradition, the woman manages the house, does everything possible to keep the family together. Whether they are intellectually gifted does not matter because most politicians are not. But I do find that women have an instinct, which men do not have. They are pretty good judges of men.'*

MILLION WOMEN PANCHAYAT PRESIDENTS

Local governments in India are called Panchayats, and since 1993, a third of the seats are reserved for women by an amendment to the Constitution. There are almost a million women Panchayat presidents today exercising their political power and taking decisions as a result of reservation for women. This constitutional mechanism has been a significant driver of increased political involvement for women. In some cases women have been re-elected even after their seats were no longer reserved. (Reserved seats rotate every five years.) They determine and ensure adequate focus on issues such as water, health, education, food security and children's welfare as well as communication facilities. A study by the International Monetary Fund (IMF) showed that political development is an important determinant of access to justice for socially disadvantaged groups. The study noted that "having female political representation at the local government level induces strong positive and significant effects on reporting of crimes against women. It also induces greater responsiveness of law enforcement officials to crimes against women, as measured by the number of arrests as well as the quality of women's interaction with police. We find a similar result in the case of SCs: despite already enjoying mandated representation at higher levels of government, representation of SCs in local councils leads to increased reporting of crimes where the victims are specifically targeted because of their caste. Most of the effects are driven by the increase in broad-based representation of women in local government councils at the district and village level, rather than women in district leadership positions."[16]

WOMEN'S RESERVATION BILL

The bill for a 33% reservation in Parliament has been passed by the Rajya Sabha, the House of Elders, but is still awaiting its passage in the Lower House. Most political parties continue to claim commitment to women reservation but the Parliament is unlikely to pass it anytime soon. Men are apprehensive of losing their seats to women and are therefore hesitant to agree on reservation. Men oppose women entering into politics mainly because they fear a change in the power balance in the family, market place and community. In addition to cultural obstacles, women also face constraints of money, time, media access and muscle power. But a consciousness has come in women that it is just not enough to vote every five years and there is a need to be involved in policy decisions. At the national level, women have never exceeded 9-10% representation in the Lok Sabha. Nicole Richardt noted: "When they do run, women are elected at comparable and better rates than their male counterparts."[17] Women also tend to be nominated and elected more often in underdeveloped and rural states rather than urban, progressive ones.[18]

One important question has been raised on whether an increase in numerical strength of women in the political decision-making bodies automatically leads to a qualitative shift in power. Another question is whether women at the helm of affairs pay greater attention to the concerns of women than male leaders do. The answer to both questions is a resounding "NO". But one thing is certain: participation of women in politics and the decision-making process is an important tool for empowerment.

MAIN FACTORS FOR WOMEN LEADING PARTIES

In a 2004 study of women running for national office in India, there were five main factors common in their backgrounds. Some were part of a political dynasty, like Sonia Gandhi. Others had a spousal connection—they were married to a politician. Many had the advantage of higher education, as is the case with daughters of middle class or wealthy families. In contrast, there were women like Mamata Banerjee and Mayawati who came from humble backgrounds and have succeeded as firebrands and opposition agitators due to their passion and charisma. Finally, women with a degree of celebrityhood also ran for office; one is reminded of Jayalalithaa, a former Tamil Nadu actress. All the women tended to be younger and better educated than their male counterparts. In general, those with higher levels of education or dynastic predecessors were concentrated in the Congress and BJP, while regional parties seemed to accept grassroots activists with inspiring rhetoric and strong personas. At the local level, female candidates and politicians represented a much wider cross-section of Indian life, including representation of the poor, uneducated, minorities and/or women with no connections.

It is interesting that Indian women attained a clear leadership position mostly after they set up their own parties (Mamata Banerjee) or through the support of their husbands, families or dynastic rule (Sonia Gandhi, Vasundhara Raje Scindia, Mehbooba Mufti, Sheila Dikshit and Rabri Devi). There have also been leaders like Mayawati and Jayalalithaa who were able to succeed their powerful mentors.

A study of these women leaders is quite fascinating. They have some commonalities and some differences. Sonia Gandhi is the widow of former Prime Minister Rajiv Gandhi. Most of them—Mayawati, Mamata and Jayalalithaa—are single women. Sheila Dikshit is a widow and Mehbooba Mufti is a divorcee. They have ample charisma and the ability to hold the attention of the public. They are vote catchers and crowd pullers with great passion and drive; they are fighters. Men pay obeisance to them. There is also some dissimilarity. Some have chosen politics out of their own free will; Mamata is a case in point. Some were chosen by mentors (Mayawati and Jayalalithaa), while others like Sonia Gandhi entered politics due to circumstances. The Congress is the grand old party and Sonia is the unifying factor. In the case of Mayawati, Jayalalithaa and Mamata there is no party without them. Most of these charismatic leaders do not want to build a second line of leadership, as they believe in a personality cult and run their parties like dictators. All three are just confined to their states but are ambitious to acquire a national role, whereas Sonia Gandhi and Sushma Swaraj are national leaders.

After being propelled by their own selves, or mentors or dynasties, these leaders have managed to survive despite fluctuating fortunes. This is in contrast to some other women leaders who arrived on the political scene but could not continue. For instance, while he was facing court cases, Rashtriya Janata Dal President Lalu Prasad Yadav installed his wife Rabri Devi as Bihar chief minister, and she ruled the state for eight years by proxy. But today she is nowhere to be seen. Urmilaben Patel, wife of Gujarat Chief Minister Chiman Bhai Patel, succeeded him and remained chief minister for some time but after that she faded away. Similarly, Janaki Ramachandran was the chief minister of Tamil Nadu for a very brief period after MGR's death, but she quit politics after realising that she did not have the ability to survive. Andhra Pradesh Chief Minister N.T. Rama Rao projected his second wife Lakshmi Parvathi but she too faded away after his death, and today she has disappeared from the political scene altogether. Therefore the ability to sustain is also very important for women leaders.

THE ROAD TO THE TOP

Today there are three broad categories of women leaders in India. The first lot has a family connection and dynastic heritage. Sonia Gandhi is a classic example. She is powerful entirely because she is the widow of Rajiv Gandhi and the daughter in-in-law of the late Indira Gandhi. Delhi Chief Minister Sheila Dikshit is yet another example, as she has a powerful family connection owing to her being the daughter-in-law of an influential Congress family from Uttar Pradesh. The People's Democratic Party's chief Mehbooba Mufti also has her father Mufti Mohammad Sayeed to thank for her entry into politics. Mufti was former Union home minister and chief minister of Jammu and Kashmir.

The second group has a mentor. It is common knowledge that a mentor or a godfather makes it easier for women to advance in politics. Tamil Nadu's Chief Minister Jayalalithaa had a powerful mentor in M.G. Ramachandran, who was an icon and founder of the All India Anna Dravida Munnetra Kazhagam (AIADMK). MGR, as he was affectionately called, brought Jaya into politics and encouraged her, taught her the intricacies of government and made her a leader, although he never acknowledged her as his political heir. Like her, MGR was a film star and a legend in Tamil Nadu's political firmament.

The Bahujan Samaj Party (BSP) chief and former chief minister of Uttar Pradesh Mayawati is yet another example of how a mentor can help. Maya, a young girl from a lower middle class family, was discovered by the BSP founder Kanshiram, who not only promoted her in the party but also made her the first Dalit chief minister of UP. Maya also has a caste identity since she hails from a Scheduled Caste family, which she has utilised to the optimum by leading a caste-based party. She has been elected the chief minister of Uttar Pradesh four times. Mayawati is ambitious and thinks of herself as a prime minister-in-waiting.

Former President Pratibha Patil also enjoyed some kind of patronage, first under the ex-chief minister of Maharashtra, the late Y.B. Chavan, and then Indira Gandhi. Her connection to the Gandhi family enabled her to get positions like the deputy chairman of the Rajya Sabha, Leader of the Opposition in the Maharashtra Assembly, Minister of State, governor of Rajasthan and finally, the presidency.

Sushma Swaraj, Leader of the Opposition in the Lok Sabha, had a mentor of sorts in Jayaprakash Narayan and was later supported by BJP leader L.K. Advani. She progressed in a male-dominated BJP because she was there at the right time—when the party was looking for effective women. She rose up the political ladder due to her talents, articulation and ambition.

West Bengal's Chief Minister Mamata Banerjee falls in a distinct third category: one with no advantage of dynastic or family connections, mentor or caste. Mamata, who has been described as "that woman" by the communists, has taught them a lesson by removing them from power in 2011 after a 34-year uninterrupted rule. She is called a superwoman today and has proved that in a democracy anyone can reach the top through perseverance, courage, ambition and devotion to the pubic cause.

DISTINCTIVE POLITICS

Is there anything distinctive in these women's mode of politics? Take the case of Sonia Gandhi; she is an Italian-born Roman Catholic. In a caste-ridden Indian society, she does not belong to any caste, which is both her weakness as well as her strength.

Sonia is unique because she hails from the First World, and, as the American official Robin Raphel points out, has transformed herself into a Second World politician effortlessly. Being a European woman, it must have been difficult to adjust to the Indian ethos, besides changing her lifestyle, clothing, food habits and other aspects. As Sonia Gandhi admits, it was Indira Gandhi who guided her and taught her how to wear Indian clothes and savour the country's food with its pungent spices and sugary sweets; it is not just a matter of clothing but also a certain level of raw political acumen which she has imbibed. Her transformation is testimony to her remarkable ability to change. As Carnegie scholar Ashley Tellis observes, first of all, Sonia had the will to do it. She had taken a conscious decision to remain in India after Rajiv Gandhi's assassination. She had the discipline to adjust to a new life even as a young girl. Secondly, India and Italy have similar customs and traditions in many ways, which might have helped her to adopt Indian standards. For instance, both believe that family comes first and the son is preferred to the daughter. Even in other cultural areas there are similarities. After all, both Indian and Roman civilisations are the oldest in the world. Thirdly, she has consciously decided to bring up her children as Indians and there is no trace of anything European in them, although she speaks to them in Italian once in a while. Fourthly, when she came into politics she had to change her way of dressing to suit the Indian public's sensibilities. They would not have appreciated a modern Indian leader wearing skirts or jeans. Even Indira Gandhi used to wear cotton sarees and full sleeved blouses in public, and elegant silk sarees while hosting banquets for foreign dignitaries or when she went abroad on state visits. Sonia saw the value of this and decided to follow suit. Fifthly, once she started interacting with other leaders in the Northern belt, she too decided to pick up their way of talking and behaving. She improved her Hindi and even speaks extempore at times.

Sonia's approach to politics, her way of looking at issues and tackling them is also unique. She sometimes reacts spontaneously but by and large her responses are carefully scripted. She never makes a political statement in a huff only to relent later or offer explanations. Hers is a cool-headed and calculated approach. She is not in a hurry to change things in the party or in the government and treads cautiously. She is not a great orator like Vajpayee, neither does she make emotional speeches like Mamata, but she has her own style of dealing with issues. She used to meet people in her party office or her residence to address their grievances but this has decreased over the years, much to the disappointment of her followers.

Sonia has established a comfortable relationship with leaders of other parties in the United Progressive Alliance (UPA). She has an excellent rapport with the rustic Bihari leader Lalu Prasad Yadav. She walked over to her neighbour Ram Vilas Paswan in 2004 before the Lok Sabha polls and sought his assistance in forming the UPA. She had a good relationship with the Left leaders, like the late Harkishen Singh Surjeet and Jyoti Basu, and now with Sitaram Yechuri. She has been able to persuade many of these leaders over big issues such as the presidential and vice-presidential elections, and the Indo-US nuclear deal. By and large she has been successful as the UPA chairperson. Moreover, she has been able to bring the Congress party to power twice consecutively since 2004.

Identity politics has worked for Mayawati more than anyone else; she has climbed up using her caste as a ladder. She has succeeded in projecting her lower caste status and building a party along with its founder Kanshiram, giving her people a sense of pride and self-respect, so much so, today a Dalit can publicly proclaim who he will vote for and go to the polling booth to exercise his franchise, which was not possible earlier because of social conditions. Mayawati has been able to provide leadership to a deprived community and expand the BSP not only in UP but also in other states.

In Mamata's case, her anti-CPI(M) stand has enabled her to get results. She has been using this strategy for more than two decades. While the Congress—the main opposition to the communists in West Bengal—declined, it was the rise of Mamata which filled up the vacuum. She consciously strove to achieve this and became a street fighter, inspiring confidence in the anti-CPI(M) forces. She not only built up and led her Trinamool Congress (TMC) to become a ruling party but also reduced the Congress to a minor partner. Her mode of politics is appealing to the youth and women, which are two big constituencies. Every minute of her public life is spent on wooing more people to her side. Her mode of politics is confrontational; she believes in agitations, strikes and protests. Though she is not a skilled orator, she is able to convey her concerns to the people even in her incoherent language. Her rise in politics is entirely through these means. After coming to power she has not been able to realise that as a ruler she cannot continue to follow her old-style politics. It may take some time for her to change in order to be on the other side of the fence.

It was her espousal of Dravidian ideology and the legacy of MGR that has brought the AIADMK chief Jayalalithaa to power. Although her mentor MGR helped her initially, it is her own intelligence, fighting spirit, sheer determination and an understanding of Tamil Nadu politics that is sustaining her. The only opposition to Jaya is the AIADMK's parent party, the Dravida

Munnetra Kazhagam (DMK), and she has been fighting it for more than two decades on equal terms. Both the DMK and the AIADMK have managed to keep the Congress on the sidelines since 1967, each with a roughly 30% vote share. They also alternately align with the Congress for elections. Jayalalithaa believes in populism to counter her opponent Karunanidhi's politics. She has developed a personality cult and often proclaims that there is no party without her. She also believes in confrontation with the centre, unlike her mentor MGR, who was on the side of the Union Government. Even when she was a partner with the Congress or the BJP, she took the path of confrontation. She has also tried to form some pressure groups with a few non-BJP and non-Congress parties.

The People's Democratic Party (PDP) chief Mehbooba Mufti is in politics because of her father, but she has cleverly taken up issues to express the sentiments of the people of Kashmir, who are sandwiched between the security forces and the militants. She arrived in politics at the right time, took up the right cause and found her niche. It is not an easy task for a young woman in a patriarchal Muslim society to find a successful place in Kashmiri politics, and she has achieved that.

The Gandhi family connection has helped both former President Pratibha Patil and Delhi Chief Minister Sheila Dikshit to reach the top. Pratibha hit the jackpot when Sonia Gandhi chose her to become the president when she was not even in the reckoning.

Sushma Swaraj moved up the political ladder because she arrived in the BJP when the party was looking for a presentable, articulate woman leader. The BJP's prospects did not look too good in 1984 when Sushma joined the party. Its leader, L.K. Advani, was impressed with her credentials since she had already made her mark in politics as a minister in Haryana.

SONIA GANDHI'S WORLD-VIEW

As Tellis points out, Sonia Gandhi's world-view has been shaped by two factors. Her upbringing and left-of-centre views with regard to the American political spectrum make up one strand. The second strand is that those views have only deepened as a result of imbibing Indira's leanings. However, she had a European liberal sentiment before she became part of the Gandhi family. While some critics believe that Indira's ideology was problematic for India, Sonia Gandhi continues to follow a similar tradition. Her political agenda is mostly populist and rather reminiscent of the 1971 Indira Gandhi agenda: *"roti, kapda aur makaan"* (food, clothing and shelter). Although her programmes like the Mahatma Gandhi National Rural Employment Guarantee Act (MNREGA) and the Food Security Bill have been updated for a new era, they still seem much the same. She may not have the middle class constituency with her. That may have gone to the BJP. 'But the way she tapped into the *"aam aadmi"* (common man) is a very strong residual desire to protect secularism even though it has become much defaced over time. But she still tapped into that, while the BJP had exceeded its sense of what an average Indian was comfortable with. She did a remarkable thing by stopping the march of the BJP. In a way, she defended the Congress tradition of secularism and cosmopolitanism,' observes Tellis.* Sonia has absorbed all this simply from her environment and partly from her genetic makeup.

HER MODE OF POLITICS

Over the years, Sonia, like her mother-in-law, has shown that she believes in populist politics. It has paid dividends for her brand of politics because she has led her party to victory not once but twice in the last nine years. As compared to her male colleagues, for instance, former Prime Minister Atal Bihari Vajpayee, she emerged better off in spite of the BJP's "India Shining" campaign, which did not return the party to power in 2004. This was despite the fact that the economy was doing well at the time and there had been many achievements credited to the Vajpayee government. Once again, in 2009 she took on BJP veteran L.K. Advani. By pitting Manmohan Singh against him, she was smart enough to ward off any criticism against herself or her family. No one would have stopped her from projecting herself as the prime ministerial candidate or putting up her son Rahul as one, but she consciously chose Singh for a second term. This ensured a victory against the (National Democratic Alliance) NDA, much to the surprise of even the Congress party.

Within the Congress, she faced challenges boldly right from the beginning. The first challenge came from the Maratha strongman Sharad Pawar, former Speaker P.A. Sangma and Tariq Anwar. They played up her foreign origin and its adverse impact on the party, but she challenged them and emerged victorious. She resigned from the presidentship of the party and got them expelled, while she came back with renewed strength and power and converted the Congress into her fiefdom. Since then the party has become the "Sonia Congress". The second challenge came from her vice-president Jitendra Prasada. Under a mistaken impression that he could challenge her, he contested the presidential elections of the party. She allowed him to do so and won a landslide victory, whereas Jitendra Prasada suffered a heart attack and died. In fact, there was a perception in the Congress ranks that whoever came in her way perished; they point out the untimely deaths of Madhavrao Scindia and Rajesh Pilot, among others. When the office of profit controversy arose, she smartly resigned from her Lok Sabha seat and contested again and came back with a larger majority.

As for dealing with leaders of other parties, it was a masterstroke when she went to each one of the UPA partners and mobilised support for its formation. She met leaders like DMK chief M. Karunanidhi, CPI(M) veterans Jyoti Basu and Surjeet, LJP chief Ram Vilas Paswan and RJD chief Lalu Prasad Yadav. Of course, she could not keep the Left parties on her side because of the differences over the economic and foreign policy, and the Indo-US nuclear deal. While some alliance partners like the Telangana Rashtra Samithi left the coalition during these nine years, Sonia added the Trinamool Congress to the UPA in 2009.

Sonia has operated in a male-dominated Congress party like a queen. Although Indira Gandhi was known as the only man in her Cabinet, Sonia Gandhi does not have that kind of "Iron Lady" image. She still controls the party with an iron hand and her male colleagues are in fear and awe of her. They are afraid to even air their views, apart from saying "yes madam, no madam". Even in the party meetings they find out beforehand what her views are and echo them. She has complete control of the party and there has been no challenge to her leadership for many years. She has many records to her credit: she was the first woman Leader of the Opposition and the first to be elected party president for four terms.

JAYALALITHAA'S WORLDVIEW

As for Jayalalithaa, she is regarded as a dictator. She had shown her control over the party when she put a first-term MLA, Panneerselvam, as the puppet chief minister after she had to resign for a few months in view of a court order. Panneerselvam was so much in awe of his leader that he would not even sit in the chief minister's chair, and she had complete control of the government and the party even while she was not chief minister. Decisions were taken at her residence and not at Fort St. George (Secretariat). She treats her male colleagues with great contempt. She has held her own and put up a good fight despite humiliations from her opponents. She has even taken a vow to finish off her main rival DMK chief M. Karunanidhi. Her allies are in awe of her. After all, Jaya is the party and the party is Jaya. Her party men know this fact and that is why they pay obeisance to her. In keeping with her style of politics, she is ready to take on anyone—the centre, the prime minister, government employees, other party leaders and whoever else comes in her way.

MAYAWATI

Mayawati's politics is much like the queen's in *Alice in Wonderland*, who declared "Off with his head!" to anyone who stood in her way. Her main opponent is Samajwadi Party leader Mulayam Singh Yadav. Together, over the past two decades these two regional leaders have sidelined the national parties—the Congress and the BJP—in UP. She has not been able to forget the guesthouse incident when she was attacked by Mulayam's men in 1995 when the BSP withdrew its support to the Mulayam Singh government. She conducts her politics in a raw manner. Her main focus is Dalit welfare and how to keep her flock together. But now, in her quest to accede to power, she is looking for backing from other sections like the minorities and upper castes. Her rainbow coalition, which gave incredible results in 2007, is worth a mention, even though she failed to retain the support of the upper castes and minorities in the 2011 Assembly polls. Like Jayalalithaa, she too treats her male colleagues with contempt. Call it sweet revenge, a triumph that even Brahmin ministers touch her feet, forgetting that for thousands of years Brahmins had kept Dalits oppressed. She is a loner and does not like to have any alliance with other parties before elections. But after the polls, she encourages ties with almost all parties. Her brand of politics is crystal clear: she will accept what is beneficial to the BSP and has no qualms in taking the support of the Congress or the BJP in order to achieve this. She has dealt with senior leaders like Narasimha Rao, Vajpayee, Advani, Sonia Gandhi and others on her own terms.

MAMATA BANERJEE

Mamata Banerjee has an altogether different style. She entered into alliances with many parties except the Left. Her brand of politics is simple: anybody against the CPI(M) is her ally. She is willing to use any strategy and any party for this purpose. That is why she had made an alliance with the BJP, and now with the Congress. She too has a dictatorial tendency, which is becoming more evident since she became chief minister. Whoever criticises her is dubbed a CPI(M) activist who is out to malign her. She treats her male colleagues just as Mayawati or Jayalalithaa treat their party men. In short, the party goes by what *"didi bolche"* (didi says). Her relationship with male leaders of other parties begins quite well but sometimes ends in a disaster. She has combined with several other regional leaders like Mulayam Singh or Lalu Prasad to create a pressure group.

MEHBOOBA MUFTI

Even though Mehbooba Mufti is the party president, she is still under the shadow of her father Mufti Mohammad Sayeed. Lately, however, she seems to be taking her own decisions. She gets along well with other women leaders like Sonia Gandhi and Mamata. (They were together in the Lok Sabha.) It was she who clinched the coalition issue with Sonia Gandhi in 2002 when her party came to power. She is a bold street fighter for the cause of the Kashmiris. She cannot afford to be dictatorial like Mamata or Mayawati because there are other senior leaders in the PDP but she is said to be arrogant.

Sushma Swaraj, Sheila Dikshit and Pratibha Patil do not have a party of their own, nor are they the top party leaders.

THEIR MODE OF COMMUNICATION

It is clear that these women have a distinct mode of communication which appeals to the public, or else they would not be where they are. They are loners and do not trust others in the party. They are also insecure despite total control of the party. A common theme which runs across the board is that they believe in direct contact with the people and talk to them about issues without any intermediaries, as Indira Gandhi was wont to do. Whenever she was challenged, Indira used to go to the people directly. This is perhaps one of the reasons why they do not pander to the media.

Take the case of Sonia Gandhi. Although she has been the president of the Congress party for more than 16 years, she hardly gives interviews or meets the media except for a few full-fledged press conferences before the elections. She has been able to keep her private and public life in watertight compartments. As a result, a certain mystique surrounds her, making people wonder what kind of person she actually is. Her inaccessibility is very much a part of her appeal.

Mayawati's mode of communication is slightly different. She too hardly ever meets the press, and even when she does, she reads out a prepared statement and confines her answers to the subject scheduled for the day. Her style of politics includes touring every nook and corner of the state and keeping in touch with the party cadre. During her rallies she takes time to explain the issues at hand directly to the people, who come in thousands to hear their leader. She knows the art of speaking the language of her supporters. She believes that the media is against her and does not give interviews. Two large volumes of her autobiography detailing the struggles in her life are the only source of information about her personal life.

Jayalalithaa has learnt some tricks from her mentor MGR, who knew how to keep his magnetism alive while also being in contact with the people. In fact, when MGR saw his party losing, he wanted somebody who could communicate with the public on his behalf, and chose Jaya. Thanks to her background in films, Jaya has mastered this art. She is a great orator and communicator and has been able to connect with the people easily. Paradoxically, she is often inaccessible and people have to wait to get a glimpse of her. Her clarity of thinking and ease with taking questions during press conferences set her apart from the other leaders.

Mamata's communicative abilities are different. She is an emotional and impulsive leader who believes in direct contact with the public but is also media savvy. She has managed to get its support right from the beginning and has loyal friends in it. However, she does not allow her party MPs and MLAs to interact with the media. She has assigned that job to select individuals whom she trusts. Her colloquial Bengali is a strength she exploits to the maximum to convey her message.

Mehbooba Mufti is a confrontationist who takes on the government over several embarrassing issues such as state security and development. Being a leader in a conflict zone, she has had to design her own brand of politics. She is a good speaker and plays the role of the Leader of the Opposition in the Jammu and Kashmir Assembly effectively. She is not media shy and she has great courage and boldness in dealing with everyone, including militants. Her mode of politics is to maintain direct contact with the people, and for this she travels all over the state to connect with them. She has painstakingly built her party using this personal touch, reaching out to those families affected by the killings of either the security forces or the militants. She even took up the cause of the surrendered militants and was even willing to engage with the separatists.

Though from the Congress stable, Sheila Dikshit had good relations with the NDA government when she took over. She did not adopt a confrontationist policy. Likewise, Pratibha Patil's term in the Rashtrapati Bhavan was without any controversy. Her predecessors, Zail Singh and Sanjiva Reddy, had differences with the government but Patil managed to sidestep these and cultivated a harmonious relationship with the prime minister.

The firebrand politician Sushma Swaraj is now in the opposition. She showed her abilities when she contested against Sonia Gandhi in 1999. She has the advantage of great oratory and communication skills in both Hindi and English.

THEIR DECISION-MAKING MECHANISM

What these leaders say is regarded as a law in their own parties; although they do go through the motions of consultations, the outcome has already been pre-determined. They depend on their own wisdom while taking decisions. In other words, they believe they know everything.

UPA president Sonia Gandhi is the perfect example of being the lone decider. In the earlier days, the party had the Parliamentary Board, which was the highest decision-making body. Today, there is the Congress Working Committee (CWC); various other bodies like the Congress Parliamentary Party (CPP) and the Pradesh Congress Committee; organisations such as the mahila and youth wings and the Seva Dal. But all these groups have become irrelevant. The Parliamentary Board does not exist. The CWC does not meet often enough. The CPP has a limited role. Since the UPA has been formed, most of the important decisions are being taken by what is called the core committee—half a dozen handpicked members, some of whom are ministers. This committee works as a kind of bridge between the party and the government. It is this body which decides everything. Sonia consults others but the final decision is hers. As for her personal decisions like resigning from presidentship of the party when Sharad Pawar and others raised the issue of her foreign origin, or her opting out of the race for the role of prime minister, or her resignation over the office of profit controversy, it is her family—she and her children—who decide.

In Jayalalithaa's case, she does not have too many advisers; she even keeps changing her friends. So when it comes to right or wrong, it is her wisdom at work, as is the case with Mayawati and Mamata. They depend entirely on their own political astuteness to take decisions.

HOW DO THEY RETAIN THEIR LEADERSHIP?

This is a most fascinating aspect. These leaders have faced ups and downs. When the chips are up, certainly, people collect around them, but the question arises what happens when they are down? It all boils down to keeping their flock together, regardless of circumstances. This is the basic rule and the most difficult thing to do.

Take the case of Sonia Gandhi. She came into politics when the party was disintegrating. When she took over, the Congress was in the opposition. Her entry itself brought immense relief and the party became united under her leadership. She managed to keep the party members together when she was in the opposition for six years. The party split only when Sharad Pawar and Sangma left to form the Nationalist Congress Party (NCP). Strangely enough, after leaving the party, they agreed to become coalition partners—first in Maharashtra and later in the UPA. Once the UPA came to power in 2004, there was no question of managing leadership because not only the leaders in the Congress, but also others in the UPA constituents accepted her leadership. Her aura, her ability to deal with the coalition partners and the unquestioned acceptance of her leadership has helped her to remain on top.

But one area where Sonia Gandhi has failed is to revitalise the party at the grassroots. After the UP election losses, both Sonia and her son Rahul had admitted this failure. The Congress party that existed as a mass mobilisation effort by Mahatma Gandhi, Pandit Jawaharlal Nehru and Sardar Vallabhbhai Patel does not exist anymore. Tellis feels that the 'problem here is that she is faced with a structural contradiction. If you are protecting the interests of the family, then you cannot revive the party at the grassroots level. If you want to revitalise the party, you have to admit that family interests should take a back seat. At best you are a caretaker, and you have to enable the rise of state leaders. It is they who would build the party. Is Sonia Gandhi ready for that?'* he asks.

Sonia has also experimented with a new idea by appointing Manmohan Singh as the prime minister while she remains the party president. The division of labour was very clear: he will look after the administration, while she will take care of the political domain. She will deal with the allies and look after the party. In this way she continues to be in the driver's seat but without taking any responsibility for the government. If the government does something wrong, the party will dissociate itself very quickly, like it did when Singh made a controversial statement on Balochistan in Sharm-el-Sheikh. There are many other such instances. But if the government programmes click, then the credit should go to the party and Sonia. This happened in the case of the Right to Information Act, MNREGA, the Women's Reservation Bill in the Rajya Sabha and now the Food Security Bill.

By and large the general opinion among the party leaders is that the arrangement has failed in UPA-2, while it worked well in UPA-1. Initially it worked well because Sonia chose Singh for his personal qualities and clean image. They complemented each other. Singh was reticent and did not take any decision which would annoy Sonia. Many analysts wonder why he did not initiate bold reforms. Was it because Sonia did not allow him to or was it because he was not sure of himself? This analysis could be endless with many ifs and buts; the bottom line is that the arrangement suited both.

When it comes to Jayalalithaa, the case is simple: there are no challengers to her position or a second line of leadership. She has not had a single contender in her party throughout these two and a half decades, even when the party lost polls.

The same applies to Mayawati; no challenger or second line of leadership is allowed to exist. She too has kept a tight leash on her party. Its members do not leave her even when her fortunes dip. Her party's vote share has increased even though there is a variation in the number of seats. She manages to retain her leadership by virtue of hard work, organisational capabilities and political acumen. Mamata has zero tolerance for criticism. At the first murmur of dissent, she either sidelines the person or suspends him. Even recently when Railway Minister Dinesh Trivedi proposed a hike in rail fares without her consent while presenting the railway budget, she taught him a lesson by getting him dropped from the Union government. Since her party men know that it is Mamata who gets them the votes, they obey her every whim and fancy.

As mentioned earlier, Mehbooba Mufti is still under the shadow of her father. The dynastic advantage of being his daughter and the way he has projected her keeps her in the driver's seat. She has further built herself up to such an extent that today she is a brand in her own right.

WHERE DO THEY GET THEIR SUPPORT? IS IT RURAL OR URBAN?

Sonia Gandhi's support is neither urban nor rural; she has a pan-national appeal. Her popularity is reflected in the popularity of the Congress. Earlier, the Congress had a more rural base than any other party because there was a party office in every district, but that has changed over the years. The BJP has managed to grab the urban base, leaving the Congress behind.

Though a city-bred girl, Mayawati's support comes from rural areas. There too, her influence is not uniform; it is in pockets and more in some regions than in others. Her party is largely confined to UP. Despite two decades of effort, she has not been able to spread the net wide enough. The BSP has managed to open electoral accounts in some states like Maharashtra, Madhya Pradesh, Punjab, Delhi and Haryana, but it has not made a mark in the South.

As for Mamata, her base began in urban areas and is now slowly growing in rural areas. The CPI(M), which had a strong rural presence, lost ground in the past few years. The Trinamool Congress (TMC) also managed to get some seats in the North East. Mamata's base in Kolkata still remains strong.

Mehbooba Mufti tirelessly strives to make a base for her party in rural Jammu and Kashmir, and has already done significant work to make that happen. She acts as a check to Chief Minister Omar Abdullah.

WILL DYNASTIC POLITICS WORK?

Some leaders like Mamata, Mayawati and Jayalalithaa have proved that dynastic politics alone will not work in India anymore. Ashley Tellis observes that it has survived in India remarkably well, as elsewhere in South Asia, until now. 'Dynastic politics will survive only to the degree that people will let it survive. It is not going to survive simply because there is a dynasty. In India, we are in a period where the critical criteria have become performance. If your dynasty fails to perform, it gets booted out. But where dynastic politics still has an advantage is that it creates certain expectations that there are natural leaders emerging from it. Where it gets really problematic is when dynasty prevents the rise of alternative power centres. That is the biggest tragedy which is happening in India. Under Nehru there were strong state leaders. He dealt with powerful chief ministers in the state, and he dealt with them as equals.'* But later, all alternative sources of power were prevented. The same thing is continuing to happen even today. Nothing seems to grow under the shadow of the Gandhi family.

The examples of these contemporary women leaders gives a glimpse of where India is heading and how such strong leaders survive in Indian democracy with their personality cults. The multiplicity of these leaders is another strange phenomenon in a country which has a diverse culture, language and politics. These women leaders have tried to connect with the public. As columnist T.V.R. Shenoy points out, 'There is an interesting aspect in the Indian context. Mahatma Gandhi was Bapu, Nehru was Chacha, Indira Gandhi was Indiramma, Sonia Gandhi is Madam, Jayalalithaa is Amma, MGR, NTR and Annadurai are Anna (elder brother), Mulayam Singh is Netaji, Balasaheb Thackeray and Sharad Pawar are known as Saheb, Mamata is Didi, Mayawati is Behenji. And the point is that these leaders want to establish some connection or intimate family relationship. All of them sit high upon their pedestals but also want to be one of us.'* They want to inspire awe among their followers, which is their main weapon to keep them under control. The lesson these leaders should learn is that when they promise the moon and do not deliver, the democratic process throws them out. These women know they will not be given a second chance, so they have to stay on their toes at all times. They have to work harder, and in the end, do better.

Women in India have a long way to go to achieve meaningful empowerment but a beginning has certainly been made. The growth of political parties led by women is a hopeful sign and the fact that the number is only growing is also important. Social changes, increasing access to education and health, growing awareness among women to fight for their due place and, above all, the determination to achieve empowerment, provide a fillip to women's dreams.

Note: All quotation marks followed by a star denote interviews conducted by the author.

NOTES

1. www.un.org/womenwatch/daw/cedaw/history.htm.
2. edition.cnn.com/2012/06/28/world/europe/women-politics-global-power/index.html? hpt=hp_c3.
3. Ibid.
4. Ibid.
5. www.businessweek.com/news/2012-05-24/hollande-gets-a-minus-on-promise-to-women.
6. www.womenscenter.emory.edu/services_resources/Womens_News_and_Narratives/election_story.html.
7. www.unicef.org/sowc07/report/report.php.
8. Joyce Gelb and Marian Lief Palley, *Women and Politics Around the World: A Comparative History and Survey*, Vol. 1, citing Robin May Schott, p. 8, ABC-CLIO, 2009.
9. Taylor Marsh, *The Hillary Effect: Politics, Sexism and the Destiny of Loss*, Premier Digital Publishing, 2011.
10. Gail Collins, "The Crying Game", *New York Times*, December 15, 2010, www.nytimes.com/2010/12/16/opinion/16collins.html?_r=1.
11. Gelb and Palley, *Women and Politics Around the World*, Vol. 1, p. 19.
12. Ibid., p. 36.
13. http://papers.ssrn.com/sol3/papers.cfm?abstract_id=288974.
14. Gelb and Palley, *Women and Politics Around the World*, Vol. 1, p. 38.
15. Peter Popham, "Nehru dynasty wilts in heat of general election", *The Independent* (London, England), September 4, 1999; *Custom 150 Online Journals*, No. 17, July 3, 2012, http://go.galegroup.com/ps/i.do?id=GALE%7CA6654 2332&v=2.1&u=wash55362&it=r&p=SPJ.SP00&sw=w.
16. Lakshmi Iyer (Harvard Business School), Anandi Mani (University of Warwick), Prachi Mishra and Petia Topalova (Research Department at the *International Monetary Fund*), "The Power of Political Voice: Women's Political Representation and Crime in India", April 5, 2011.
17. Gelb and Palley, *Women and Politics Around the World*, Vol. 1, Chapter: "India's Women: Problems, Prospects, and Progress", p. 385.
18. Ibid., p. 384.

Sonia Gandhi

WHAT IS THE MYSTIQUE surrounding Congress President Sonia Gandhi? Despite being in public life for more than 16 years no one knows her. What are her likes and dislikes, her vision for India, her views on various issues? Is she a rightist, a leftist or a left of centre? There is no clear picture. Some call her an enigma, although her daughter Priyanka Gandhi is not comfortable with this description. "Enigmas are really built around people who are sometimes very simple. People don't understand that there can be simplicity in her," she explained in an interview.[1]

Some call her arrogant, others call her the "Cinderella of Orbassano", but she has proved to be an extraordinary woman—hailing from Italy, she has come to rule the one billion plus people of India. The British came with their army, as did the Dutch and the Portuguese, but Gandhi came all alone as a twenty-one year old and transformed herself as she moved from the First World to the Third World. A US embassy telegram from New Delhi points out: "Despite her carefully erected Indian persona, her basic Italian personality is clearly evident in her mannerisms, speech and interests. She presents an intriguing enigma of a warm private personality that remains concealed and is available only to her closest confidants and family members."[2] This telegram was sent from the American Embassy after Sonia's meeting with Maria Shriver, the First Lady of California.

Sonia Gandhi was named the third most powerful woman in the world by *Forbes* magazine in the year 2004 and the sixth in 2007. She ranked ninth on the list of the world's most powerful persons in 2011 and twelfth in

2012. She also featured in *Time* magazine's list of "The 100 Most influential People in The World" in 2008. The British magazine *New Statesman* listed her at number 29 in their annual survey of "The World's 50 Most Influential Figures" in the year 2010. Gandhi has also been ranked sixth, a notch above US First lady Michelle Obama in *Forbes'* list of "The 100 Most Powerful Women" in August 2012.

In an article dated April 30, 2009, Indian minister Shashi Tharoor notes that Sonia Gandhi's story is remarkable at every level, and the fairy-tale metaphor barely begins to scratch the surface of its extraordinariness. "But which story is one to tell? That of the Italian who became the most powerful figure in a land of a billion Indians? That of the reluctant politician who led her party to power? That of the parliamentary leader who rejected the highest office in her adoptive land, one she had earned by her hard work and political courage? That of the woman of principle who demonstrated that one could stand for right values even in a profession corroded by cynicism and cant? That of the novice in politics who became a master of the art, trusted her own instincts and discovered she could be right more often than her jaded rivals could ever have imagined? The story of Sonia Gandhi must be all these stories, and more."[3]

From her modest origins in Italy, to becoming one of the most powerful politicians in India, Sonia Gandhi has overcome the chauvinism and xenophobia of Indian politics and emerged as a charismatic global leader in her own right. Her rise to power is like the Cinderella story. "When Sonia entered India on a cold January evening as the fiancée of Rajiv Gandhi little did she expect that her destiny would be dovetailed with that of the strange country she was coming to?"[4] Born in a middle-class family in Turin, she would not have expected to rule India when she first met Rajiv Gandhi, the son of Prime Minister Indira Gandhi in a Cambridge café. Theirs was love at first sight and it blossomed into marriage. Though her father was not in favour of this match initially, she married Rajiv Gandhi in 1968. After that there was no turning back. She joined Prime Minister Indira Gandhi's family and became the wife of Prime Minister Rajiv Gandhi, who succeeded his mother after her assassination. It is vital that the story of Sonia Gandhi and her leadership is understood, in its true spirit.

It is very difficult to get a glimpse of Sonia's personal life behind her mask. Those who are close to her do not open up for fear of losing her trust and others have no clue about her personality. As former minister Natwar Singh, who was once close to her, puts it, her story is like a Greek tragedy. She has been through the assassination of two of her closest relatives—her mother-in-law Indira Gandhi and husband Rajiv Gandhi—both former prime ministers. Singh adds that she has come to understand the psyche of India and also that of the Congress. 'The main thing is not to get familiar; you keep your distance in order to raise the necessary awe and respect. In Indian politics, accessibility is an asset. In her case, inaccessibility makes her politics and is her asset. She would make you feel that meeting her is a great occasion and she has used this to her advantage.'*

Former Information and Broadcasting Minister Ambika Soni agrees that Sonia is a very private person. 'You can't know her. I have seen her evolve as a political entity. She has a very clear distinction between her private life and personal affairs and her pubic life.'* Close family friend and Delhi Chief Minister Sheila Dikshit confirms this: 'Sonia Gandhi is very simple. On the other hand, she is also not easy to understand. She has the capacity to keep to herself and express herself when she thinks she should.'* Priyanka admires her mother's metamorphosis into a confident leader. On the campaign trail in Sonia Gandhi's constituency of Rae Bareli during the Uttar Pradesh elections in 2012, Priyanka Gandhi told a television channel that her mother was doing a great job. "I really admire her evolution," she said, referring to her mother as a 'shy person'. "If I look at her today, she doesn't need a paper to read (speech) to say what she needs. She makes decisions beautifully with advice from everybody. I think she is doing a wonderful job."[5]

It is perhaps a Gandhi family trait to be perceived as shy and reluctant to enter politics. Rajiv was a reluctant entrant when his younger brother Sanjay died in a helicopter crash in 1980. He joined politics to help his mother at that time, and later, donned the prime minister's mantle when she was assassinated in October 1984. Even Indira Gandhi was tongue-tied and bashful in her earlier days. She was referred to as a *goongi gudia,* a dumb doll. Sonia took her time in deciding whether to enter politics or not; it actually took seven years for her to make up her mind. Since she has entered politics, she has converted her shyness into an advantage. Her son Rahul Gandhi is still a reluctant politician. Perhaps the Gandhi family thinks that people of India like those who renounce power.

THE PIVOTAL MOMENT

Although Sonia had been in the public eye since the day she married Rajiv Gandhi in 1968, her decisive moment in politics came in 1998, when she took over the reins of the Grand Old Congress Party. She cut her political teeth then; this was at a time when the Congress's fortunes were at their lowest. The party's efforts to support the United Front government from 1996 onwards, first under Deve Gowda and then under I.K. Gujral, were gambles that failed. It was at this time of crisis that Sonia was persuaded to take over the party. Ambika Soni recalls how Congressmen were leaving the party in search of a better future. 'In December 1997, there was an exodus. People like Mani Shankar Aiyar and Suresh Kalmadi were all leaving the party. Congress people from all over the country were asking her (Gandhi) to take over. Thrice, the Congress Working Committee had asked her to take over the party, which she refused. She had declined for reasons best known to her. I am not privy to all that. Then she came out and campaigned for the party.'*

In a television interview, Mrs. Gandhi herself reveals that she was a reluctant politician to begin with. "It's just that circumstances compelled me to enter politics, but I think I've got used to it. I am quite comfortable in politics, and yes, I am a rather private, shy person, though I think I have progressed. I am certainly less shy than I used to be."[6]

Sonia's entry upset the calculations of not only the then Congress President Sitaram Kesri, but also of the BJP and other opposition parties. Kesri was not keen to encourage her, as he knew that it would be the end of his long political career. He was fully aware of her hold on the party and was surprised when one evening on December 28, 1997, the announcement came from her residence that she would campaign. He could do nothing except grin and bear it.

Once Sonia came into the political arena, the party was quite relieved by the way she conducted herself and the favourable response from the media and the public. The initial apprehension was whether she would be a successful political campaigner, but they had no doubt about her crowd-pulling capacity. Gandhi's understanding of political issues was not clear, nor were her capabilities in dealing with them. Sitaram Kesri and other senior leaders were apprehensive that she might only focus on the Jain

Commission's interim report. (The Jain Commission investigated Rajiv Gandhi's assassination). However, she did not mention the commission in any of her early meetings. Their second worry was her foreign origin, which the BJP had raised and made into an election issue. With regard to the Bofors controversy, Sonia challenged the government to release all the papers pertaining to it and claimed that Rajiv Gandhi became the victim of malicious propaganda. As for her foreign origin, she contended that since the time she came to India, she had adopted this country as her own. Even after her husband's death, she had decided to live and die in India. To the relief of the Congress, the public did not pay heed to the foreigner issue. So within days, she became the only national campaigner of the Congress to match stalwarts like BJP leader Atal Bihari Vajpayee. She addressed meetings wearing pastel-coloured sarees and often covering her head with her *pallu* (the loose end of her saree). She depicted herself as a traditional Indian woman and kept her children with her during meetings to expose them to the family legacy.

I had covered several of her election meetings. During the 1998 campaign, she travelled 60,000 kilometres and spoke to 138 constituencies in 34 days, hopping from one place to another by helicopter. During the campaign, she played the secular card and declared to the crowds that the Congress Party would restore secularism. She was referring to the flight of Muslims from the Congress Party after the demolition of the Babri Masjid in Ayodhya by a mob in 1992. The BJP raised religious passions into a frenzy by organising a congregation for the building of a Ram temple in Ayodhya on December 6, 1992, which ended up in the demolition of the adjacent *masjid* (mosque) dome, to the shock of the entire nation. Several people were killed and injured in the nation-wide riots that followed. The Narasimha Rao government at the Centre received flak for not being able to prevent the demolition.

The *New York Times* reported on February 27, 1998: "After 34 days of hectic campaigning in India's general election, the woman who started life as Sonia Maino, the Roman Catholic daughter of a building contractor from a small town near Turin, is today the undisputed star of the domain she once shunned. At 51, Mrs. Gandhi has added an astonishing new chapter to the story of the Nehrus and Gandhis, the family that has done more to write the political history of India in the 20th century than any other."[7]

Thousands gathered to catch a glimpse of Sonia even though she spoke in a soft voice and in heavily accented Hindi. Many also came out of curiosity to see the Italian woman addressing meetings. Others saw her as a grieving widow and a reminder of the party's past glory; the result was that the Congress Party got re-energised. Sonia's first-ever campaign speech was made to a packed audience on January 11, 1998 at Sriperumbudur, where her husband was assassinated in 1991. Her private secretary Vincent George, along with a handful of Rajiv Gandhi loyalists, carefully chose the venues for her campaign trail. Sonia and her children handpicked speech writers and the speeches were finally vetted by the family. She rehearsed before the mirror and modelled her style of walking and talking on her late mother-in-law.

However, given the party's poor organisation, there was no ground level support to convert her popularity into votes. There is no doubt that the Congress would have done much worse without her campaign. She had prevented its disintegration. The Congress got only 141 seats, as against 140 seats in 1996, while the BJP-led NDA with its 24 partners staked claim to form the government.

WHY DID SONIA DECIDE TO JOIN POLITICS?

The indications of Sonia Gandhi's entry into politics came when, unknown to many, she first became a primary member of the Congress in 1997. She later attended the AICC (All India Congress Committee) session in Kolkata. In fact, some suspect that she had already been meeting several party members who called on her to air their grievances, which meant she had been keeping her options open since 1991. But she never indicated that she was even considering the idea of jumping into politics for seven years.

The timing of her entry was perfect for the Gandhis, as the Congress Party needed some direction and a charismatic leader to take charge. The Congress, though in Opposition, had the power to influence the United Front government headed by Deve Gowda and later by Gujral, because it was supporting it from outside. However, Kesri became ambitious and decided to pull the Gujral government down using the Jain Commission report as an excuse. The Congress held that the Jain Commission, which had gone into the Rajiv Gandhi assassination, indicated the DMK's involvement; therefore, Gujral should drop the DMK ministers from his Cabinet. Gujral refused to do so and his government fell, leading to the 1998 Lok Sabha polls.

It was in this scenario that Sonia made up her mind to campaign for the party. The Gandhi family deliberated over this decision and finally made the announcement around Christmas time. Sonia clarifies, "I had opposed my husband's joining politics. And I had opposed it because I feared I might lose him. I was right. So when I took the decision, this was one of the main factors my children were concerned about. Both my son and daughter were very worried about this aspect but eventually they said they would go along with any decision I took."[8]

Sonia claims that her duty to the family she had married into was one of the reasons for the decision. She explained her predicament to veteran journalist Shekhar Gupta during a television interview: "I have photographs of my husband and mother-in-law in my office. And each time I walked past these photographs, I felt that I wasn't responding to my duty, the duty to this family and to the country. I felt I was being just cowardly to just sit and watch things deteriorate in the Congress for which my mother-in-law and the whole family lived and died. So at that point I took the decision."[9]

The announcement on December 28, 1997, took many leaders, including Kesri, by surprise. Mamata Banerjee, Mani Shankar Aiyar and Suresh Kalmadi, who had left the party, were stunned. Later, they said had they known her intention, they would not have hastened their departure. Mamata Banerjee was particularly hurt that Sonia did not reveal her mind even a day before her launching the Trinamool Congress. Mani Shankar, who had gone to Sonia several times to plead with her to take over the party, came back with the impression that she was not interested. 'We had a long conversation and in the end I told her this was the last time I was seeing her as a Congressman but she did not indicate her intention of joining politics even at that time.'* Suresh Kalmadi, too, had faced similar disappointment.

THE CRUCIAL MOMENT

Meanwhile, efforts were on to make Sonia the Congress president. In fact, the exercise began as early as December 1997 when Vincent George announced on her behalf her intention to play an active role in the party. When she casually asked Madhya Pradesh Chief Minister Digvijay Singh what would happen were she to campaign for the party, Singh immediately understood the implication and replied, 'Madam, it will electrify the party.'*

AS CONGRESS PRESIDENT

After the poor showing of the Congress in the 1998 polls, the first casualty was its president Sitaram Kesri. There was clamour and discontent within the party to throw him out of office. Senior leaders like Arjun Singh, Makhan Lal Fotedar and Natwar Singh got together to put pressure on Gandhi. Fotedar remembers their telling Kesri that Sonia Gandhi should be brought in, but he was not willing to go along. 'We persisted and she agreed at last. She realized that the party was disintegrating fast and felt it was her duty to stop that.'*

Natwar Singh confirms that Sonia was slowly coming round. She was keenly aware of the Nehru-Gandhi family legacy. 'Seven of us, including Arjun Singh, Fotedar and Ghulam Nabi Azad, pleaded with her after the AICC session in Kolkata, which turned out to be a fiasco. The Kolkata session made her realize that something was wrong. Despite his substantial experience in the party and as an ideal treasurer, Kesri was not able to make a mark as the Congress president.'* The Kolkata AICC session showed the real state of affairs: there were signs of a split, with Congress leader Mamata Banerjee holding an outdoor rally while the session was in progress; there were rumblings about the Congress Working Committee (CWC) elections which took place just before the session, with senior leaders complaining of rigging.

Inder Malhotra, columnist and Indira Gandhi's biographer, asserts that people believed that Sonia Gandhi was not interested in politics. 'I think it is absolutely wrong; she kept it open. When she decided to oust Kesri and take over the Congress Party, or when Sharad Pawar and Sangma raised the issue of her foreign origin, the way she handled the Congress Working Committee was astounding.'*

CONSPIRACY TO OUST KESRI

And then came the coup. Kesri was not aware of what was brewing at 10 Janpath (Sonia Gandhi's residence). He became nervous soon after the Kolkata session. "There was something in her eyes which made me feel uneasy but I had no idea that she was going to take the plunge or dump me so unceremoniously," Kesri told his inner circle.[10] The plot to overthrow him thickened over the next few days. As Inder Malhotra points out, 'On her part, Sonia seemed to have interpreted the election results as a mandate to seize the party's leadership she had been consistently declining for so long. Throwing aside her emphatic denials of ever wanting to hold any political office, she almost literally grabbed the office of the Congress president, though she left the necessary dirty work to the coterie surrounding her.'*

After getting Sonia's nod, some of the CWC members hatched a plan to install her. Ahmed Patel and Ghulam Nabi Azad informed Kesri about the goings-on, but he would not believe that Sonia wanted him out. He insisted that people like Arjun Singh and George were behind the plot. Then Kesri called on Sonia and told her bluntly that he was ready to step down whenever she chose. Sonia shocked him by asking when he could do so. A dejected Kesri announced on March 9 that he was stepping down. However, he revised his decision and announced that he would formally resign at an AICC session that he would soon convene. But the Sonia camp was getting restless. After consulting astrologers, March 14 was fixed as the date for Sonia taking over the party and Kesri's removal. Since Kesri was not convening a CWC meeting, some senor committee members drafted a resolution on March 13, asking him to convene the Congress Working Committee meeting the next day.

There was high drama at the AICC headquarters on March 14. It was the day of the coup, which was conducted with the active help of most CWC members, including Arjun Singh, Fotedar, Manmohan Singh, Pranab Mukherjee and Sharad Pawar. Since morning there was hectic activity in preparation for the CWC meeting. An unsuspecting Kesri arrived at the party office and chaired the meeting at 11 am. Many scribes, myself included, were standing around, sensing something was going to happen.

Even before Kesri could mention the first item on the agenda, the customary approval of the minutes of the earlier meeting, Pranab Mukherjee rose and thanked him eloquently for his "valuable services to the party" and moved a resolution to make Sonia Gandhi the new president. Other members joined him. This provoked Kesri, who walked out, adjourning the meeting abruptly. Senior members like Pranab Mukherjee, Manmohan Singh and Azad followed him and tried to persuade him to come back. Kesri left in a huff. Hanging around the party office, we (reporters) found that within half an hour the CWC meeting was reconvened by Vice-President Jitendra Prasada, this time without Kesri. As expected, Sonia Gandhi was unanimously elected as the new Congress president. Kesri loyalist Tariq

Anwar was the only one who walked out. Thus began Sonia Gandhi's regime in the Congress, which she has dominated for the past 16 years.

What happened after the CWC meeting was still more surprising. Even as we kept a vigil on the Congress president's office, we found that a shining brass nameplate with the name Sonia Gandhi had replaced Kesri's within an hour, making it more than clear that the Kesri era was over. The deposed Congress president was keeping a close watch on these developments and decided to hold a press conference at 4 pm at his Purana Quila Road residence to expose the way he was ousted. Several Congress leaders went to his house to dissuade him from taking any hasty action. Perhaps wise counsel prevailed, or maybe it was the pressure, or the realization that he had no supporters; Kesri did not hold the press conference though he did meet with the reporters. Meanwhile Sonia Gandhi arrived at the party office at 5.30 pm, addressed her first CWC meeting, thanking all the members. To assuage Kesri's hurt feelings and to seek his cooperation, she also called on him immediately after taking over, which ended the drama for the day.

Thus March 14, 1998, was the day Sonia Gandhi became the Congress president after a successful bloodless coup. *The Hindu* wrote an opinion piece which read: "It was claimed that the party had been purged of its recently acquired unnaturalness: the usurpers—non-Nehru-Gandhi family leaders, Narasimha Rao and Sitaram Kesri—had been scratched from the escutcheon, and now the leadership had been restored to its natural and only claimants: the Nehru-Gandhi family. There was much celebration; this stage-managed euphoria notwithstanding, those who participated in this unprecedented conspiracy—the new leader and her plotters—were mindful of the grand organisational sin they had committed. Each one of them knew that the deposed president had been elected only less than a year ago in a democratically contested election, the first of its kind in more than two decades. The coup had abruptly stopped the party's gradual rediscovery of democratic ways of conducting its internal affairs. That day the Congress opted to move against the grain of a democratic India."[11] The op-ed further argued: "For better or for worse, the party would be given no other leadership choice, and its leaders must reconcile to this format. The only alternative to Sonia Gandhi would be her children; you, dear Congressman, are free to exercise your democratic choice between the daughter or the son. The top leadership was not negotiable, nor questionable, nor accountable."[12]

Harish Khare, former press adviser to Prime Minister Manmohan Singh, observes that the party was looking for a leader. 'The moment P.V. Narasimha Rao lost the elections he was dumped. Kesri failed to deliver. In the Congress Party only Sonia Gandhi was acceptable. Kesri's presidentship was only a stop-gap arrangement. It was decided that he had to go; he was old and seventy-five at the time.'*

On March 16,1998, an AICC meeting was held at the Siri Fort Auditorium in which Sonia made her first speech to the Congress delegates. Natwar Singh recalls that she was terrified of speaking that day. 'She arrived at the venue with Priyanka and called me over. We were sitting in the anteroom and she was looking very nervous. Anyway she read out the speech prepared by Jairam Ramesh and two others. For the next two or three years, her speeches were her biggest anxiety. I used to prepare them along with Jairam and a few others. She did not use Mani Shankar Aiyar, who used to prepare Rajiv Gandhi's speeches. When I used to hand over a speech to her, she would read it out but confess that she could not do so in public. She is a perfectionist. She used to read it over and over again. She was very shy and you could see she was very nervous. Now she is not. Gradually she began doing well.'

SONIA'S ORIGINS

UXL Newsmakers begins the Sonia story like this: "The story should have had a fairy-tale ending: a beautiful young girl meets her handsome Prince Charming, has two children and lives happily ever after. In 1968, however, when Sonia Maino married Rajiv Gandhi of India, the fairy tale was only half realized. She snagged a handsome prince, but she also inherited the troubled history of his country. Rajiv Gandhi was a member of a family that had ruled India since the 1940s."[13]

Sonia reminisces about her meeting with Rajiv in Cambridge, where she had gone to study English language in 1965. Feeling homesick, she was looking for some good food and would often go to a Greek restaurant called Varsity. It was there that she met her future husband Rajiv Gandhi. "As our eyes met for the first time I could feel my heart pounding. We greeted each other and, as far as I was concerned, it was love at first sight. It was for him, too, as he later told me."[14]

Rajiv studied at Cambridge University while Sonia did a language course from February 1965 to July 1966. She returned to her parent's house and Rajiv continued his flying lessons in London. After getting his license, Rajiv travelled to Italy to meet Sonia's parents. Her father had doubts about how Sonia would adjust in a strange country and also felt that she was too young (barely 20 years old) to know her mind. He stipulated that if the two of them decided to wait for a year and, if they found they were of the same mind then, he might agree to the marriage, thinking that the whole thing would die in a few months. When she turned 21 in December, her father allowed her to go to India. Landing on a cold January night, she felt reassured when she saw Rajiv along with his brother Sanjay and Amitabh Bachchan, who went on to become a legendary film star. Indira Gandhi made her stay with the Bachchans until the wedding on February 25, which was a simple ceremony, even though Mrs. Gandhi was the prime minister then. Sonia remembers how she felt strange initially. "Everything around me was new and strange: the colours, the smells, the flavours, the people. Strongest of all were people's eyes—that gaze of curiosity which followed me everywhere. It was an exasperating experience—the total lack of privacy, the compulsion to constantly check myself and repress my feelings."[15] After marriage, Sonia settled down to the Indian way of life and remembers, "I was allowed to be myself, and to find my own way of fitting into Rajiv's world. I began gradually to take an interest in the running of the household."[16]

RAJIV GANDHI'S ENTRY INTO POLITICS

Things carried on smoothly for a few years, but when Sanjay Gandhi, Rajiv's younger brother who was being groomed as Indira's successor, died in a plane crash in 1980, Sonia's world changed overnight. Naturally, Indira Gandhi expected Rajiv to assist her in her political work, which had been previously handled by Sanjay. "For the first time in the fifteen years that we had known each other, there was tension between Rajiv and me. I fought like a tigress—for him, for us and our children, for the life we had made together, his flying which he loved, our uncomplicated easy friendships and, above all, for our freedom: that simple human right that we had so carefully and consistently preserved."[17] Sonia confirms that from the time Rajiv chose to go into politics, their lives transformed. "His time was no longer flexible and each hour he could spend with us became all the more precious."[18] The family soon adjusted to Rajiv's new life.

INDIRA GANDHI ASSASSINATED

The next watershed moment was when Indira Gandhi was assassinated on October 31, 1984, by two of her security guards at her residence. Recalling the event, Sonia observes "I had started my bath when I heard what sounded like an unusually close burst of Diwali crackers—but with a peculiar difference. I called out to the children's nanny to see what it was. I heard her screams. I knew at once something terrible had happened. I rushed out. My mother-in-law had been placed in the back seat of an Ambassador car—stretched out lifeless. I knelt by her. It was a nightmarish drive to the hospital, slowly, through heavy traffic. Frantic, scattered thoughts: Was she just unconscious? Could she be saved somehow? Where was Rajiv? Where were the children? That strong refusal to believe that the worst had happened, that it was all over for her."[19] Indira Gandhi's assassination changed Sonia and Rajiv's life further.

RAJIV GANDHI BECOMES PRIME MINISTER

P.C. Alexander, who was then the principal secretary to Prime Minister Indira Gandhi, describes how Rajiv became the prime minister. Discussions were on whether there should be an interim PM, similar to what happened when Nehru's successor Lal Bahadur Shastri died. The common view that emerged among the chief ministers and the senior Congress leaders was that Rajiv Gandhi should be sworn in immediately. Some felt that since President Giani Zail Singh was abroad, the Vice-President should be asked to swear Rajiv in. Alexander recollects a poignant moment when he went to speak with Rajiv Gandhi, who was closeted inside with Sonia. "Rajiv was clasping Sonia by both hands in a corner of that room and talking to her very animatedly. Sonia was holding him tightly and with tears rolling down her cheeks was ardently pleading with him not to agree to be Prime Minister. Rajiv was kissing her forehead and trying to convince her that he had to accept the office as it was his duty to do so in that hour of grave crisis."[20] That same evening at 6.45 pm Rajiv Gandhi was sworn-in by President Giani Zail Singh, who had cut short his trip.

When Rajiv became the prime minister, his schedule again underwent a change, with most of his time spent on national, international and party affairs. His time for the family shrunk further. Sonia travelled with him the length and breadth of the country and also visited 57 countries as his wife.

She played the hostess to perfection, taking interest in the details of the menu and the requirements of their State guests. Rajiv's five-year regime was marked by ups and downs. He squandered the goodwill of the people and ultimately lost power in 1989. All the while, Sonia Gandhi kept aloof from politics and remained a silent spectator.

Rasheed Kidwai, Sonia Gandhi's unofficial biographer, points out that during the times she was the prime minister's wife, her photographs depict her as an inscrutable person, constantly tense, aloof and cold. Rajiv Gandhi's detractors were quick to brand her as the power behind the throne. "Someone described her as Noor Jahan of Turin, while others linked her to a Sphinx, the mythical Greek monster with a woman's head and lion's body who waited outside Thebes, asking travellers a riddle and killing them when they failed to answer it."[21]

The 1987 Bofors controversy was an indirect attack on Sonia Gandhi; the Opposition alleged that a substantial kickback was given to Sonia and Rajiv Gandhi's family friend, Italian businessman Ottavio Quattrocchi, for facilitating the gun deal. On April 16, 1987, a startling announcement made on Swedish Radio that Bofors paid kickbacks to top Indian politicians and key defence officials, galvanised the Opposition. This was the biggest contract won by the Swedish arms company AB Bofors. From then on, Sonia became a target and Rajiv spent the next two years defending himself before the public and in Parliament. Subsequent events connected with Bofors have been even more mysterious and inexplicable.

The Opposition was belligerent and insisted on a Joint Parliamentary Committee (JPC) to probe into the allegations of kickbacks. When the JPC was announced, the Opposition boycotted it. The Bofors taint stuck to Rajiv Gandhi despite his insistence that neither he nor anyone in his family was involved in the deal.

TRAGEDY STRIKES AGAIN

As prime minister, Rajiv's life was always at risk. In 1986, while he was on his way to attend a prayer meeting at Mahatma Gandhi's Samadhi at Raj Ghat on October 2, a gunman hiding in a nearby thicket shot at him with a revolver. Police later found out that he had been waiting for days to attack him. Six other people who were walking with the prime minister were injured. The next year in 1987, when Rajiv and Sonia had gone to sign the Indo-Sri Lankan Peace Accord in Colombo, there was another attack while he was inspecting the guard of honour in front of the Presidential Palace. The intense feelings of the Sri Lankans against the accord was evident when a naval cadet reversed his rifle and struck Rajiv with its butt. Luckily, Rajiv ducked and the blow aimed at the back of his head injured his shoulder instead.

The Congress party triggered off the 1991 Lok Sabha polls by withdrawing support to the Chandra Shekhar government, which it had propped up for a few months after the fall of the V.P. Singh government. The party members was impatient to capture power and forced a mid-term election. Furthermore, the first Gulf War had created a misunderstanding when the Chandra Shekhar government allowed refuelling facilities to the US in Mumbai, which the Congress had vehemently opposed. The Congress used a flimsy excuse to withdraw its support, claiming that two policemen were keeping a watch over Rajiv Gandhi's residence on the government's instructions. The party's calculations would have gone awry, as the poll pundits had predicted a poor show. But Rajiv Gandhi's tragic assassination on May 21, just before the polls, resulted in sympathy votes and the party won 242 seats.

Sonia had always been tense about Rajiv Gandhi's security. When the final blow came, she was not even with him. LTTE militants assassinated Rajiv Gandhi at Sriperumbudur in Tamil Nadu, where he had gone to campaign. They were upset that Rajiv had sent the Indian Peace Keeping Force (IPKF) to help the Sri Lankan government disarm the rebels. India's role in the Sri Lankan ethnic conflict was baffling because it was during the time of Indira Gandhi that the LTTE got covert support from the Indian government. LTTE supremo Prabhakaran was also upset about the Indo-Sri Lankan Peace Accord signed in 1987.

I was working for the *Hindustan Times* then and had just reached home around 9.30 pm. As I sat down to dinner, I got a call from my office asking me to come back immediately as Rajiv Gandhi had been assassinated. I rushed to the AICC headquarters at Akbar Road along with a colleague. The party office was just getting active and Janardhan Dwivedi, now the AICC General Secretary, was struggling with a statement on behalf of the party. There was a sense of shock and bystanders were getting angry with the journalists present there. No one was allowed near Rajiv Gandhi's residence. Even when President Venkataraman came to meet Sonia Gandhi, he was booed away.

It was only later that I learned about what had unfolded inside 10 Janpath that night. Sonia Gandhi and daughter Priyanka had already retired for the day when a friend called asking her diplomatically whether everything was all right; she got suspicious. Rahul was returning from abroad the next day. She called her private secretary Vincent George on the intercom to find out what was happening. George had, in the meantime, called Congress leader P. Chidambaram's lawyer wife Nalini in Chennai and found out about the blast but could not bring himself to inform Sonia. After some time, when another caller from Chennai announced that Rajiv was no more, George went inside and informed Sonia that there had been a blast. A stunned Sonia remained speechless for a few minutes before going to Priyanka's room to tell her the tragic news.

Fotedar and other Congress leaders rushed to Rajiv Gandhi's house after hearing the news. The bungalow was soon barricaded to stop the stream of mourners. Huge crowds gathered in front of the residence shouting angry slogans against the assassins. The next morning Sonia and Priyanka went to Chennai to bring back Rajiv's mortal remains. Natwar Singh, who was at the airport when they returned to Delhi, recalls how grief-stricken Sonia and Priyanka were. 'At the airport there were very few of us. Sonia Gandhi's eyes were red and for the first time I saw her lose composure. For the cremation, several world leaders came. Olof Palme, Prince Charles, Yasser Arafat, Benazir Bhutto, Nawaz Sharif and several others. After the cremation, most of them called on her. I was with her in all these meetings. Rahul and Priyanka were also present. I remember Benazir told her, "You must not join politics after this tragedy." Rahul said that at that moment there was no question. Benazir appealed again. I said, "You are asking her not to do something that you have yourself done." I was referring to her taking over the mantle after her father Zulfikar Ali Bhutto's execution.'*

SONIA DECLINES TO BECOME PARTY PRESIDENT

The Congress Party, though badly jolted by the assassination, began to consider their options. Beginning the next morning, the Congress leaders met to deliberate on who should replace Rajiv Gandhi as the Congress president since a vacuum at the top was not desirable. M L Fotedar, Arjun

Singh and others wanted to install Sonia Gandhi on the post. P.V. Narasimha Rao, who was campaigning in Ramtek, returned the next morning. The CWC assembled at 24 Akbar Road, the party headquarters, 18 hours later and decided to induct Sonia Gandhi as the party president. We scribes were surprised when Pranab Mukherjee came out and announced the decision in the evening. He had no answer to many questions posed by the journalists present. Questions like when had Sonia Gandhi become a Congress member or had she been consulted before the decision were left unaddressed.

Fotedar remembers that he had gone to the CWC meeting wanting to ensure a smooth transition. To prepare the ground, he took Sharad Pawar aside before the meeting and requested him not to oppose Sonia's name, even if he did not support her. Pawar, to his surprise, agreed to second Sonia Gandhi's name. Senior CWC member Narasimha Rao chaired the meeting. It was a solemn assembly and the resolution to make Sonia president was unanimously passed. Fotedar adds, 'Then we, along with Ghulam Nabi Azad, Pranab Mukherjee and Arjun Singh, went to Sonia Gandhi's residence with the resolution. I told Vincent George that there was no urgency. She should take her time to reply the next day. But Sonia Gandhi declined the same night.'* Sonia issued a cryptic statement that read: "The tragedy that has befallen me and my children does not make it possible for me to accept the presidentship of the Congress." Many Congress leaders saw the point but still envisaged a role for her in the party in the future. That was why, after the mourning period of one year was over, they made a beeline for her residence. Sonia's assent to meet them gave them hope that some day she might agree to join politics and take over the party, which she did after seven years.

NARASIMHA RAO BECOMES PM

Shortly after the meeting during which Congressmen nominated Sonia Gandhi as the party president, I had gone to see Narasimha Rao at his residence and asked him about his future plans. He seemed to be in a mood to pack up and go back to Hyderabad, as there was nothing for him in Delhi. Within 24 hours, his fortunes changed and he was chosen as the party president, and later, as prime minister.

There is a background to Rao's choice as the leader of the Congress. Natwar Singh recollected the sequence of events for me. When the various world leaders who had come for the cremation had returned, he spoke to Sonia

Gandhi and requested her to decide who should become the Congress president. 'I said, "Please call P.N. Haksar (Indira Gandhi's principal secretary) and ask for his advice." She replied, "I will let you know." Then, she must have consulted Haksar and others. Haksar, apparently, suggested that freedom fighter Aruna Asaf Ali should try to convince Vice-President Shankar Dayal Sharma to take over the post. Sonia asked me to meet Sharma with Aruna. We went and told Sharma that Sonia Gandhi wanted him to take over. He immediately excused himself and said, "Considering my age and health, I will not be in a position to do this 24/7 work. So please tell Sonia Gandhi I cannot accept the offer." It was only after this that Narasimha Rao's name came up and, after much discussion, he was chosen.'*

The leadership tussle continued for four days. Sharad Pawar, along with at least half a dozen others, threw his hat in the ring too. His main supporter Suresh Kalmadi organised a dinner which was attended by several MPs who supported Pawar. Meanwhile, the group which was keen on Sonia's selection, thought that Rao, who was in his seventies, could be a stop-gap prime minister until Sonia decided to take over. Leaders like Fotedar and Sitaram Kesri had suggested Rao's name to Sonia. The then chief minister of Kerala, Karunakaran, and former West Bengal Chief Minister Siddhartha Shankar Ray called each MP and ultimately declared Rao as a consensus candidate. His selection became easy as the other contenders cancelled each other out. So Rao became the prime minister without being a member of either House, as he had not contested the elections. The Indian Constitution makes it incumbent on the President to swear-in any Indian citizen to the prime minister's post, provided he gets elected within six months after proving his majority.

This was the first occasion when Sonia declined the prime minister's job. Had she agreed, she would undoubtedly have become the Congress president and the country's prime minister without any opposition. Insiders say that she declined the offer due to her concern about the security of her children and over the fact that they were very young. Her close friends also advised her against jumping into politics at that point of time.

ON THE SIDELINES

Sonia was in mourning for a year. During Rao's regime, she kept aloof from the affairs of the government and the party and confined herself to activities related to the Rajiv Gandhi Foundation and other Gandhi family trusts like the Nehru Memorial Trust. She was controlling various trusts worth Rs. 5000 crore. Sonia received a stream of foreign dignitaries who called on her—first to pay their condolences, and later, as courtesy calls. Throughout this period, she did not evince any interest in political issues.

Rao knew Sonia Gandhi's potential and did not want any clash with her. Both were congenial towards each other, and for the first few months everything went off well. Two months after his appointment, there was a meeting of the Rajiv Gandhi Foundation, of which Rao was a member. In the normal course of events, the meeting would have taken place at the prime minister's official residence. However, Natwar Singh called and expressed Sonia Gandhi's reservation about visiting the official residence of the prime minister since she had lived there during Rajiv's tenure. Security agencies suggested holding the meeting at Hyderabad House, where foreign delegations are hosted. Ultimately, Rao resolved the matter by offering to go to Gandhi's house for the meeting. Thus began his visits to 10 Janpath, which were virtual monologues; Sonia passively listened to him without expressing any opinions. For some reason, senior party leaders, including Sitaram Kesri, did not want Rao to have direct access to her. It seems some party members were averse to the possibility of a close interaction between the two leaders.

Rao had to face humiliation when Sonia Gandhi declined a Rs. 100 crore allocation for the Rajiv Gandhi Foundation in his first Union Budget. The generous bonanza suffered extensive criticism both from the media and the Opposition. Sonia wanted to avoid any embarrassment and refused the funds. Gradually, Rao's visits to Gandhi's house became infrequent. Various emissaries would come to him claiming that Gandhi wanted such and such thing to be done. Rao could not call her to confirm the claims. She would also not check the veracity of allegations made by detractors like Arjun Singh—that Rao was not interested in investigating the Rajiv Gandhi assassination case. Slowly, the misunderstandings began to increase. On one occasion, Vincent George was being considered for the Rajya Sabha. Captain Satish Sharma, a close friend of the Gandhi family and a minister in Rao's Cabinet, was one of the channels Rao used to get her opinion on an issue. He asked Sharma to find out if Sonia supported George's candidacy. Gandhi did not commit either way and George was not given a ticket. George was naturally upset about it.

Meanwhile, Congressmen did not give up hope of getting Sonia Gandhi to play a bigger role. They were encouraged by her willingness to meet them, although she did not say anything to them. Eventually, Rao devised a method to keep in touch with Gandhi: through her close aides. Natwar Singh was one of them. He explains: 'One day Rao asked Sonia whether he could install a RAX (an internal phone meant only for the government) to keep in touch with her but Mrs. Gandhi refused.'* The strain in their relationship continued throughout Rao's term as prime minister.

CONGRESS SPLITS

Within a year, Arjun Singh began to show his true colours. Rao had made him the Leader of the Lok Sabha until he was elected to the Lok Sabha, and Singh was consulted on every issue. For all purposes, he was number two in the party as well as in the government. But Arjun Singh had other ambitions. He wanted to become the party president, or even the prime minister. Singh soon began to write several embarrassing letters to Rao and would leak them to the press even before they reached him. He formed a group of disgruntled leaders, including N.D. Tiwari, Natwar Singh, K.N. Singh, B.P Maurya and Sheila Dikshit, and voiced their grievances against Rao. At the Surajkund AICC session on 27 March 1993, this group demanded the revival of the "one man, one post" concept and that the PM should not hold the post of party president. Eventually, in 1995, they organised a meeting to announce a new party under the chairmanship of N.D. Tiwari, a four-time chief minister of UP. Sheila Dikshit recalls, 'Arjun Singh, Tiwari and others somehow felt they were not given the importance they deserved. There was a general atmosphere of innuendo and mistrust. They were pushing me to come along. Those days Sonia used to keep very quiet. She was a wonderful listener. She understood everything but spoke very little. I can't say that she was the one who had given the signal to break away. She never said anything to me, but these people claimed they had her blessings. I had no reason to believe that I should check the facts.'*

Ultimately, the Congress split and a section of disgruntled leaders left the party. On the day of the formation of the new party, it was rumoured that Sonia Gandhi was going to be present. Rao confided to a friend that she called him when the meeting had already begun and told him to stop the split. Rao had conveyed to her that he would confer with them soon, but they should first call off the meeting. But by then, the breakaway faction was in no position to reverse what had been done. The decision was further sealed by all the hype over the rift. And so, Congress (Tiwari) was formed.

The first signs of discord between Rao and Sonia surfaced over the Jain Commission investigating Rajiv Gandhi's assassination. Rao's detractors led Sonia to believe that the government was dragging its feet on it. Natwar Singh notes, 'One day P.V. (Rao) called me over to 5 Race Course Road, where he met people for confidential talks. I could see that he was very agitated. He said, "I can take on others but I can't take on Sonia Gandhi. I don't want to. If she is unhappy, I am willing to quit citing health reasons. (Rao did not keep good health). But what does she have against me?" So I explained, "She has been given the impression that you are dragging your feet on the Rajiv Gandhi assassination case." To which he replied, "Listen Natwar, I went to her myself. I sent S.B. Chavan (Home Minister) to her with the case files. What more can I do?" I said, "I can't talk to her. You must talk to her." Anyway, there was no patch up.'*

The Sonia–Rao equation deteriorated to such an extent that on August 26, 1995, while addressing a public rally in Amethi, she chided the government and lamented to the assembled crowds: "You can understand my anguish. My husband has been dead for four years and three months, but the inquiry into his assassination is moving at such a slow pace."[22] The message was meant for Rao and he winced.

CONGRESS LOSES ELECTIONS

The Congress lost the elections in 1996 and had to sit in the Opposition. Rao got embroiled in several court cases and the party promptly dumped him, forcing him to choose his successor as the party president. Since Rao had to appear in court for the hearings, he thought it would be better to find someone who could carry on until he was free of the cases. There were several aspirants and it was difficult to choose between them. Sitaram Kesri suited Rao since Kesri made him believe that he was loyal to him. The other leaders thought that they could manipulate Kesri and he was not a threat to them. Rao later admitted that it was a mistake when Kesri started treating his predecessor very shabbily.

Even during Kesri's two-year tenure as the Congress president, disgruntled Congressmen continued to call on Sonia Gandhi and increasingly pleaded with her to take charge of the party. When the Congress lost the 1998 Lok Sabha elections, Sonia was pressurised to take over, even as several second-rung leaders had begun to abandon ship.

The process of installing Sonia had begun several months earlier. In 1997, when she attended the Kolkata AICC session in August. There were a lot of excitement in the party leading up to the CWC elections, in which Kesri tried to push his panel through. To his disappointment, three party leaders, who were not on his list—Arjun Singh, Ghulam Nabi Azad and Sharad Pawar—got elected. Gandhi's presence at the AICC session further added to his discomfiture. While she was sitting in the audience, there was a clamour for her to come to the dais. Kesri reluctantly called her and she made a short speech which received a standing ovation. Those of us who had gone to cover the session could feel the expectations within the party rank and file. The media then speculated that it was only a matter of time before she decided to enter politics.

Sonia's attendance at the Kolkata AICC session was the second indication to Congressmen that they should not give up hope, and that she would join politics soon. From then on, the tempo for Sonia Gandhi's political induction escalated until December 28, when she decided to campaign for the 1998 elections. A few months prior to that, in 1997, there was another writing on the wall when Sonia quietly enrolled herself as an ordinary member of the Congress Party. When the decision was announced, Congressmen were jubilant. Her entry into politics not only revived the Gandhi dynasty but also helped check the growth of the BJP.

"[The Congress Party] did subscribe to the party's collective credo: 'Sonia is best and then there's the rest.' In a faction-ridden party, she stood above the fray, in a polity increasingly dominated by caste, she had no such affiliations; and her appeal spanned the entire country, which is more than what could be said of any other Congress leader, then or now," observes Inder Malhotra.[23]

While Sonia has modelled herself on her mother-in-law Indira Gandhi, there are several similarities and differences in their style of functioning. Insiders often used to say that Sonia would practice before the mirror. Inder Malhotra points out that Indira Gandhi had been in politics since she was four years old. She had the unparalleled experience of observing her father Jawaharlal Nehru work, attending meetings with him, hosting and interacting with international leaders. As Nehru's daughter, she even campaigned in the first general elections, and by the second Lok Sabha polls, she had become a Working Committee member, Parliamentary Board member and Congress president. Yet when she was elevated as prime minister, she made a tentative, nervous beginning as she had no administrative experience. 'But she moved from being a *goongi gudia* (dumb doll) to Goddess Durga (after the Bangladesh War). Her direct connect with the people, over the heads of leaders like Kumarswamy Kamaraj, Morarji Desai and Sanjiva Reddy, was her biggest asset. She could choose a cause, dissolve the house and go to the people. This is a quality Sonia has not acquired. She has acquired political skill but does not have the same kind of popularity like Indira,' explains Malhotra.* He also notes that due to her European roots, Sonia has not grasped the intricacies of Indian culture and its problems. In order to get a better understanding as a leader, she ought to meet a lot of people but this is where she is found lacking. All access to her is being controlled by the few around her.

Indira Gandhi used to direct her officers in the execution of her decisions and assured them that she would take care of their political fallout. Sonia does not do that. She has not said a word on issues, except on populist policies like the Mahatma Gandhi National Rural Employment Guarantee Act (MGNREGA) and the Food Security Bill. While Indira had a point of view on everything, Sonia has not spoken on any major foreign policy or economic matter apart from the Indo-US nuclear deal.

In the initial years, Sonia was more diffident and took time to find her feet. Indian politics has changed over the years, and so has the Congress. The emergence of regional satraps and players has reduced the Congress' influence and the grand old party has had to even reconcile to coalition politics both at the states and the Centre.

While Indira Gandhi depended on a kitchen Cabinet and Rajiv Gandhi on his coterie, Sonia consults her family on all important decisions that she takes and keeps changing her small group of advisors.

Amar Singh, who had interacted with her on behalf of the Samajwadi Party as a supporting partner, claims that 'people think that she does not talk much, but she talks. People think that she is unaware of what is going on. I think that at times looks are deceptive. When I did not have any interaction with her earlier, I also used to think that her silence might have been her strategy. But when I started interacting with her, I was amazed to find that she was very well informed about politicians not only in her party but also in other parties. She may not show it, but she is very well informed.'*

SONIA CONSOLIDATES

After Sonia Gandhi took over the Congress' reins on March 14, 1998, after ousting Kesri, she began to consolidate the party and her position. Her record since the 1998 coup has not been dismal at all and luck has favoured her. First of all, she has revived the dynasty. Secondly, her leadership certainly prevented the fragmentation of the Congress. As a result, the party has been able to reclaim its natural political space. Within months of her taking over, the Congress won three states—Delhi, Rajasthan and Madhya Pradesh—boosting Sonia's image.

One important milestone in Congress' revival journey was the soul-searching exercise at Pachmarhi, a beautiful hill station in Madhya Pradesh. Taking a leaf out of her mother-in-law Indira Gandhi's book, Sonia organised a conclave in September 1998, a few months after she took over. Congress policy issues were discussed threadbare and shaped at this meeting. Several senior Congress leaders participated in the free-for-all discussions. Sonia appointed several committees after this conclave to get micro-level reports. Manmohan Singh was asked to head a committee to repackage the economic reforms with a human face. The conclave also sent a signal that the Congress would go it alone in the next elections and would return to power on its own, rejecting coalition politics. However, the party had to revise this decision later at the Shimla Conclave in July 2003, which brought the Congress back to power in 2004 and 2009 as the leader of the UPA coalition.

SONIA PLOTS AGAINST VAJPAYEE GOVERNMENT

Since Sonia was not a Member of Parliament, senior Congress leader Sharad Pawar was made the Leader of the Opposition. She became the Congress Parliamentary Party (CPP) chairperson, which gave her overall authority without being an MP. She continued to keep her distance from the media and hardly ever interacted with them except granting an occasional byte to a TV channel, keeping the aura of mystery around her intact. In the first year of her Congress presidentship, she did not mingle much with the Opposition either. That task was left to Sharad Pawar in the Lok Sabha and Manmohan Singh in the Rajya Sabha, who were the floor leaders for the Congress.

Meanwhile, the NDA government led by Vajpayee was finding it difficult to pander to the whims and fancies of the 24 alliance partners. The differences began to grow, reaching a height when AIADMK chief Jayalalithaa decided to pull the government down within 13 months. Since she could not do so on her own, she needed Sonia Gandhi's support. Janata Party President Dr. Subramanian Swamy brought them together. Swamy recalls, 'Jayalalithaa was pressing me to bring the Vajpayee government down. She was emotionally hurt in those days as the BJP was taking her for granted. I kept buying time and tried to convince her that the time was not right. I asked her, "Do you want an election?" and she said elections were better than continuing this way. I said there is only one catch: without the help of the Congress, we cannot do anything. She agreed. I talked to Sonia in November 1998; her reply was "not now". Suddenly she called me in March and told me to go ahead. In the confidence vote, the Bahujan Samaj Party (BSP) also did not vote for the NDA and Vajpayee lost by one vote.'*

CONGRESS STAKES CLAIM

When the Vajpayee government fell, Sonia took the lead in forming an alternate government. She consulted the Left and other parties. The Congress was jubilant that the party may capture power again. She was misled about the numbers before she went to President K.R. Narayanan to stake the party's claim. She came out of the meeting, faced the cameras and informed the waiting media that she had told President Narayanan that she did not have the numbers at that point of time but had informed him that within two days, they will have 272 [the minimum majority required to form a government] with them, with more coming in. However, the Congress could not form the government because Samajwadi Party chief Mulayam Singh Yadav would not support it. All efforts to persuade him failed. Amar Singh, a Samajwadi Party leader and a close associate of Mulayam Singh, explains that 'it was not a decision of the heart but a decision of the mind. He (Mulayam) promised support and did not give it later. He has done this many times on other issues. He was not very categorical with Arjun

Singh that he would definitely support her but neither did he say that he would not. Given the communal–secular divide, Arjun Singh might have thought he would. I don't know if Sonia Gandhi wanted to become the prime minister.'*

Two of the Left parties also refused to support Sonia as prime minister. Gandhi later clarified in an interview, "I obviously did not mean that I, Sonia Gandhi, have 272. For God's sake, grant me a little more sense than that! What I meant was the Opposition had constituted a majority of the House because the government had just been defeated in a confidence vote."[24] This was perhaps the only time during that period when her body language betrayed something which her statements did not. All efforts to form any other alternative government also failed.

Sometime later, Gandhi told an interviewer it was a mistake to have brought the Vajpayee government down. "Yes, I think it was. But we didn't bring them down. Their coalition collapsed. Nevertheless, it was a miscalculation on our part. We were depending on assurances given by certain persons and those assurances were not fulfilled."[25] Thus, the three women—Sonia, Jayalalithaa and Mayawati—imposed yet another general election on the nation, the third in three years, sending shivers down the spines of the Lok Sabha MPs, who would have liked to avoid facing the electorate so soon. Vajpayee continued for some more months because elections could not be held during the monsoon. So 1999 was yet another occasion (the second after 1991) when Sonia Gandhi could have become the prime minister but missed it narrowly.

CONGRESS SPLITS AGAIN

Just a few months before the 1999 election, the Congress suffered another revolt. This time is was led by the troika of Sharad Pawar, P.A. Sangma and Tariq Anwar. The rebellion had been brewing for some time; the rebel leaders met to define their strategy to confront Sonia Gandhi on her foreign origins so that she could not stake her claim to be prime minister. The Congress Working Committee (CWC) meeting, which convened on May 15 to discuss certain issues, turned out to be turbulent, leaving Gandhi stunned. When the Pawar camp raised the issue of her foreign antecedents, she could not believe her ears. She thought that the matter had been resolved and that people had accepted her. She did not expect her own party men to make it a talking point again. When the meeting began, Sangma, whom Sonia had continuously promoted in the party, bluntly told her that the party did not know about her background, pointing out that the BJP had been able to spread negative sentiments about her foreign origin. Sharad Pawar, diplomatically praising her first for her contribution to the party, added that Congressmen did not know how to counter BJP's allegations. Rajesh Pilot joined in, acknowledging that there was some merit in what Pawar and Sangma were saying and that the party should discuss the issue. R.K. Dhawan, a Gandhi family loyalist, rose to defend her but before he could finish, a furious Sonia Gandhi walked out of the room, leaving everyone shocked. Pawar, Sangma and Anwar had come prepared to leave the party; Pawar had even made arrangements to launch the Nationalist Congress Party (NCP). He was keen to get more seats in the Maharashtra Assembly to teach Sonia a lesson. And Sangma, who hailed from the North East, was confident of the voters' support in Meghalaya. It seems they had lofty ambitions of joining a coalition of non-Congress and non-BJP parties and to form the government in the event that either party did not fare well.

Sonia Gandhi, who was deeply hurt by the revolt, sent her resignation letter to the party the next day, plunging the Congress into a crisis. Ambika Soni points out, 'Soniaji was hurt because of the personal attack on her… She was very upset.'* The CWC met again, this time without Sonia, and expelled the rebels. A huge drama unfurled over the next few days, in true Congress style. Several Congressmen had landed up in Delhi and laid siege to Gandhi's residence and the AICC headquarters, demanding that she take back her resignation. Many other Congress office bearers across the country also sent in their resignations. Several leaders competed with each other and brought along huge crowds to sit in front of Sonia's house for almost a week, demanding that she reconsider her decision.

Nine days later, on May 24, after daily visits from Congress leaders, the sulking Gandhi relented. The next day she addressed an AICC session at the Talkatora Stadium. She maintained an aggressive tone throughout her speech, pointing out that she did not want to join politics, but they had urged her to do so. She warned: "Those who want to walk with me should do so with their heads and their hearts… Those who have an iota of uncertainty are free to choose their own course."[26] Her words made it clear that from that day the Congress was hers. The way she handled the rebels was stunning. She emerged much stronger after that speech.

KARGIL WAR

In May 1999, the Kargil War broke out between India and Pakistan. The Pakistani army had infiltrated across the Line of Control (LOC) and tried to occupy some parts of the mountainous region in Kashmir. The Indian army and the government were caught unawares. Prime Minister Vajpayee, who had been trying to extend a hand of friendship to Pakistan and had taken a busload of people to Lahore, where a friendly Nawaz Sharif met him, felt betrayed. Nawaz Sharif later claimed that the operation had been led by his army chief, General Pervez Musharraf, without his knowledge. The Indian army, despite the provocation, decided not to cross the LOC. Ultimately, it was US President Bill Clinton who forced Sharif to withdraw from Kargil, thus ending the war. Within months, Musharraf orchestrated a coup; he deposed Nawaz Sharif and took over the reins of the government.

Sonia Gandhi essayed her role as the opposition leader aggressively, attacking the government whenever she could. The BJP accused her of playing politics over national security issues. The Congress Party's pushy stance as the Opposition did not seem to go down well with the Indian people and it had to face the repercussions in the 1999 elections.

SONIA BECOMES AN MP

The BJP, after losing the government by one vote in 1999, resumed its attack on Sonia with renewed vigour while campaigning for the next general elections. The "foreigner" tag was revived as an election issue when Sonia contested the polls. Janata Dal (United) leader George Fernandes, who was the defence minister in the NDA government, highlighted the fact that Sonia did not become an Indian citizen until 1983, although she married Rajiv Gandhi in 1968. The BJP launched a virulent attack on her Italian background, contrasting "Ram Raj" (the rule of Lord Ram) with "Rome Raj" and assured the voters that on winning the elections, it would set up a Constitution Review Commission to ensure that only people of Indian origin could become president, vice-president and prime minister. However, when the commission was formed, this issue was bypassed.

Sonia contested the Lok Sabha polls in 1999 from Bellary and Amethi (Rajiv's constituency) and won both. Until then she had fought the BJP from behind the scenes, but her entry into Parliament gave her an opportunity to lead from the front and face the government head-on.

While Sonia chose Amethi before the elections, she did not reveal the second constituency she planned to contest from until the last moment. The reason for choosing one constituency from the North and the other from the South was to show that she was a pan-Indian leader who was acceptable to the entire country. The BJP, which was smarting after losing the government by a single vote, was keen to put up a good fight and chose firebrand Sushma Swaraj to take on Gandhi. The Sushma–Sonia contest was interesting, as both were trying to woo different constituents—the former reached out to traditional conservative voters, while the latter claimed the legacy of Indira Gandhi. Sushma fought well and lost by just 58,000 votes, although she campaigned for only 14 days. Sonia won both Amethi and Bellary. Afterwards, she only retained Amethi since she cannot represent two constituencies. Later, to her surprise, the Congress candidate doubled the majority she had won, proving that Bellary was a Congress bastion.

The 1999 election results disappointed Sonia Gandhi as the Congress tally came down to 112 from 141. Her leadership did not get seats although it drew large crowds. But Congressmen continued to support her and justified that the party's vote share had gone up from 25.8% in the previous year to 28.5% in 1999. The NDA won a comfortable majority of 296 seats and had the largest number of partners—24 in all, from across the country. Vajpayee, once again, became the prime minister.

AS OPPOSITION LEADER

After the polls, Sonia set a record by becoming the first woman Leader of Opposition (LOP) in the Lok Sabha. This Cabinet rank position came with its fair share of responsibilities: she was expected to provide spontaneous responses to issues in the House, decide on the strategy against the government, meet foreign delegations and, above all, speak in the House. She had a battery of senior Congress leaders to assist her in these parliamentary responsibilities. Although she was the LOP, she delegated power to her deputy leaders: first to Madhavrao Scindia until his accidental death, and then to Shivraj Patil, the erstwhile Lok Sabha Speaker. Gandhi's maiden speech on October 29, 1999, was prepared with great care and she read it out while the entire House, including anxious Congressmen, watched her performance. Instead of the leader assessing her MPs' performance, the party men gauged her capacity to deliver speeches. Manmohan Singh and Pranab Mukherjee tackled the Rajya Sabha. As leader of the Congress Parliamentary Party, she had an overall responsibility, which she tried to fulfil with the help of these leaders.

During this period, Sonia was able to develop a good rapport with Prime Minister Vajpayee. When militants attacked the Parliament on December 13, 2001, the first thing they did was telephone each other to find out if they were all right. Natwar Singh recalls accompanying Gandhi to New York and finding, to his horror, that the security arrangements were inadequate. 'I called up Vajpayee in the middle of the night. He came on line; I told him that if something were to happen to her, he would be responsible. He said he would do something right away. Within an hour, the Indian Ambassador to the US Lalit Mansingh called, informing that all arrangements had been made.'* Natwar Singh and Brajesh Mishra, Vajpayee's principal secretary, coordinated with each other to see to Gandhi's needs. After all, Vajpayee also needed the cooperation of the Congress.

Despite these acts of reciprocity, Sonia led the Opposition aggressively. The Congress was belligerent about issues such as the *Tehelka* expose, which alleged that bribes were taken at the defence minister's residence, and "Coffin–gate", a major scam involving fraud transactions in the purchase of coffins during the Kargil War. With Sonia at the helm of affairs, the Congress would not allow Parliament to function for days. Initially, Gandhi was not comfortable with the other opposition leaders and operated through her deputies, but she slowly got to know leaders like Lalu Prasad Yadav, Somnath Chatterjee, and others. By the time the 2004 elections were around the corner, she was in a position to form partnerships with several parties to create the United Progressive Alliance (UPA).

Sonia also began meeting international delegations visiting India and interacting with foreign dignitaries who called on her. However, during these gatherings, she mostly listened and spoke little. Natwar Singh recollects her success in interacting with international leaders. When she went to New York in 2001 to speak at the Asia Society and the Council on Foreign Relations, she handled her audiences well. 'She spoke about how a meeting between her husband and Vice-President George H.W. Bush in 1985 had resulted in the Indian city of Bangalore being developed into an international Information Technology hub. During the question-answer sessions, she tackled the sensitive issue of relations with Pakistan and China, and spoke with clarity about Kashmir. Her address to the United Nations General Assembly on the same day on HIV/AIDS was also appreciated. In addition, she spoke at the Congressional India Caucus. All these interactions raised her international profile.'*

RE-ELECTED AS PARTY PRESIDENT

Two years after taking over the Congress, in the year 2000, Sonia ordered organisational elections again and followed a democratic process. Possible contenders propped up by her detractors in the party were Rajesh Pilot, but he died in a car accident, and party Vice-President Jitendra Prasada. She graciously allowed him to contest against her, aware of her own strength in a party which would not accept a non-Gandhi member as its leader. The Congress, over the years, had grown into an organisation which would leave it to the leadership to nominate even the district presidents. Prasada knew that contesting against a Gandhi was an uphill task, but he went ahead and filed his nomination papers. Assured by her aides, Sonia was confident that she would get elected without a hitch. The loyalists in the party ensured that even the voters' list was not shared with Prasada. No Congress leader was willing to receive him when he went around the country seeking votes. As expected, Sonia was elected Congress president for the second time on November 20, 2000, with an overwhelming majority. She garnered 98.88% of the votes; Prasada was left with only 94 votes. Some felt that Prasada did not stand a chance because the state units were exceptionally eager to prove their loyalty to the "queen"; the leaders openly showed their ballot papers with Sonia's name selected. Prasada was not a heavy weight, but the loyalists wanted to send a message that no one in future could dare contest against the Gandhi family. *The Economist* commented on the election: "If the strength of a system could be gauged by electoral landslides, communism would still be around. The election for the presidency of India's venerable Congress party, say many Indians, was as farcical as those under communism."[27]

Gandhi showed magnanimity towards Prasada after his defeat: she refused to listen to her close advisers who insisted that he ought to be punished. But Prasada was a broken man and eventually died of a heart attack. Sonia continued to be patronising and gave his widow a ticket to contest. She later fielded his son Jitin Prasada, made him a junior minister in the Manmohan Singh government and also allowed him to become a part of Rahul Gandhi's brigade. However, no one in the party dared to oppose Sonia after the Prasada episode. When Gandhi got elected as party president for the third and the fourth time, it was a unanimous choice.

PDP AND THE CONGRESS IN KASHMIR

Sonia played her cards well in Kashmir when the Vajpayee government tried to make the Jammu and Kashmir Assembly elections a showpiece for the international community in November 2002. Vajpayee allowed free access to those who wanted to observe the election, which was by and large considered free and fair. No party won a majority in the much-publicised election. The People's Democratic Party (PDP) won 16 seats, while the Congress bagged 20, emerging as the single largest party. After trying out several permutations and combinations, the Congress agreed to form a coalition government led by the PDP. This deal was clinched over a telephone call; PDP chief Mufti Mohammad Sayeed's daughter Mehbooba Mufti called Sonia Gandhi, resulting in his being made the chief minister for three years. As agreed upon, the second half of the term would be ruled by a Congress chief minister chosen by Sonia. The two parties also agreed on a Common Minimum Programme (CMP), on the basis of which the government functioned. This was a masterstroke, as Kashmir achieved some stability during Mufti's rule. Since his main focus was to bring a sense of normalcy to the state, he adopted a "healing touch" policy to assuage the people's hurt sentiments—this not only had Sonia Gandhi's support, but also Prime Minister Atal Bihari Vajpayee's. Had she not agreed to the Mufti rule, Governor's rule would have been re-imposed in Kashmir .

SONIA ATTACKS BJP AFTER GODHRA

Sonia was aggressive and led the Opposition in Gujarat when the Godhra carnage took place. What transpired was, on February 27, 2002, a trainload of Hindu volunteers, known as *karsevaks*, mostly belonging to the BJP, were returning to Gujarat from Ayodhya in Uttar Pradesh (where anti-Muslim riots had taken place in 1992 after the demolition of the Babri Masjid). These *karsevaks* had gone to put pressure to construct the Ram temple. Just after dawn, when the train left Godhra in Gujarat, a number of Muslim attackers hurled bottles of petrol inside the coaches, setting them alight. Nearly 67 charred bodies were found on the train. In retaliation, Hindu mobs targeted Muslim neighbourhoods. They attacked the residents, raped women and burnt families alive. The government was slow to act; as a result, at least 300 people, most of whom were Muslims, were killed in the riots within ten days. Sonia, being the main Opposition leader, visited hospitals and relief camps in Gujarat. She sat in protest, sent emergency supplies and deployed Congress workers to help with the relief operations.

Contrary to expectations, Sonia decided to play the soft *Hindutva* card in Gujarat, putting up less number of Muslim candidates in the 2002 Assembly polls. The election results, however, went in favour of Chief Minister Narendra Modi, who returned to power triumphantly. In his campaign, he bashed Pakistani President General Musharraf, whom he called "Mia Musharraf", and asked his constituents to ensure the general's efforts to create tension on the border were defeated. The BJP got 124 seats, as compared to the Congress tally of 51. After the 2002 Assembly polls, Modi became an icon of *Hindutva*; he continues to rule Gujarat uninterruptedly since the past ten years. He won a third term in 2012—a clear sign that the people of Gujarat appreciated his developmental work. The Congress improved its position, while Modi got two seats less than what he had earlier. After his third-time win, the BJP clamoured to make him the prime ministerial candidate. As for the Congress, it is ready with Rahul Gandhi as its trump card.

Sonia considers her term as LOP "eventful and educative". She claims that the Congress party was a constructive and responsible Opposition, much more than the BJP was when it sat in Opposition. "We extended our support to the government on major political, economic and foreign policy issues when we felt that it was in the national interest. I have been criticised by some of my own colleagues for this approach but I stuck to my position. We extended full support to the government on its peace initiatives in J&K and with Pakistan. I was in regular touch with the Prime Minister on many issues like drought relief, PDS (public distribution system), employment guarantee and security in the North-east. But I hardly received any response from the PM. We took a firm and principled stand against sending Indian troops to Iraq and it is this that forced the government not to send troops when it had already decided to do so."[28]

SONIA EMERGES SUPREME

Under the BJP rule, the economy seemed to prosper, and by 2004, Vajpayee was claiming credit for turning the economy around. True, big business was booming and India was advancing technologically, but millions of rural Indians living in poverty were not benefiting from the BJP's reforms. However, Vajpayee was so confidant that the voters were behind him that he called for polls six months ahead of the end of his five-year term.

The NDA began a campaign called "India Shining", projecting its achievements of the past six years, but this message boomeranged unexpectedly. The campaign and the money which the ruling coalition spent stunned the Congress; it had no hopes of matching it. The Congress' mood during the elections was low. There was demoralisation among the ranks due to poll reverses in some Assembly elections. The BJP, on the other hand, was upbeat. The NDA was convinced that it would return to power and did not take the Congress seriously. Almost all pre-poll surveys predicted a victory for the NDA, further lulling the BJP into a sense of security. In addition, Vajpayee won credit as a good statesman when India won the Kargil War. The Congress, on its part, made the then Defence Minister George Fernandes a target over the "Coffin-gate" scam and turned it into an election issue.

Sonia Gandhi went back to her mother-in-law's strategy of wooing the common man and engaged a prominent advertising agency, Leo Burnett. It coined the slogan: "Congress ke haath aam aadmi ke saath" (The Congress' hand is with the common man). The common man depicted as the skinny basket-carrying mango man (the aam admi) became the mascot of the election campaign. The Congress identified many issues pertaining to the woes of the ordinary citizen. This clicked instead of the "India Shining" hype of the BJP.

The most effective strategy was Sonia's efforts to form the UPA coalition. It was at the Shimla Conclave of the Congress in 2003 that she signalled that the party was ready to work within a coalition—a major departure for a party used to having a free hand in running the country. Sonia and the Congress realized that the party alone would not be able to form the government after the 2004 elections. Taking a leaf from the success of Congress coalitions in some states like Maharashtra, in a swift change of strategy, the party decided to look for coalition partners. Making a significant policy statement at the conclusion of the party's three-day meeting on July 9, Sonia Gandhi said: "Taking into account the present political scenario, the Congress would be prepared to enter into appropriate electoral coalition arrangements with secular parties on the basis of mutual understanding but without compromising its basic ideologies."[29]

She explained that the strategy shift was necessary to defeat the BJP and its allies, which were bent upon destroying Hinduism and its liberal tenets. She asserted that no sacrifice would be too great to ensure their defeat in the 2004 polls. The coalition offer came with a rider: she must be accepted as the leader. The Shimla declaration was unlike those of earlier party conclaves at Pachmarhi, Bangalore and Mount Abu, where the preference was to strive to regain power on its own and enter into alliances only when absolutely necessary.

Sonia began the exercise much earlier when she invited a few prospective allies to her house for dinner to sound them out on February 16, 2003. This group became larger when other smaller parties also agreed to join. Sonia forged alliances with the Left parties, the Dravida Munnetra Kazhagam (DMK), the Nationalist Congress Party (NCP), the Rashtriya Janata Dal (RJD) and other smaller parties. She personally approached most of the regional parties and the Left, forming a loose coalition which ultimately provided the required arithmetic. As a new experiment, Sonia set up a war room to monitor the poll exercise round the clock. From December 23, 2003, she travelled nearly 30,000 miles, addressing a total of 148 rallies. She also spoke at some joint rallies along with her allies. Ambika Soni recalls, 'In the 2004 elections, we fought as Congress and got 144 seats, but the emergence of other secular groups and parties made her go that extra mile and reach out to people like Ram Vilas Paswan and Lalu Prasad Yadav (other regional party leaders). We did not fight the elections with them but we formed the UPA. It was Sonia Gandhi's idea to have a secular polity. It was important that the Congress led the front in order to form a larger group.'* Allying with the Left was a masterstroke, as it won an unprecedented 62 seats in that election, becoming the single largest block after the Congress and the BJP.

Gandhi brought in her son Rahul, who contested from Amethi and won the seat, sending the signal that the dynasty would continue. The Gandhi family mostly conducted the campaign; the other leaders were not given a prominent role. Though a few film stars were drafted to attract the crowds. Sonia travelled about 70,000 kilometres in a gruelling campaign comprising of rallies and road shows. The month-long campaign ended on May 10, 2004. She had been campaigning relentlessly for nearly five months.

SONIA DECLINES TO BE PM

The number 13 proved to be lucky for Sonia Gandhi and the Congress when the poll results began pouring in on May 13, 2004. To everyone's surprise, including the Congress, the UPA coalition got 278 seats, and was poised to form the government. The Congress itself bagged 145 seats, emerging as the single largest party. The BJP followed closely behind with 136 seats. There was jubilation in the Congress headquarters as several Congressmen visited Gandhi's house to congratulate her on her success. Then the question of prime ministership arose. The Congress had not projected anyone as its candidate since Sonia did not want her foreign origin to become an issue. She was elected the leader of the Congress Parliamentary Party (CPP) on May 15. The next day the allies met at her residence and asked her to lead the new coalition government—the United Progressive Alliance (UPA). The party, as well as the coalition partners and the Opposition, assumed that Sonia would be the prime minister.

Two days later I witnessed the drama at 10 Janpath. A number of scribes, including myself, arrived at her residence where all the newly elected MPs had been invited to assemble. We waited for about four hours in the evening but there was no sign of Gandhi or the top Congress echelon. The gathered MPs were getting restless amid reports that Gandhi was not going to become the prime minister. The alliance party leaders who had been invited to her residence were also trying to persuade her to change her mind. After four hours, Manmohan Singh came out and read a two-line statement, informing them that Sonia Gandhi would call on President Kalam the next day. The MPs dispersed with doubts lingering in their minds.

At the *Hindustan Times* Conclave held six months later, Sonia reiterated that she had already decided from the beginning that she would never occupy that chair in any event. She had even spoken to her children regarding this. Priyanka later told a television interviewer, "Rahul and I would have these discussions with her where we would say: 'Why don't you just say so now?' But she didn't…"[30]

The next day, 18 May, all the Congress MPs assembled in the Central Hall of Parliament to elect their leader. By this time it was known that Gandhi was not going to be the prime minister. Those of us who were covering the meeting saw that the MPs were not very enthusiastic: they were not sure how the new government would function without Sonia Gandhi. In the evening, at the appointed time, Sonia arrived with Manmohan Singh. Her children, Rahul and Priyanka, and son-in-law Robert Vadra were also there, which was unusual, considering the CPP meeting was only meant for MPs. The leaders watched her anxiously until she opened a small piece of paper and read out a statement. In a nutshell, she said: "... as I have often stated, the post of the prime minister is not my aim. I was always certain that if ever I found myself in the position that I am today, I would follow my own inner voice. Today, that voice tells me I must humbly decline this post."[31] There was a lot of commotion and several MPs urged her with tears in their eyes to reconsider her decision, but she refused to do so. Then the CPP amended its constitution, making her its chairperson and giving her the power to appoint someone as the prime ministerial candidate. This was to ensure that Sonia retained all the powers and the prime minister was only appointed, not elected. She chose Manmohan Singh. On May 19, the duo emerged from the Rashtrapati Bhavan and Singh announced that the President of India had invited him to form the government.

Meanwhile, the BJP, smarting from the humiliation of defeat, launched a campaign against Gandhi. It made it clear that if Sonia became the prime minister, she would have to pay a very heavy price, as it would launch an attack, beginning with a boycott of the swearing-in ceremony. Sushma Swaraj led the campaign, with other BJP leaders like Uma Bharti joining the chorus. They started chanting "Rome Raj"—referring to Sonia's Italian origin. Sushma threatened that if Sonia were to become the prime minister she would go into mourning for the country. She declared, "The day she takes oath, I will tonsure my head (a ritual associated with widows), put on white clothes (widows in India wear white), sleep on the floor and eat only bhuna *chana* (roasted chickpeas)."[32]

Dr. Subramanian Swamy also launched his own campaign against Sonia becoming prime minister. He had fallen out with her after the 1999 fiasco of pulling down the Vajpayee government. He claimed that in his petition to President Kalam, he had pointed out that according to the Italian government rules, Sonia could still have her Italian passport anytime she wanted, therefore, she should not be sworn in. President Kalam has set the record straight in his book titled *Turning Points: A Journey Through Challenges*. He recalls "that had Gandhi staked a claim herself he would have appointed her as it was the only 'constitutionally tenable' option available to him." Kalam further adds in the book: "During this time there were many political leaders who came to meet me to request me not to succumb to any pressure and appoint Mrs. Gandhi as the Prime Minister, a request that would not have been constitutionally tenable. If she had made any claim for herself, I would have had no option but to appoint her."[33]

Sonia realised that the Opposition would raise the twin issues of her foreign origin and Bofors after she became the prime minister and she did not want to spend her entire term defending herself. Inder Malhotra affirms, 'She was afraid of the BJP propaganda. She was aware of the implications. In 2009, when the party came back to power, she had found the perfect equation. Look at her advantage! Whatever goes right, the party gets the credit. Whatever goes wrong is to the government's discredit.'*

Ultimately, the UPA coalition government was formed with the DMK, PDP, NCP, and other smaller parties; the Left supported it from outside. External support was also promised by several minor parties that were not members of any coalition: the Samajwadi Party (39), Bahujan Samaj Party (19), Marumalarchi Dravida Munnetra Kazhagam (4) and Janata Dal (Secular) (3). Nevertheless, these parties were not a part of the government. The UPA thus had 335 MPs out of 543 supporting it at the time of its formation. Sonia Gandhi scored a mark when senior leaders like DMK chief Karunanidhi and the Left stalwarts H.S. Surjeet and Jyoti Basu were willing to accept her leadership of the UPA.

Gandhi's decision not to become prime minister was a masterstroke which dumbfounded the BJP. Today there are some who feel that the BJP should have allowed Gandhi to take responsibility instead of becoming the power behind the throne. Now she is not accountable to anyone, while the entire power remains with her. Prime Minister Manmohan Singh holds the position but he has to look to the party president to ratify each of his actions. This experiment of power without responsibility has not proved to be beneficial to the country over these nine years of UPA rule. Many critics claim that the scams and the lack of governance are partly due to this anomaly.

WHY MANMOHAN SINGH?

Did Sonia decide against becoming the prime minister right from the beginning or did she change her mind? There were doubts because the letters of support for staking claim to form the government were first taken in her name. There were no consultations with the allies about appointing someone else as the prime minister as it was presumed she would hold the post. The UPA had to wait for one more day to change the letters in her name to that of the Congress Party. But Gandhi claimed in an interview to a TV channel: "I have answered this question. I've answered it with my actions. In 1991, when my husband was assassinated, the Congress Party asked me to take his place. It would have been easy for me to become Congress President, and as you know, the Congress then formed the government. But I refused all offers to join politics. When I did join, I did it only because I felt that the party my husband, my mother-in-law and so many members of his family had given their lives to was becoming weak. And because of this, communal and divisive forces were on the ascendant. At that time, when there was no question of becoming prime minister, I decided that it was cowardice for me to sit back and stay at home. I owed it to the family I married into to do whatever I could. It is hard for some people to understand why anyone would join politics except to become prime minister. But that's not why I joined. I joined because I couldn't have faced my own conscience otherwise."[34] Gandhi's critics are not fully convinced by this answer. They wonder why she entered politics and allowed her son to join politics when she did not want her husband Rajiv Gandhi to do so in 1980.

The citizens of the country appreciated Sonia, who had renounced her crown twice (1991 and 2004) and missed it narrowly once (1999). They now saw her in a different light. The foreign media went gaga about her renunciation. But her critics claim that actually she did not renounce anything except the position and emerged much stronger and more powerful after this decision. At the end of the day, she knew the last word would be hers on every matter in the government and the party. Even the UPA coalition partners know where the actual power lies.

Sonia chose Singh because she felt comfortable working with him. She also trusted him as the Leader of the Opposition in the Rajya Sabha during the NDA regime. Secondly, he had a clean image and was internationally known—the very reasons why Rao chose him as his finance minister in 1991.

Thirdly, Singh did not have a political base; therefore he would not challenge her or her family. He was completely dependent on the Gandhis for his position. He was a bureaucrat who knew the workings of administration thoroughly. Above all, he was fully aware that his continuance depended entirely on her. If she had appointed him prime minister, she could also remove him any time she chose. All she had to do was to send a signal to the Congress, and her sycophants would do the rest.

Sonia told a TV interviewer: "Ours [she and Manmohan Singh] is a relationship of mutual trust.... We are not competitors. We work together."[35] The two leaders did work together but Manmohan Singh was no more than a CEO, while Sonia Gandhi was the proprietor. *The Washington Post* notes, "In him [Singh] she saw not only the perfect figurehead for her government but also a man of unquestioning loyalty, party insiders say, someone she could both trust and control."[36] He would do nothing that would annoy her. Their division of labour was quite clear: he would run the government while she would deal with the party and the allies and look after the complete political management. There were several issues which needed political sagacity like the disinvestment of Public Sector Undertakings and the second-generation economic reforms. Singh did not have to tackle the allies—that was Sonia's job. When the Indo-US nuclear deal was to be clinched, he could only manage with the support of Sonia Gandhi and her son Rahul. The Congress took a risk when the Left parties pulled out their support over the nuclear deal. It was Sonia who talked to every partner and succeeded in mobilising support so that the government survived.

Singh had to agree to all the populist schemes that the Sonia Gandhi-headed National Advisory Council (NAC) came up with, despite his disinclination. This includes the Right to Information Act, the Right to Education Act, the Mahatma Gandhi National Rural Employment Guarantee Act (MGNREGA) and the Food Security Bill, among others. During UPA-I, when the DMK protested against disinvestment in the Neyveli Lignite Corporation, Singh had to abandon the idea to please the ally. All appointments of governors, CBI directors, Intelligence Bureau chiefs, secretaries (Cabinet, Finance, Foreign, Home and Principal), had to be made with Gandhi's concurrence.

However, many analysts point out that this dual power centre worked in UPA-I, but when the coalition came back to power in 2009, it did not do so well. The cohesiveness was not visible in the second term since the government was unable to face a series of scams, although most of them had occurred during UPA-I. Singh came across as a weak prime minister who presided over a corrupt regime and closed his eyes while his ministers were looting the country. The main problem was that the prime minister was accountable, whereas Sonia Gandhi, who was the "super PM", had all the power. She also distanced herself and the Congress Party from any decision that got flak from the public or the Opposition. The price rise, inflation and other embarrassing issues were left to the government to deal with. Sonia wrote letters to the prime minister (98 in the first four years) on various issues, sometimes differing from the government's viewpoint.

Secondly, even the Congress ministers, particularly senior ministers like Arjun Singh, Pranab Mukherjee, Natwar Singh, P. Chidambaram, and some junior ministers close to Sonia Gandhi, made it evident that they owed their position to Sonia Gandhi, not Mr. Singh. This was because when the Cabinet list was drawn up, the calls to the ministers went from Sonia, not from the prime minister. Similarly, the decision to sack a minister was taken by her, rather than Singh, be it Natwar Singh over the Volcker Report; Shashi Tharoor for his alleged involvement in some financial irregularities in the cricket match scam; or A. Raja of the DMK over the telecom spectrum allocation in the 2G scam. Even in foreign policy matters, when Prime Minister Manmohan Singh took the initiative to sign a joint statement with his Pakistani counterpart at Sharm-el-Sheikh in July 2009, the party conveniently distanced itself, embarrassing Singh publicly. He was also in no position to exert his authority with his Cabinet colleagues from other parties like Sharad Pawar (NCP) Lalu Prasad Yadav (RJD) or the DMK ministers. Each of them became autonomous in their functioning.

As for pushing economic reforms, Singh could not do much during his first term since the Left parties, and sometimes even the DMK, put a spoke in the wheel. During his second term, it was the Trinamool Congress (TMC) led by Mamata Banerjee that opposed the reforms. With such coalition compulsions, Singh could not implement much of the second-generation reforms. These were some behind-the-scene challenges which rendered the prime minister ineffectual.

India's growth rate of 9%, which Singh took full credit for, fell to 5% in 2013, further weakening his image. While he was eager to take credit for the high growth, he was not willing to take the blame for the low growth, spinning a theory that it was because of the international situation. His popularity graph began to dip internationally. The prestigious *Time* magazine portrayed him as an underachiever in its July 12, 2012 issue. Similar sentiments were echoed in the September 3, 2012, *Washington Post* article. Perhaps peeved by the criticism, Singh began to persuade Sonia and Rahul Gandhi to accept the reforms. They acquiesced and openly supported his bold measures. Sonia also went out of her way to back Foreign Direct Investment (FDI) in multi-brand retail, and even mobilised the support of other parties in Parliament in December 2012. Subsequently, she supported Singh in the petrol and diesel price hike, which both the UPA allies and the Opposition were against. His crowning moment came during the Jaipur AICC session when the party endorsed the reforms and ended the debate on the issue once and for all.

Carnegie scholar Ashley Tellis is not sure why the arrangement did not work in UPA-II. 'On the prime minister's part, there is an unwillingness to take tough decisions. But has Gandhi restrained him in any way? I am willing to be convinced that she has not formally restrained him in the second term. She has a certain vision about what makes the Congress succeed. Singh, due to his temperament and his being an economist, has not been comfortable with some of her decisions. However, even when he thinks populist schemes like the MGNREGA are not feasible, he finds it difficult to oppose them. But why did he not confront his party men and tell them that these schemes are untenable?' he wonders.* There are others who think the constraints equally stem from his own reticence. If there was someone else with a stronger political base and more confidence, he could have pushed for the economic reforms.

As Manmohan Singh's term is coming to an end, even some Congress leaders like Digvijay Singh have raised questions about the success of this dual power centre and demanded that in future it should be vested in one individual. His real intention was to make sure that when Rahul Gandhi became the prime minister, he would have all the powers. Even some of the scams are being attributed to this dual power centre.

SONIA HEADS NAC

Setting up the National Advisory Council and heading it was yet another masterstroke by Sonia, as this became the instrument through which she could implement her populist schemes. As the NAC chief, she had a Cabinet rank, and through this institutional framework, she imposed her schemes on the government. Gandhi filled this super body with experts from NGOs, civil society and social scientists. Since this panel is not comprised of UPA members, it is not beholden to the government and functions independently.

She took the NAC seriously, using it to translate her projects into policy implementation. Once the NAC sent its report, the government could suggest some modifications, but ultimately it had to by and large agree with Sonia's pet schemes: the Right to Information Act, the Food Security Bill and MGNREGA, among others. Within one year of the UPA-I coming to power, the Right to Information Act was passed. This instrument enabled many ordinary citizens to obtain the information they sought. When the government felt too much information, that too, classified documents, was filtering out, and suggested amendments, she indirectly made it clear that she would not welcome them.

Another important gift of the NAC was the Mahatma Gandhi National Rural Employment Guarantee Act (MGNREGA), which guarantees 100 days of work to jobless agricultural labourers. This is the flagship programme of the government which has brought benefits to the poor, despite its critics' claims that there is more abuse than use. They point out the increasing number of farmers' suicides in rural areas and the fact that the scheme is not free of corruption. Of late, however, there are criticisms about the scheme and also some leakages.

The third scheme, the Food Security Bill, is meant to ensure adequate quantity of food to those below the poverty line. Aimed at wooing the poor, this would be Sonia's trump card and she is keen to get it implemented before the 2014 elections. The Land Acquisition Bill and the Communal Harmony Bill are other populist measures which are yet to be passed by Parliament. All these left-of-centre policies are being implemented through the NAC, which acts as a super government.

RESIGNATION OVER CONTROVERSY

Sonia has never lost an opportunity to take on the Opposition, and when it came to personal vilification campaigns, she was all the more assertive and aggressive. It was evident from the way she handled her foreign origin issue or took on Pawar and Sangma when they raised it within the Congress.

The NAC was disbanded on March 31, 2006, and was revived after the Congress returned to power in 2009. Since then, its role has only grown. It continues to formulate bills for the government, including the controversial Communal Violence Bill and the Food Security Bill.

In 2006 Sonia ran into another controversy; this time it was about her holding the position of the chairperson of the NAC. As per Article 102 (1) (A) of the Indian Constitution, an MP or an MLA is barred from holding any office of profit under the Government of India or any state government other than an office declared by Parliament by law as not disqualifying its holder. Sonia was an MP and the NAC chief, which had not been exempted by Parliament. On March 25, she dropped a bombshell by resigning from the NAC as well as the Lok Sabha, responding to her "call of conscience".

The controversy started when actress-turned-politician Jaya Bachchan, the wife of superstar Amitabh Bachchan, a one-time close friend of the Gandhis, was disqualified from the Rajya Sabha on the grounds that she was the chairperson of the UP Film Development Corporation. About 62 other MPs were clubbed in the same category of holding an office of profit. Although there were rumours that Sonia was behind Jaya's disqualification, as the Bachchans and the Gandhis had fallen out with each other, Sonia denied these allegations. Had Jaya not been disqualified by the Congress' manipulations, Sonia too would have escaped, but the episode backfired on her. The NDA and Samajwadi Party chief Mulayam Singh Yadav did not let go of this opportunity to attack Sonia Gandhi. While some legal experts held that the NAC was not an office of profit, the Opposition insisted otherwise.

The Indian Express wrote on 23rd March: "With one swift stroke Sonia Gandhi has turned the tables on her opponents. By resigning from the Lok Sabha and the chairmanship of the NAC, she has made the best of the bargain."[37] The BJP-led Opposition was in the process of urging the President of India to disqualify Gandhi since she was holding an "office of profit" by being the NAC chief. She chose her moment well and resigned on the day the BJP was proposing to appeal to the president. Gandhi issued a statement to explain herself: "In the last few days, some opposition parties are trying to create an impression that the Congress and the United Progressive Alliance are using Parliament and the government only to protect me. This has hurt me very much. I have stated earlier also that I am in politics and public life not for my selfish ends. I have taken a pledge to serve the people of the country and protect secular ideals. So, in keeping with my public life and political principles and according to my belief, I resign as member of the Lok Sabha and chairperson of the National Advisory Council. I have full faith that brothers and sisters of Rae Bareilly and the whole nation will understand this feeling of mine."[38] Two days later, the *International Herald Tribune* wrote: "Political martyr or cunning strategist? The fallout from Sonia Gandhi's unexpected resignation from Parliament has concentrated India's attention once again on the elusive head of its governing political dynasty."[39]

Yet again, the party was taken by surprise, as Gandhi took the decision entirely on her own, after consulting her children. Within three months, Sonia contested the by-election from Rae Bareilly and won with a 4,17,888 margin of votes, creating a record. The BJP-led Opposition was silenced by this smart move. The Manmohan Singh government tried to bring an ordinance to protect her but she declined. Gandhi told a TV interviewer later: "Because of me, the government found itself in a very awkward position, and I didn't like that feeling."[40] Much later, the government introduced a bill to exempt 56 posts, including the chairpersonship of the NAC, from being considered as office of profit.

VOLCKER REPORT

Within the first two years of UPA-I, Sonia and the Congress faced another embarrassment when the Volcker Committee—set up by the United Nations to enquire into irregularities in the Oil-for-Food Programme—released its report. It made pubic a list of corporations and politicians across the world that had benefitted from an elaborate "oil-for-food" scam devised by the late Iraqi dictator Saddam Hussein.

The Volcker Committee named K. Natwar Singh (who resigned from the Manmohan Singh Cabinet on December 6), the Congress party and several Indian companies, as beneficiaries of the scheme. Natwar Singh put up a stout defence but Sonia decided to let this close Gandhi–Nehru loyalist, who had served three generations of the family, go. He had worked hard to build up Sonia Gandhi internationally. Natwar's exit shocked the party because it exposed Sonia's ruthlessness. She was unforgiving when she spoke to an interviewer on NDTV: "As it became clearer that it was true that my colleague had misused the name of the party in some ways, I felt extremely betrayed.... He was a colleague in whom I had placed trust..."[41] Thus ended the Natwar saga.

SONIA PLAYS A ROLE IN PRESIDENTIAL ELECTIONS

The next important thing on Gandhi's agenda was to select the Congress nominee for President of India. She could do this not once but twice—in 2007 and 2012. Although a figurehead, the President's post is prestigious and so far the ruling party has had an upper hand in getting its candidate installed at the Rashtrapati Bhavan. In July 2007, before the presidential elections were held, the political atmosphere became murky and vicious, with different political players pulling in different directions. Sonia's first choice was Home Minister Shivraj Patil, who has been loyal to her and taught her a lot about Parliament, as he was the former Speaker. Patil's image was clean and he had no skeletons in his cupboard. There were several other hopefuls like former Maharashtra Chief Minister Sushilkumar Shinde and ex-Union Minister Karan Singh. The Left parties had first suggested the name of External Affairs Minister Pranab Mukherjee, but Sonia shot it down by asking, "Who would run the government?" It was clear that she did not trust him. While Sonia staunchly supported Shivraj Patil, the Left parties opposed his name on the grounds that he was not secular and was a disciple of Sai Baba of Puttaparthi. When there was no consensus on any name during the Coordination Committee meeting, CPI veteran A.B. Bardhan suddenly suggested, "Why not a woman?" Sonia saw an opportunity: to get the credit for installing the first woman President at Raisina Hill. She immediately agreed to select a woman presidential nominee. So, Rajasthan Governor Pratibha Patil was chosen instead of Shivraj Patil—Gandhi did not think twice before switching one Patil for the other. The Opposition was taken aback when Sonia sprang this surprise. The BJP was not sure how to oppose a woman candidate; therefore, it dug up whatever dirt it could find on Pratibha Patil, including irregularities in the names of the educational institutions she had attended. While Sonia and the Left touted the gender advantage, the BJP made personal attacks on the presidential candidate. Never before had a presidential election became so sordid, but ultimately Patil was elected, defeating the Opposition-supported Bhairon Singh Shekhawat, the sitting Vice-President. A month later, Sonia also managed to get Congress nominee Hamid Ansari elected as the Vice-President of India.

When the country chose the President in 2012, Sonia managed to get Congress nominee Pranab Mukherjee into the highest office. Mukherjee was a heavy weight and the Congress was able to split the ranks of the Opposition when the Shiv Sena, JD(U) and other parties voted for

Mukherjee in view of his long-standing political connections. As expected, the UPA candidate won the presidential race with a huge margin, defeating his rival, former Speaker P.A. Sangma. In a bitterly contested election, Mukherjee secured a value vote of 713,763, well beyond the half-way mark of 525,140 in an electoral college of over 10.5 lakh votes. Sangma could only secure a vote value of 315,987. While UPA ally and Trinamool Congress chief Mamata Banerjee did not support Mukherjee initially, she later fell in line and voted for him. In 2012, Ansari was re-elected as Vice-President for the second time, clearly demonstrating that Sonia had the upper hand.

THE INDO-US NUCLEAR BILL

Sonia showed that she is not averse to risk-taking. Her gamble during the last few days of the nuclear bill's passage in 2008 highlighted the fact that she was willing to even risk the survival of the government. Since 2005, most of the government's time was taken up by the controversial Indo-US nuclear deal. It took three years and several rounds of persuasion to get it passed. The Left parties and the Samajwadi Party were opposing it due to what they perceived as the UPA's pro-US leanings. Prime Minister Singh held that India needed energy; nuclear energy was the cleanest; the country was getting access to advanced scientific knowledge; and the deal would end the nuclear isolation imposed over India after the 1998 Pokhran II nuclear blasts. India's neighbours, China and Pakistan, were against the deal, but the then US President George W. Bush stood firm in his resolve to make the nuclear agreement happen. The politics at play was that Washington was trying to check the rise of China in the region by encouraging India's rise.

Several rounds of debate and defence by the government did not convince those who were opposing it. Even the BJP had reservations on the bill. When the prime minister stood by his commitment to the deal and was even willing to resign, Sonia came to the rescue. She made a forceful argument in its favour by pointing out its benefits at the Congress Parliamentary Party meeting in August 2007. Soon Rahul Gandhi also came out and expressed his full support. With the Gandhi family on board, the Congress Party became united on the issue.

But Sonia was unable to convince her Left allies, who insisted on abandoning the bill. Several meetings took place, but in vain. The Left had made up its mind to pull out right from the beginning. It did not support the government on the nuclear bill in the Lok Sabha on July 22, 2008, but to its surprise the government did not fall. The Left made its own calculations and in the next Lok Sabha polls in 2009, the communists took a risk. The Congress was resigned and looked around to replace the Left Front's 64 votes. The Samajwadi Party came to its rescue finally and the UPA survived. The very same Mulayam Singh—a staunch ally of the Left parties and the man who stopped Sonia Gandhi from becoming the prime minister in 1999—influenced by his close aide Amar Singh and foreign-educated son Akhilesh Yadav, switched sides at the last minute to bail out the Manmohan Singh government. While the Congress promoted the growing Indo-US ties, it also balanced the Moscow–New Delhi relationship by signing an agreement with Russian President Medvedev to build four civilian nuclear reactors in India.

UPA WINS A SECOND TERM

Sonia surprised the party and the country once again when the 2009 Lok Sabha elections were round the corner. Everyone expected her to project her son Rahul as the prime ministerial candidate, but she made it clear that Manmohan Singh would be the prime minister again if the party came back to power. Obviously the Gandhi family had discussed the issue. With the poll prospects not looking too bright, she probably did not want to expose Rahul Gandhi. Perhaps she thought that this was not the right time for him to take over, or Rahul himself had not shown any inclination to do so. Given the muddled and uncertain political environment, Gandhi did not want to risk tying him to a Congress Party setback in the elections. However, the two main campaigners were Sonia and Rahul. They crisscrossed the country and addressed several meetings. Her confidence in Singh also reflected the fact that she had enough faith that the prime minister would not put up any resistance to a Singh–Rahul transition in the future. Ambika Soni points out that 'at the press conference where the party's manifesto was being released, when Sonia showed the manifesto covering her face and revealing only Manmohan Singh's face, it put an end to all the whispering that she and Singh were not getting along.'* She was trying to imply that Manmohan Singh would be the prime minister if the party came back to power. This seemed to have paid dividends as the Congress won 206 seats. There are some who give credit to Singh for this increase since his appeal to the middle class continued.

In the election campaign, Sonia Gandhi dwelt on three broad issues: safeguarding secularism, ensuring inclusive economic growth and fighting terror. She highlighted the UPA's economic achievements, including the farm loan waiver scheme. Her only foreign policy statement (besides Pakistan) was to laud the Indo-US nuclear deal. She attacked Pakistan and said that Pakistan-sponsored terrorism should end. The campaign, on the whole, did not have any controversial issue. The "aam admi" continued to be the Congress mascot.

The UPA came back to power in 2009, winning 205 seats—an increase of 56 seats from 2004, much to the Congress' surprise. As a US embassy telegram from New Delhi reveals, "Even the party's internal polling going into the final weekend only showed a range of 160–180 seats.... The BJP's attack on Singh as the lapdog of Congress Party President Sonia Gandhi failed to resonate."[42] The BJP finished second; it was clear that in the Manmohan Singh vs. L.K. Advani contest, the people had chosen Singh. The voters decimated the Left Front. In 2004, the Left combine won 64 seats, as compared to the 20 in 2009.

The telegram concluded: "The overwhelming victory for the Congress Party represents the best result the US could have anticipated. With approximately 200 seats, the victory is a clear mandate for the leadership of Manmohan Singh and Sonia Gandhi, which has been very friendly towards the US. And now that it appears the shorn Left Front parties will not be in the coalition, those with the most virulent anti-US attitude in India will no longer hold a veto over Indian government policy."[43]

THE UPA'S SECOND TERM

While the Manmohan Singh government was able to show some results in its first term, UPA-II has not gone too well, although it is in its last leg of the second term. Two of its big allies—the DMK and the TMC—parted company, reducing the UPA to a minority in its fourth year. The regime's uncertainty over the passage of key economic legislations and decisions is perceived as weakness. It faces tough challenges in the run up to 2014. Hopping from crisis to crisis, UPA-II comes across as a helpless government, in stark contrast to UPA-I. Adding to its discomfiture is the slide in the growth rate, rising prices, food inflation and falling image of the country for overselling itself abroad. The overall economic situation is also cause for concern since there has been less tax collections. The prime minister, who has touted his clean image all these years, is now facing scam after scam: 2G, CWG and Coalgate—all originating from the UPA's first term.

The coalition is also not cohesive, with the DMK unhappy after its minister Raja and chief Karunanidhi's daughter Kanimozhi were sent to jail over the 2G scam. Since then, the government had been struggling to find the numbers on the floor of the House to push through the bill on foreign direct investment (FDI) in multi-brand retail. It had to strike a bargain with the regional Samajwadi Party and Bahujan Samaj Party to get their votes. West Bengal Chief Minister Mamata Banerjee broke away, giving an excuse about the FDI in retail, whereas the real reason was that the Congress had not obliged her with a financial package for her state.

Gandhian Anna Hazare and Yoga guru Baba Ramdev hogged the limelight in 2011 by launching an anti-corruption movement which caught the imagination of the people. They wanted a strong Lokpal (independent body) to investigate various corruption cases but the Jan Lokpal Bill is still in Parliament. Baba Ramdev also demanded the repatriation of black money deposited abroad. The government mishandled the movement while Sonia Gandhi had gone overseas for surgery. The movement fizzled out; Anna's team also split, with Arvind Kejriwal forming his own political outfit. However, the bigger problem was to pacify middle-class outrage, which later took the form of flash crowds after the Delhi gang rape incident of a 23-year-old medical student. Angry youth laid siege to Raisina Hill, where the government offices are located, and demanded justice. Even the promise of speedy justice and harsh punishment to the culprits did not pacify them. Initially, the government made the mistake of not responding to the pubic anger in a befitting manner. The Congress Party has realized the importance of growing middle-class concerns and finally decided to address the issue during its AICC session in Jaipur on 20 January, 2013.

The opposition parties are of the opinion that the government has performed miserably in the last four years. Even some of its allies have reservations. The BJP-led Opposition was up in arms over the Coalgate scandal. It alleged that the government had allocated 142 national coal blocks to state-run and private companies without going in for competitive bidding. The Opposition demanded that the PM should resign since he was the coal minister for five years during the UPA's eight-year rule.

Prime Minister Singh has gradually lost his image. Today the impression is that he has presided over a corrupt regime and did nothing to control his ministers. He had to let go of Railway Minister Pawan Kumar Bansal and Law Minister Ashwani Kumar for irregularities. There are more than 11 vacancies in his Cabinet after the TMC and the DMK ministers quit.

The division of power between Sonia and Singh seems to have failed in UPA-II. His future seems bleak since he might not be projected as the prime ministerial candidate in the 2014 elections. Sonia Gandhi is aware that it is going to be an uphill task to get the UPA re-elected for the third time in 2014 although the party is ruling in 14 states now.

The odd thing is that the party has not accepted any responsibility for the failures of the government. Sonia wants to keep the party aloof from its shortcomings. Moreover, the UPA seems to lack unity. Even when it came to pushing the second-generation economic reforms, there were divided opinions within the party. Since this issue was finally settled at the Jaipur AICC, there is no going back on the reforms now. Then there is the strange fact that the prime minister is not involved in the political management of the allies or the Opposition, leaving it to Sonia Gandhi.

A LOOK AT UPA-II'S ACHIEVEMENTS

Sonia was jubilant when the Rajya Sabha passed the controversial Women's Reservation Bill in 2010. She remained committed to getting the bill passed despite resistance from some opposition parties and finally managed to persuade the BJP and the Left parties to support it.

Gandhi has been vocal about reservation for women in legislatures. The bill ensures 33% reservation to women in Parliament, as against the current 10%. This percentage has remained unchanged since Independence and the bill has been pending since 1997. Several attempts have been made to introduce it but political parties like the Samajwadi Party, Rashtriya Janata Dal and Janata Dal (United) are not fully convinced that the reservation quota needs to be increased; almost all parties are divided on the issue. The BJP, the Congress, the AIADMK, the Telugu Desam Party and the Left Front are supporting the bill, but a consensus has yet to be reached in the Lok Sabha.

Another achievement is that the Congress managed to get its candidate Pranab Mukherjee elected as President by making full use of the division among the Opposition's ranks. Although Sonia did not reveal her hand until the last minute, her choice proved to be good, as even opposition parties like the Shiv Sena voted for Mukherjee, thereby increasing his margin against his opponent, former Speaker P.A. Sangma. The Congress was also able to persuade its ally, the Trinamool Congress (TMC), to come on board at the eleventh hour. TMC chief Mamata Banerjee was supporting former President Abdul Kalam's candidature and was reluctant to support Mukherjee in spite of the fact that he, too, hails from Bengal. But she was brought around.

Sonia also succeeded in getting Vice-President Hamid Ansari elected for another five years. She managed to mobilise votes for his election against the NDA's candidate, Jaswant Singh, who fared poorly. Gandhi played a critical role in the political management of the presidential and vice-presidential elections.

AS LEADER OF THE CONGRESS

While Sonia earned kudos for getting the Congress-led UPA back to power for the second time in 2009, the party organisation needs a lot of attention. She has been elected president for a record fourth time and has led the party for the past sixteen years.

What kind of a political boss is she? Her political secretary Ahmed Patel claims that she never tried to impose herself as a boss. "She is as democratic as our leaders have been in the past. She believes in democracy," he told an interviewer.[44] He also mentioned that when a decision had to be taken, she would discuss the matter with other party leaders and friends as well. She would also talk to general secretaries and to those in charge of the states. According to Patel, she has never cultivated her image as a boss. Generally, she observes protocol and maintains the kind of relationship that must exist between the Congress president and other senior colleagues. He described Sonia Gandhi as a boss who can be a tough taskmaster. "On occasions she has expressed her anger too when a job is not done the way it should be. She expresses her disappointments too."[45]

But on the organisational side, Sonia could not achieve much. In the Hindi heartland, particularly UP and Bihar, the Congress Party is yet to revive since it lacks organisational coherence, as revealed by the Assembly poll results. Sonia and Rahul admitted this after the 2012 UP elections. The party has lost its primacy in Tamil Nadu, UP, Bihar, Orissa, West Bengal, Madhya Pradesh, Chhattisgarh, Goa and Gujarat, where the opposition parties have been ruling for the past decade. Digvijay Singh, the Congress Party's general secretary, contends that it has not slipped back: 'See our results. The Congress has certainly improved its vote share in elections. As far as the states are concerned, we have neither done badly nor better, but Mrs. Gandhi has made honest efforts to improve our national structure. The Congress is basically a mass party, not a cadre-based party. To fight the cadre-based and regional parties like the Left and the BJP, it has to mould itself to the requirements.'* Rahul Gandhi made efforts to make inroads in UP but could not succeed. Digvijay Singh admits, 'We were able to convince the voters that we want a change but we have not convinced them that we have the capacity to form our own government. So the polarisation again took place between the two regional parties (SP and BSP), and the two national parties (Congress and BJP) did not fare well.'*

One reason for this state of affairs could be that second-rung leaders have not emerged in many states. Rahul mentioned this in his speech at the Jaipur AICC. The family dominates the party; there has been no effort to build the leadership as the party chief nominates most chief ministers and state leaders. This is in contrast to the way Nehru functioned: he would deal with several strong state leaders. He was able to function harmoniously with stalwarts like C. Rajagopalachari and B.C. Roy. It was Indira Gandhi who introduced this "nomination culture" in the Congress, and it has been continued by Rajiv and Sonia Gandhi. Unless the states have good leaders, the party organisation cannot be effective.

Added to this is the grass root level growth of the party. There is more and more disconnect between the party and the people, which is one of the reasons why the Congress is losing ground. There is no democracy at the ground level as leaders are thrust from above, with the result, those with money power buy positions, be it district or block level president. When the late Rajiv Gandhi addressed the Congress Centenary Session in Mumbai on 28th December, 1985, he mentioned the power brokers who were thriving in the party and reiterated that he wanted to get rid of them. But the system did not allow him to. Similarly, Rahul Gandhi is now talking of democracy within the party and wants to bring about several changes to give the ordinary worker a chance to rise. He spoke of changes and democratisation in the party but his efforts to do so in the Indian Youth Congress, which he was heading, did not yield results. The National Students' Union of India (NSUI) also faced the same fate. In several states, the idea of inner-party democracy met with stiff resistance. It went against the present culture of the Congress, where the leadership nominated even district level office-bearers. Rahul also attempted to bring corporate culture into the party by recruiting young, bright, foreign-educated men and women. Now that he has become the number two in the party officially, it is to be seen whether he will deliver. Elections are no longer held in the party since a nomination culture has taken its place. The filling up of all posts, including Congress Working Committee members, is now the prerogative of the president.

The highest policy-making body of the Congress, the Parliamentary Board, was done away with in the nineties, while the other top body, the Congress Working Committee, meets infrequently. The CWC has not even analysed the election losses. Sonia announced that there should be at least one CWC meeting every month but gradually the frequency decreased. She appointed several committees to revive the party, but their recommendations have not been implemented, despite the dire need for sweeping changes in the organisation.

As for the decision-making process, a disgruntled Arjun Singh had this to say in an interview: "Earlier, there were many opportunities to contribute to the decisions, and even major decisions of the Congress were taken after going through the process of consultations and people used to accept it. But now this process has fallen into a bit of disarray and when people do not have the feeling that they have contributed to the decision-making process, then they have no hassles in defying it."[46] Although one could dismiss his angry remarks, as he was sidelined, the fact is that only a handful of individuals decide even the most serious issues. The Congress Core Committee that serves as a bridge between the party and the government—consisting of half a dozen people including Sonia Gandhi, Manmohan Singh, Home Minister Sushilkumar Shinde, Defence Minister A.K. Antony and Sonia's political secretary Ahmed Patel—functions as the top decision-making body today, although there is no provision for such an organisation in the party constitution. Ambika Soni explains that the 'Core Committee is not connected to the party constitution because it is part of the coalition and the Congress wants to know what the government is doing. It has nothing to do with the Congress, except for the fact that its president presides over it. The Congress Party is also a constituent of the UPA. All of us have our own respective agendas. The government informs the party of its plans, and the Congress, too, must have a mechanism to interact with the government.'*

Even during the infrequent AICC sessions, only a chosen few are allowed to speak; the other delegates go home disappointed. Overall, the workers have no access to the leaders at these sessions. They can only get a glimpse of them, because they are segregated by barricades. At the Jaipur Chintan Shivir, pride of place was given to the youth delegates, while several old-timers felt left out as they were not part of the 350-odd delegates.

Sonia did try to involve the party leaders in chalking out the future strategy of the Congress at the Pachmarhi, Bangalore, Mount Abu and Shimla conclaves. The latest conclave—held at Jaipur from January 18–20, 2013—called to endorse the resolutions of the Chintan Shivir as a fait accompli, was significant since that was when Sonia Gandhi appointed her son Rahul Gandhi as the vice-president of the party. This ensured the continuance of the dynasty and the family's hold on the Congress Party. It also puts the onus on the young Gandhi to prove his leadership qualities.

No serious effort has been made towards building up the party in the states where it is weak. Even after the disastrous results in the UP Assembly polls in 2007 and 2012, neither the AICC nor the CWC discussed this issue. The same inertia was evident when the party was routed in the Bihar Assembly polls. There is no accountability or responsibility vis-à-vis the poor state of affairs in these states. Yet another important problem is the lack of communication as no one has a clue about what goes on in the minds of the leaders.

But Sonia Gandhi deserves kudos for having united the party. She has three major achievements under her belt. First, she brought a languishing party to power in 2004 and then again in 2009. Secondly, she has kept the flock together this past decade. Thirdly, as political analyst Harish Khare observes, 'She also broke the anti-Congress-ism in other parties, including the Left, to the extent that they joined the UPA coalition. Anti-Congress-ism was not only against the party but also against the Gandhi family.'*

When Sonia took over, the party's fortunes had hit rock-bottom. It had already lost its traditional base of Dalits, Brahmins and minorities. It is indeed a fact that she kept the Congress in power by stringing together a so-called secular coalition. In the past 13 years, the party's vote share has oscillated between 20–29%. In 1998, it was 28%, while the next year it came down to 25%. In 2004, it rose to 28% and 2009 saw a 0.5% increase. In terms of seats, in 1998 the party got 141, while the next year the number fell to 112. In 2004, it won 146 seats and 2009 saw a jump to 206 seats.

At the political level, Sonia has grown over the years, getting recognition from other parties as well. Even her bitter critics acknowledge that in today's political scenario, there is no other leader comparable to her on the national scene. This is a huge jump for a novice who entered politics 16 years ago. Another significant aspect is her style of functioning. As Khare points out, 'The Congress no longer pursues a policy of confrontation. After taking over, Sonia admitted that the party did not have the numbers and her personality is a reflection of this non-confrontational stance. Her policy is, if you are reasonable, I will be reasonable. If you respect me, I will respect you.'*

While Sonia has delivered a creditable performance at the Centre, it is a different story in the states. Gandhi has failed to increase the number of Congress-ruled states. She has also not allowed the state leaders to grow. This is big minus point. T.V.R. Shenoy observes that after 2009, she failed to look at the broader picture. 'Instead of the party, she began to think of how to strengthen her son's position. Do you have to weaken others in the bargain? She did exactly that. Which is the biggest state? Uttar Pradesh. And that is where she wanted Rahul to be number one. It was the same in Bihar. She could not revive the party in these two states.'* Overall, when one looks at the Congress' prospects, it does not look very encouraging. It is presently ruling in Assam, Haryana, Delhi, Andhra Pradesh, Kerala, Maharashtra, Jammu and Kashmir and Himachal Pradesh. It has lost power in Tamil Nadu since 1967 and has been riding piggyback on either of the two Dravidian parties—the DMK or the AIADMK. From 1995 onwards, the BJP has dominated in Gujarat, with the exception of an 18-month period. In Bengal, the Trinamool Congress, along with the Congress as a minor partner, removed the 34-year rule of the communists. Kerala alternates between a CPI(M)-led Left Democratic Front regime and a Congress-led rule. The party has been sidelined in Orissa since 2000. In general, the Congress has not been able to consolidate its presence in the past two decades.

Its frontal organisations like the Indian Youth Congress, National Students' Union of India and Mahila Congress have also not been doing well. There has even been a demand to wind up the Mahila Congress (the women's wing). Despite a young man like Rahul Gandhi heading the Youth Congress, not many young people seem enthusiastic about joining the party.

THE FUTURE OF THE GANDHI DYNASTY

A US diplomatic cable from New Delhi comments that as one of the world's oldest and largest political parties, the Congress has evolved an elaborate culture aimed at protecting the Gandhi dynasty. "Mrs. Gandhi's inner circle carefully controls her access to information, and inoculates her from criticism, while her carefully scripted public appearances protect her from making gaffes or missteps. This has the advantage of preserving the 'sanctity' of Mrs. Gandhi and the dynasty, but can also complicate her efforts to wield power. This system prevents Mrs. Gandhi from asserting herself and reduces her charisma, and makes her overly reliant on a selected group, which may not always have her or the party's best interests at heart."[47]

Some political analysts are of the opinion that Sonia Gandhi's decline has already set in. They cite the fact that the Congress did not get a single Assembly seat in her Parliamentary constituency (Rae Bareli) and only two from Rahul Gandhi's constituency (Amethi) in the recent UP Assembly elections. This was in spite of intense campaigning by Priyanka Gandhi. Sonia's critics claim that the Gandhi magic is slowly ebbing away. Present indications are that her popularity, as well as that of the Congress Party, will decline further as the people are angry over the huge scams which have tumbled out of the closet in the last two or three years. Recent opinion polls have shown that the Congress may lose five to six per cent of its vote share in the next Lok Sabha elections.

Ashley Tellis observes that dynastic politics will survive only to the extent people let it survive. 'It is not going to survive because there is a dynasty. In India, we are at an age where the critical criterion has become performance. If your dynasty fails to perform, you get booted out.'*

Sonia has now officially made Rahul Gandhi the number two in the party, signalling the continuance of the dynasty. The Jaipur Chintan Shivir has made sure that the continuance of the family's rule now rests with Rahul. This has its negative and positive aspects. While holding an official position, he can no longer disclaim any responsibility in the party's electoral fortunes. He has to prove his leadership qualities and has to ensure that the dynasty continues. There are many who believe that had he become a minister in 2004, by now he could have gained some experience in administration. Even within the party, he has not taken on any other responsibilities other than heading the Youth Congress and NSUI. Even when Sonia Gandhi was abroad for a surgery in 2011, he did not lead the party from the front, although she had set up a committee which included Rahul to look after party affairs.

There are many who believe that Sonia Gandhi has successfully passed on the baton to her son after keeping the seat warm for 16 years. She has had to face several anxious moments during this period but has proved her political mettle all through.

Amar Singh sums up her political journey succinctly. 'I think she was not a politician but she was not averse to politics. She was living in a political family and was watching what was happening around her. People were in and out of her mother-in-law and her husband's house. She has seen Siddhartha Shankar Ray giving evidence against her mother-in-law before the Shah Commission; she has seen tragic assassinations in her family and she has seen close friends leave her. She has seen many ups and downs. It is not correct to say she does not understand or she is not pragmatic. If there was nothing in her, she could not have achieved all this.'*

In balance, despite her minus points, Sonia Gandhi has adapted well to Indian conditions, and has proved herself to be an extraordinary woman, effectively steering the Grand Old Party for more than a decade. When she joined politics, she faced the dual challenges of transitioning from a housewife to a politician and transforming from a European to an Indian. She has come out with flying colours on both counts. Once her son Rahul takes over the reins from her, chances are that she may still remain in the Congress as Queen Mother and not retire from politics. It is for Rahul to continue the dynasty, and if Rahul fails, Priyanka is always the trump card.

NOTES

1. "Priyanka admires Sonia for becoming confident leader", Indo Asian News Service, April 15, 2009.
3. http://wikileaks.org/cable/2006/08/06NEWDELHI5495.html.

3. Shashi Tharoor, "Sonia Gandhi", *TIME*, May 12, 2008.
4. www.encyclopedia.com.
5. "Priyanka admires Sonia for becoming confident leader", Indo Asian News Service, April 15, 2009.
6. Interview with Barkha Dutt on NDTV, http://www.aicc.org.in/new/interview-by-barkha-dutt.php.
7. John F. Burns, "Sonia Gandhi, the 'Foreigner,' Startles the Political Pundits", *New York Times*, February 27, 1998.
8. Interview with Vir Sanghvi, *Hindustan Times*, April 17, 2004.
9. Interview with Shekhar Gupta on "Walk the Talk", aired on NDTV24x7, February 27, 2004.
10. Rasheed Kidwai, *Sonia: A Biography*, p. 91, Penguin Books, 2010.
11. Harish Khare, *The Hindu*, 1998.
12. Ibid.
13. "Gandhi, Sonia", *UXL Newsmakers*, 2005, http://www.encyclopedia.com/topic/Sonia_Gandhi.aspx.
14. Sonia Gandhi, *Rajiv*, p. 1, South Asia Books, 1992.
15. Ibid., pp. 2.
16. Ibid., p. 3.
17. Ibid., p. 6.
18. Ibid., p. 7.
19. Ibid., p. 9.
20. P.C. Alexander, *My Years with Indira Gandhi*, p. 154, Vision Books, 2007.
21. Rasheed Kidwai, *Sonia: A Biography*, p. 28, Penguin Books, 2010.
22. Rani Singh, *Sonia Gandhi: An Extraordinary Life, An Indian Destiny*, p. 160, Pan Macmillan, 2011.
23. Inder Malhotra, *Dynasties of India and Beyond: Pakistan, Sri Lanka, Bangladesh*, p. 172, HarperCollins, 2008.
24. Interview with Vir Sanghvi, *Hindustan Times*, April 17, 2004.
25. Ibid.
26. Speech at the Talkatora Stadium.
27. "Sonia, of course", *The Economist*, November 16, 2000.
28. Interview with Vir Sanghvi, *Hindustan Times*, April 17, 2004, http://www.aicc.org.in/new/interview-with-soniaji.php.
29. Purnima S. Tripathi, "Coalition offer, with a rider", *Frontline*, July 9, 2003.
30. Interview with Barkha Dutt, NDTV, March 11, 2010.
31. Sonia Gandhi's statement at a Congress Parliamentary Party meeting, May 18, 2004.
32. TV Today news report, May 18, 2004.
33. "Abdul Kalam was ready to swear Sonia Gandhi in as PM in 2004", *Times of India*, June 30, 2012.
34. Interview with Vir Sanghvi, *Hindustan Times*, April 17, 2004.
35. Interview with Vir Sanghvi on "One on One" aired on NDTV24x7, 2006.

36. Simon Denyer, "India's 'silent' prime minister becomes a tragic figure", *The Washington Post,* September 3, 2012.
37. Neerja Chowdhury, "Gamble of a daughter-in-law", *The Indian Express,* March 23, 2005; *Custom 150 Online Journals,* July 16, 2012.
38. Inder Malhotra, *Dynasties of India and Beyond: Pakistan, Sri Lanka, Bangladesh,* p. 171.
39. Amelia Gentleman, "By leaving, Gandhi might gain. Indian party leader plays sacrifice card", *International Herald Tribune,* March 25, 2006; *Custom 150 Online Journals,* July 16, 2012.
40. Interview with Vir Sanghvi on "One on One" aired on NDTV24x7, 2006.
41. Rasheed Kidwai, *Sonia: A Biography,* p. 138.
42. http://wikileaks.org/cable/2009/05/09NEWDELHI998.html.
43. Ibid.
44. Interview with Sheela Bhatt, rediff.com, January 24, 2013.
45. Ibid.
46. Kidwai, *Sonia: A Biography,* p. 205.
47. http://www.thehindu.com/news/the indiacables/article1574328.ece.

Mayawati

IT IS NO MEAN achievement for a poor Scheduled Caste woman to become the chief minister of India's largest and most populous state, Uttar Pradesh, four times or to make it to the cover of *Newsweek* magazine. Former Uttar Pradesh Chief Minister Mayawati has done just that: the magazine listed her as one of the eight top women achievers in the world. It also referred to her as India's anti-Obama in April 2009. Comparing the two leaders, *Newsweek* stated, "Mayawati is both a bigger underdog and a potentially bigger threat to the established order than Obama was.... But unlike Obama who promised a new politics that would transcend not only race but traditional ideology and the corrupt Washington ways, Mayawati has built her power on demagogic class warfare."[1]

Mayawati is known as the "Dalit queen" because she has empowered the weaker economic sections, which was unthinkable two or three decades ago. The untouchables in Hindu society belong to the lowest castes. They remain on the periphery of society and are not allowed to have any social interaction with the rest of the village. In rural India, these sections were barred from using wells used by non-Dalits, forbidden from walking in the village streets and entering temples. In jobs, they were paid less, ordered to perform the most menial tasks and were rarely promoted, except in the government jobs reserved for them. Even at school, Dalit children were often asked to eat separately, although the government came down heavily and punished the offenders. Marriage with a partner from a higher caste was unthinkable for them. Members from the other three castes—Brahmins (priests and scholars), Kshatriyas (rulers) and Vaishyas (traders)—have exploited the Dalits for thousands of years. It was after independence that these weaker sections were given protection by the Constitution and are now assured reservations in jobs, education and legislatures. Still these sections of society have a long way to go to be at par with the other castes.

Mayawati comes from one of these disadvantaged sections. Being a city girl, she has used her education and her awareness to fight for Dalit upliftment. A teacher in a government school, Mayawati realised the importance of political power at an early age. For India's 170 million Scheduled Castes, she is a symbol of hope and has used caste as a mobiliser, building on a social and political revolution since independence. Her answer to those who criticise her—and many do—is that they are after a "Dalit *ki beti*" (a poor Dalit's daughter). For many Dalits, she is an icon of upward mobility that they are unlikely to ever match, but whom they are proud of.

Mayawati does not depend on the media for her or her party's projection. She says, 'We don't get votes through media publicity. The media has its own responsibilities and I have my own. Why should we pursue the media?'* If other women leaders have transformed themselves to look simpler to appeal to the common man, Mayawati has adopted a different image to lure her voters. Though she used to be a simple woman—plump and plainly dressed with oiled plaits—today Mayawati flashes her diamonds, Gucci handbags and imported sandals to display her upward mobility to her Dalit constituency. Her supporters like their leader to look rich and flashy because it makes them feel good. Mayawati also used the services of beauticians for an image makeover, which included a trendy hairstyle and a new wardrobe. Radhika Ramaseshan, a senior journalist and Uttar Pradesh (UP) observer, recalls Mayawati telling her about her cropped hair and how she finds it convenient to manage. 'This was before the 2007 polls. She had consciously lost weight and seemed to be exercising or might have been on a special diet. Before the 2007 polls, she had tried to acquire a softer image to woo the upper castes, who thought she was rustic and uncouth.'*

On January 15, 2006, to mark her 50th birthday, Mayawati appeared at a function wearing a pink garland of 1,000 rupee notes and beaming at her "subjects" who had to wait for hours to get a glimpse of her. 'I don't give away money or vehicles or food but people think their leader is good and that is why they spend their own money and come to listen to me. They have faith in me,' she claims.* Her supporters, mostly from lower classes, travel vast distances on foot, by bicycle and on tractors and scooters. They bring their own food and wait patiently for their leader to arrive. Through her larger-than-life presence on the Indian political scene, Mayawati has become a folk heroine for her supporters and a threat to her rivals. Janata Party president Dr. Subramanian Swamy notes, 'Of all the women political leaders I know, she is the most liberated. So, realistically speaking, I found her the most normal. She has experienced economic hardships and her supporters also suffer from lack of money. And so her new style appeals to them.'*

Mayawati behaves like the queen from *Alice in Wonderland*; when someone comes in her way, she almost orders "Off with his head!" Playing by her own rules, she became the chief minister of UP three times leading a coalition, and the fourth time singlehandedly brought her party to power with a massive majority. Mayawati believes that she has reached a stage where she may be criticised, even condemned, but not ignored. She believes that political power is the key to success and is in a hurry to capture as much of it as she can and retain it. Mayawati also believes that the secret of her success is her struggle. "Life cannot be imagined without struggles," she says.[2]

DIFFERENT FROM OTHER DALIT LEADERS

What is the difference between Mayawati and the other Dalit leaders in the country? There are Dalit leaders in the Congress, the Bharatiya Janata Party, the Lok Janshakti Party, the Republican Party of India and others. Mayawati claims there is a difference. "Everyone talks about the upliftment of the Dalits. If there are no differences in the politics of Dalit leaders, why don't they get together and pool their efforts to wage a sustained campaign against an unjust social and political order?... Without going into the merits and demerits of these questions, my simple and straight reply is that my life and policies are as much in contrast with those of the other Dalit leaders in the way that Bharat Ratna Babasaheb Dr. Ambedkar's thinking, sacrifice, political ideology and dedication were from Babu Jagjivan Ram's politics of power."[3] She alleges that the so-called successful politics of the "so-called Dalit leaders" must have served their personal interests and those of their families, friends and relatives but they cannot claim to have made any momentous societal changes.

A LANDMARK

Mayawati's golden moment came when she became the first Dalit chief minister of Uttar Pradesh. UP is important to any political party because several prime ministers, including Jawaharlal Nehru, India's first post-independence prime minister, hailed from the state. It has the largest number of seats in the Lok Sabha (80) and whoever gets a majority in UP becomes the "king" or the kingmaker in national politics. Even though it has been blessed with substantial natural resources and scientific wealth, none of the political parties have been able to develop the state. It has the largest Scheduled Caste population, numbering about 35.1 million, and also has the highest rate of atrocities against the Dalits in the country. The state has the largest number of women and children suffering from malnutrition and the highest number of polio cases. UP, besides being one of the least developed states, also has the dubious distinction of being the most corrupt in the nation.

Until the mid-1980s, it was the Congress party which ruled the state. By the early 1990s, the party's influence waned as a result of social upliftment of the backward castes, which allied themselves with the Muslims. In UP, the Muslims hold the key in at least 114 constituencies. The base of the Congress party was the upper castes, supported by the Dalits and Muslims, but the Congress was unable to retain their support over the years. Slowly both the Scheduled Castes and the Muslims were weaned away by the two caste-based parties, the Samajwadi Party (SP) and the Bahujan Samaj Party (BSP). Meanwhile, the upper castes moved to the BJP. With the Congress party in a structural crisis, parties like the BJP, SP and the BSP gradually gained ground in the eighties. The formation of the BSP was perfectly timed with a growth in awareness among the lower castes as a result of improved educational facilities. Prof. Sudha Pai, an avid Dalit watcher, points out that the emergence of the BSP was an outcome of the twin processes of affirmative action and democratisation that accelerated in the 1980s. She notes, "These processes, combined with the economic development and educational progress in parts of UP, have been instrumental in creating a more identity conscious, socially and politically aware Dalit community, no longer expected to accept upper caste domination or remain an appendage of the Congress party. Kanshi Ram's success lay in realising this and using this to create a strong party."[4]

The motto of the BSP, as enunciated by its founder Kanshi Ram, was to capture power through ballots, not bullets. In other words, for him political power is the master key which opens all the locked doors of progress. Except for caste, the BSP had no other political platform. Kanshi Ram began his quest for a new party in the 1970s in Maharashtra. Initially, he formed a social group, the All India Backward and Minority Communities Employees Federation (BAMCEF), which was transformed into a reformist political party. Kanshi Ram formed his Bahujan Samaj Party on April 14, 1984, a few months before the assassination of Prime Minister Indira Gandhi. Indira's son, Rajiv, succeeded her and won a landslide victory in 1984 because of the sympathy votes.

The ambitious BSP contested the 1984 polls but its candidates, including founding members Kanshi Ram and Mayawati, lost the elections. In the 1985 UP Assembly polls, the Congress did not fare well, while the BSP got 4% of the vote share, proving it could draw the Dalits away from the Congress fold even though it did not win any seats. Soon Rajiv Gandhi got embroiled in the Bofors controversy with a belligerent Opposition demanding a probe into the Rs. 64-crore gun deal. While Rajiv declared that neither he nor his family members were involved in the kickback, the Opposition would have none of it. The corruption tag stuck to him and the 1989 elections saw the Congress crumble. By then Rajiv Gandhi had realised the importance of the BSP and, through intermediaries like industrialist Jayant Malhotra, Congress MP Chinta Mohan, ministers Ghulam Nabi Azad and Rajesh Pilot, was trying to forge an understanding with Kanshi Ram. Several secret meetings were held between the two leaders but nothing tangible materialised and it was only later, after some wooing, that an electoral alliance was forged with the BSP under Rajiv's successor, Narasimha Rao. The National Front government headed by Janata Dal leader V. P. Singh, supported by the right and left parties, took over in 1989. Singh opened up a Pandora's Box by wanting to implement the Mandal Commission report, which recommended quotas in education and jobs for the backward classes. It became a contentious issue with the other castes who opposed it, arguing that reservations based on caste were not right. From then on a power struggle began among the caste-based parties in UP. Each held office for a while through a number of coalitions and minority governments.

By 1989, the BSP gained 9% of the popular vote and today it has about 27% of the vote share. Mayawati had worked relentlessly with Kanshi Ram to build the party. Recalling Mayawati in her early days, Shahid Siddiqui, a former BSP member and editor of an Urdu newspaper, points out that in her younger years she was a simple girl. 'I never thought that she could become such a powerful, autocratic and dictatorial leader because she just used to follow Kanshi Ram wherever he went. She was like his house manager, looking after his needs because he did not have a family. But what was remarkable was that she was hard working even then. She would often sit some leaders down and instruct them on the do's and don'ts. Kanshi Ram invariably indulged her. He used to say, "Let her do what she wants." What Kanshi Ram really gave her was the knowledge and discipline.'*

Sudha Pai states that prior to the 1993 UP Assembly elections, the BSP did not attempt a strategy of forming alliances to attain political power and empower the Dalits. The decision to do so came out of a realisation that Dalits alone could not get a legislative majority. The 1993 polls demonstrated that an alliance between the SP (backward castes) and the BSP (Scheduled Castes) could be a winning combination. Before the polls, Kanshi Ram and Samajwadi Party leader Mulayam Singh Yadav thought it would be mutually beneficial to form an alliance. The BSP moved closer to the SP and tried to create a caste coalition centred on Dalits, Other Backward Castes (OBCs) and minorities. The V.P. Singh government's efforts at "Mandalisation"—reserving seats for the backward classes based on the recommendation of the Mandal Commission report—also helped the SP grow. The BSP, on its part, benefited by the increased assertion by the Dalits. The two lower caste parties were able to halt the progress of the BJP in UP in those elections. The BSP came to power in 1993 as a junior coalition partner with the SP. Providing outside support, both Kanshi Ram and Mayawati did not join the government led by Mulayam Singh.

Though the coalition began well, constant friction between the partners led to its collapse within 18 months. Personality clashes and political rivalry were central to the coalition's demise. Mayawati, now in a position to assert herself, began to interfere in the government. Mulayam Singh, averse to women politicians, left it to his principal secretary P.L. Punia to deal with her. Punia later became Mayawati's principal secretary during her three terms as chief minister. Punia recalls, 'She used to call me every evening asking for the transfer of some low-level policemen. She did not ask for IAS or IPS officers' transfers. If I referred her back to the chief minister, she used to get angry. But she would come back to me again and again with such requests. She was just an MP at that time. She used to say, "Mulayam Singh may be the CM but I am the super CM." The SP-BSP coalition began to fall apart as "super chief minister" Mayawati tried to call the shots, which was resented by Mulayam Singh. Kanshi Ram tried to restrain her but could not succeed and thought she was spoiling the show. He started coming for meetings with the chief minister to review the administration without Mayawati. I used to be present at these meetings.'* All these issues led to the break-up of the alliance though the BSP blamed it on Mulayam Singh Yadav's anti-Dalit stance.

Circumstances helped Mayawati in succeeding Mulayam Singh. Kanshi Ram used to narrate the developments leading to Mayawati becoming the chief minister. He had travelled to South India to broaden the base of the BSP movement and to give it a national presence. Before leaving Delhi, he told Mulayam Singh that Mayawati would coordinate the affairs of the alliance government with him. "I told him that the BSP's purpose in running the government would be to check atrocities on the Scheduled Castes and Scheduled Tribes.... During my absence from UP, atrocities on the SC and ST communities continued. In spite of protests from Mayawati, Mulayam Singh could not control the situation. As a result, all parties approached me to replace Mulayam Singh with a more capable chief minister. It was under these circumstances that I got the opportunity to make Mayawati the chief minister."[5]

It all began on June 1, 1995, when the BSP decided to withdraw support to Mulayam Singh's government. According to Sudha Pai, "The leadership of the BSP remained unhappy over its inability to convert its votes into seats despite forming a government and implementing welfare policies under the leadership of Mayawati."[6] This was one of the reasons for the BSP going in for an alliance with the Congress in 1996. The BSP, since its inception, has been through many phases and at every stage has reinvented itself to suit the political conditions and its transition to a more liberal and modern party. It was in 1992 that the BSP transformed itself from a Dalit movement into a political party.

To understand the Dalit assertion and its ascendancy, one has to look into its background during the eighties. Many thought that the BSP would become a flash in the pan like the erstwhile Republican Party of India, which stayed limited to Maharashtra. After the collapse of the SP-BSP alliance, Kanshi Ram changed his strategy and began to gravitate towards the two national parties—the BJP and the Congress—for gaining power.

Explaining the alliance with the right-wing BJP, Kanshi Ram once noted, "At any given point, I'll enter into a tactical alliance with another party if I feel it will strengthen the BSP. And it is what I have done in the past. I did not enter into an alliance with the BJP because of any ideological common ground—in fact, we are poles apart. […] We entered into an understanding with the BJP last year to increase the base of the BSP and when we feel we are not benefitting any longer we'll end it."[7]

Mayawati's chance came as a result of the coalition break-up. She was made chief minister under stormy circumstances. Unlike Mulayam Singh, who was already a senior politician, Mayawati was a novice. She considered her appointment as a first step towards Dalit empowerment, pointing out, "My coming to power and that too by unseating Mulayam Singh Yadav was the first major victory in our power struggle."[8]

Mulayam Singh resented the withdrawal of the BSP's backing. The BJP was keen to end the SP rule and therefore got into a secret understanding with the BSP. It gave a letter of support to Kanshi Ram much before the final act of the political drama. Sensing this, Mulayam tried to divide the BSP to avert a collapse of his government. When Kanshi Ram came to know of these moves, he decided to pull out of the coalition. A still rattled Mayawati recalls, "Nobody knew then that the power struggle would acquire such a horrendous form that attempts would be made to even kill me and all the pillars of democracy would shirk their constitutional responsibility of extending help to me, a legal claimant of an alternative government."[9]

Meanwhile, Mulayam Singh was making all efforts to save his government; this is when the "abduction drama" took place. Mayawati alleged that legislators from her party were taken away to a guesthouse where she too was confined while relentless attempts were made to kill her on June 2, 1995. She claimed that all this was orchestrated to thwart the withdrawal of support by the BSP.

Looking back, Mayawati is appalled at the extent to which Mulayam Singh was willing to go to save his government. She recollects: 'There were two telephones in the guesthouse. When Mulayam Singh let the criminals loose on us, the press was keeping vigil. When the goons started raising slogans, I was fortunately in a room with some other people. As I was talking to them there was a lot of noise outside. I told the guests to leave and locked the door behind me. Within a few minutes, the goons were trying to break down the door. Had the door opened, they would have shot me dead. It was because of the blessings of the poor that I had a providential escape. After this incident, I never lock my door. Guesthouse doors are normally not very strong but somehow that day the doors and windows did not give way. Mulayam Singh made a BSP leader file an FIR (First Information Report) with the police claiming that I had kidnapped his son and insisted on having the door opened so that his goons could shoot me dead. Fortunately a Dalit sub-inspector called me and warned me not to open the door at any cost. Meanwhile, from the other telephone in my room, I had already spoken to Prime Minister Rao, BJP leaders Vajpayee and Advani, Janata Dal leader Bommai and others. A Samajwadi MLA was trying to plant two gas cylinders next to my room; BJP leader Tripathi saw this and shouted. Then some other people also arrived and surrounded the guesthouse. I was in the room for hours without food or water. Ultimately forces were sent to rescue me.'* This incident hardened Mayawati's attitude towards Mulayam Singh, a position which continues to this day. Since that day she has not been able to forgive the Yadav chieftain.

"But democracy finally triumphed when on the evening of June 3, 1995, Governor Motilal Vora dismissed the minority government," claims Mayawati.[10] Former Prime Minister P.V. Narasimha Rao described her installation as chief minister as a "miracle of democracy". Giving a detailed account of what happened, former UP Governor Motilal Vora recollects that the BJP sent him a letter stating that it would support the BSP government and the party's top leaders also met him. 'So I invited Mayawati to form the government. Mayawati phoned me soon after the BJP leaders left. She said she was afraid of her security and asked me to send some of my security staff to the guesthouse where she was staying. When she reached Raj Bhavan, I gave her my letter. She asked me if she could telephone Kanshi Ram, who was at a hospital in Delhi. I said yes; after speaking to Kanshi Ram she said he wanted to speak to me. I told him that I have already given the letter to Mayawati and that the swearing-in could take place around 10.30pm but she told me it should be at 11.05pm. I administered the oath to her in the lawns of the Raj Bhavan. Many people, including Mulayam Singh, came for the function. After that she said she was afraid to go out and would stay the night at the Raj Bhavan. I agreed and made arrangements for her overnight stay. Next morning, after breakfast, I told her that now she was the chief minister, she should not fear for her security. So she went away. Her government lasted just four and a half months and then the BJP pulled out. After that, President's rule was imposed, keeping the Assembly in suspended animation. '*

Praising her first term, Kanshi Ram observed that the immediate agenda before the BSP was to check atrocities on Scheduled Castes and Scheduled Tribes, the most vulnerable sections of society. The lawlessness in Uttar Pradesh was so widespread that Mayawati had nearly 1.4 lakh criminals placed behind bars. "By this act, she earned the sobriquet 'Iron Lady'. During her short first tenure of four and a half months, she left her mark."[11] The first statement that Mayawati made at a press conference after taking over was that she would not spare Mulayam Singh's goons. The next day she ordered the release of all those arrested under fictitious cases relating to the Babri mosque demolition on December 6, 1992.

The immediate benefit of Mayawati's first term was that it provided the Dalits the courage to assert themselves. Symbolically, she also assigned posts in her office and in other important ministries to Dalit officers. As soon as she took over, she asked P.L. Punia, a Scheduled Caste civil servant who served as Mulayam Singh's principal secretary, to continue. Punia recalls, 'I told her every chief minister should have his or her confidant at the post but she pointed out that I was from her caste and why should I not help her in running the government. That was how I became her principal secretary.'*
She appointed Scheduled Caste magistrates in several districts who would hear Dalit cases sympathetically. She gave them the confidence to feel equal to the other castes and not be apologetic. Since 1993, the Dalits have gone on strike on several occasions and asserted their land rights. Punia, used to regularly chair review meetings to implement programmes for the betterment of the Dalits. Mayawati also tried to perpetuate the memory of Scheduled Caste leaders. Dalit icon Dr. B.R. Ambedkar's statues were erected all over Uttar Pradesh. She began naming universities and other public institutions after Dalit leaders and also tried to woo other backward classes (OBCs) and Muslims by offering sops of all kinds.

The relationship between the BSP and the BJP, however, soon became strained. Local BJP leaders were critical of Mayawati's Dalit agenda. The BJP decided to withdraw its support within four and a half months. "Giving a long list of reasons, Kalraj Mishra, UP BJP president, listed several irregularities in government deals, including the grant of distillery licenses, the sale of sugar mills, deliberate insults heaped on Lord Rama—in whose name a temple was sought to have been built as an election issue during the BJP's two successful election campaigns in the past—through the Periyar Mela, the clash with the Vishwa Hindu Parishad (a sister organisation of the BJP) on the Krishna Janmabhoomi (birth place of Lord Krishna) issue in Mathura, the government's refusal to grant permission to prosecute police personnel involved in the rape of some activists in Uttarakhand (UP) and the brazen policies on transfers of officials in the state. While most of these charges have not been substantiated, there is no denying the provocative gestures towards some of the BJP's most venerated icons and symbols."[12] The abrasive style of the two BSP leaders was also one of the reasons for the break-up. So the brief bonhomie between the two parties ended in a bitter parting of ways. But Mayawati and Kanshi Ram were happy that the party's profile improved during this short period.

Meanwhile, 1996 saw many changes in the political arena. The Narasimha Rao government lost power and Rao himself was embroiled in several court cases. The Congress Party dumped him when it saw he could not get them back to power. The BSP moved forward by winning six Lok Sabha seats from UP and increasing its vote percentage to equal that of the SP. There was more good news for the BSP when it got one seat each from Punjab and Madhya Pradesh, enhancing its national presence.

Sensing the growing importance of the BSP and its ability to transfer votes to other parties, Rao sought a pre-poll alliance with it in the 1996 UP Assembly elections. Kanshi Ram was flattered that Rao sought his help and that the BSP could have an alliance with the "Grand Old Party" although he had not yielded to the overtures of Rajiv Gandhi earlier. The BSP chief thought that tactically aligning with the Congress might widen its base. During the 1996 Assembly polls, for the first time the Congress became a minor partner, leaving 300 seats for the BSP. There were joint campaigns where leaders of both parties shared a platform. The BSP faced the Assembly polls with confidence in view of its doubling of vote share in the 1996 Lok Sabha polls to almost 20 per cent. It won 67 seats while the Congress got 30 seats. The BJP emerged as the single largest party once again (180) and the SP got 110 seats. Facing criticism for aligning with the BSP, Rao defended his decision: "I thought, and many of my colleagues in Congress agreed, that this would be a natural alliance in the sense that the Dalit votes had been with the Congress solidly for a long time and so Dalits would vouch for this alliance. The result was also, to my mind, good since, despite the Congress winning only 30 seats, not a single Congress candidate forfeited his deposit. The margins were also narrower than before."[13] His critics, however, did not agree with his analysis.

After the Assembly elections, Uttar Pradesh underwent another spell of President's rule because no political combination could form the government. Kanshi Ram realised that although the Dalits voted in large numbers for the BSP, it was not enough to garner more seats. He realised that the party needed to get votes from other castes as well. It was for this reason that later he was willing to get help from other sections of society, including the Brahmins.

KANSHI RAM DISCOVERS MAYAWATI

Before going any further, there is a need to understand Mayawati's personality and her roots. Once, in jest, she asked her father why she had been named Mayawati. He reportedly disclosed that he never consulted a priest, which was ordained by the Manuwadi traditions for naming children. According to him, her naming had to do with events that occurred on the day she was born; on that very day, her family received three happy tidings. She recalls, "My father, who was employed as a lower division clerk in the postal department, was promoted to an upper division clerk. Along with that, he received his pending salary arrears. That day, he was also posted to a better department. My father was so happy that he christened me Mayawati, which symbolises mundane happiness and wealth."[14]

Born into a large, poor family with eight siblings, Mayawati grew up in a city but maintained links with her ancestral village in UP, as she used to visit her grandparents during holidays. It was during those visits that she began to understand the caste system and the plight of the Dalits. The intensity of caste discrimination and ghettoisation of the communities shocked her. Since her childhood, she was influenced by the Scheduled Caste freedom fighter and the father of the Indian Constitution, Babasaheb Ambedkar.

After her graduation, Mayawati took a teacher training course and started working in a government school. As for her introduction to politics, a chance meeting with BSP founder Kanshi Ram in 1977 changed her life. "It marked the beginning of my political career and I deem it very important," she reminisces.[15] Mayawati had been invited to a *jaati todo* [break the caste] function, presided over by Health Minister Raj Narain. Indira Gandhi's Congress government had recently lost the elections comprehensively, paving the way for a Janata Party government in which Raj Narain was an important minister. In that meeting, Mayawati opposed Narain's use of the term Harijan, originally coined by the father of the nation, Mahatma Gandhi, for the Scheduled Castes. Kanshi Ram, who was in the audience, was impressed by Mayawati's oratorical skills and courage. So one winter evening, he visited her at her house. Mayawati's family had retired for the day and she was preparing for her IAS [Indian Administrative Service] exams. Glancing at her books, Kanshi Ram asked her, "What is your ambition in life?" Mayawati replied she wanted to become an IAS officer to serve the people. He told her that she would be able to do better service by becoming a political leader. "Shri Kanshi Ramji's words affected me. I dropped the idea of becoming an IAS officer and thought of becoming a great leader," explains Mayawati.[16] After that day's fateful decision, she went on to become the chief minister of UP four times.

Mayawati's father, Prabhu Das, did not like Kanshi Ram's influence on his young daughter. He tried to dissuade her but she was adamant. Kanshi Ram once observed, "Initially her father opposed her joining the BSP movement. He didn't think that the BSP movement would pick up and so his daughter might fail in life. He had suggested that she should play it safe and go in for a lucrative government job. If at all she wanted a political career, she should join an already successful party and not one yet to be launched. Mayawati discussed the matter with me. I told her that it is a matter of ideology for me; it should be a matter of ideology to her too. Success or failure comes later. And she opted for the BSP movement."[17] Mayawati's differences with her father over the issue led to her leaving home and moving into Kanshi Ram's house. She completed her law degree and plunged into politics from 1984. Despite opposition from other leaders, Kanshi Ram promoted her in the party.

HER ELECTORAL DEBUT

Mayawati was groomed by her mentor, as promised, to become the leader. The two had different personalities but could work together harmoniously. There was an unexplainable bond between them. Unlike Kanshi Ram who was an extrovert, Mayawati is suspicious by nature and trusts only a handful of close associates. He put her in charge of UP while he travelled around the country to expand the BSP base. Mayawati, too, plunged into her work wholeheartedly, building the party from scratch in UP, which she considered her fiefdom.

Her rise in politics was related to the rise of the BSP, which Kanshi Ram launched on April 14, 1984. It has been a long journey for the party, which started small, with hardly any money, cadre or influential personalities. Its success lies in its capacity to reinvent itself, constantly shifting policy and capitalising on every opportunity. Over the years, whenever threatened by others, the BSP has transformed itself from a party practicing conservative, identity politics to one with a more liberal outlook. It grew from a movement in the 1990s to a political party, acquiring power as a coalition partner not once but thrice, which made Mayawati the chief minister. The fourth time the BSP came to power on its own. In the beginning of the 21st century, it seized the advantage of the fall in influence of the two national parties—the BJP and the Congress—and emerged as a challenger to SP, the other significant regional party in UP. Since 2007, it has become a Bahujan Samaj Party, including all castes.

Mayawati made her debut in electoral politics in 1984, when she contested for the first time from the Kairana Lok Sabha constituency. Her well-wishers advised her against it but she took a risk, resigned from her job and contested the polls. There was no chance of anyone other than the Congress wining the elections then because of the sympathy wave for the Congress after the assassination of Prime Minister Indira Gandhi. She did not win, but stood third. Nobody took the young woman in ordinary attire and going around on a bicycle while campaigning for a Lok Sabha seat on a modest fund, seriously. When she became jobless, Kanshi Ram gave her more opportunities to progress in the organisation. Mayawati was not disheartened by her failures and continued to contest elections, still riding her bicycle. Dr. Subramanian Swamy remembers an incident soon after her defeat: 'Kanshi Ram used to call her tenacious. One day I asked him if she was dejected over losing the elections. He said, "Oh no, she has got guts." When Mayawati came, she was already talking about the next elections.'*

Undaunted, she contested the 1985 Lok Sabha by-elections from Bijnore, a reserved constituency for the Scheduled Castes. She walked and cycled from village to village and managed to increase her votes from 5,700 in the 1984 elections to 65,000 votes within a year. She rallied against formidable opponents; one was the well-known Dalit leader Ram Vilas Paswan. The other was the present Lok Sabha Speaker Meira Kumar, who made her debut in politics and won as a Congress candidate, benefiting from the legacy of her father, Babu Jagjivan Ram, a veteran Congress leader.

Even though Mayawati's increased vote tally in the Bijnore elections was proof of the party's growing strength, senior leaders and the media began to notice the gains made by the BSP. She came under attack from senior BSP leaders. Kanshi Ram observed, "The seniors in the party put pressure on me to curtail the opportunities I was giving her. On my refusal to do so, most of the seniors left the BSP movement and started out on their own. But none of them are visible today, whereas Mayawati has become a success as chief minister of the largest state in India."[18]

Two years later, Mayawati contested from the Hardwar constituency (again a reserved seat) and secured more than 1,00,000 votes, fetching the second place, while former minister Ram Singh of the Congress got elected. He recollects the dignified way Mayawati conducted her election campaign. By this time, the BSP was recognized by the Election Commission and had its own symbol. Kanshi Ram and Mayawati used the period from 1984 to 1989 to consolidate the party. He contested against V.P. Singh—who would become the prime minister after the polls—from Allahabad in 1989 and secured the third position. He cut into Congress votes, weakening it significantly in the crucial state. After these polls, the national media began to take note of the BSP and its chief.

AS MEMBER OF PARLIAMENT

Mayawati made her debut in the Lok Sabha by winning the Bijnore seat in the 1989 polls when she got 1,83,189 votes and won by a comfortable margin of nearly 10,000 votes over her nearest rival from the Janata Dal. She had also contested from Hardwar but lost the seat and her only consolation was that she secured more than 1,00,000 votes. In UP, the party won nearly ten per cent vote share, overtaking the BJP, which obtained 7.5 per cent. Though Kanshi Ram himself lost the election, the overall performance of the BSP was quite encouraging. At last, Mayawati's dream of entering Parliament had become a reality. Attending Parliament was a new experience for her and she began to take interest in its proceedings and participated in the debates. She often rushed to the Well of the House to make a point, protesting especially against any atrocities on Dalits. Her plain, unglamorous and shabby appearance evoked rude comments from other smart women members of the Congress and the BJP. Undeterred, she continued being herself, often sitting in the Central Hall of the Parliament or the members' lounge, relishing toast and coffee. Through this entire phase, her focus on

Dalits never wavered. During her first term in Parliament, Mayawati got media attention because of her aggressive posture and unruly behaviour in the House.

When the V.P. Singh regime fell in November 1990 and the Chandra Shekhar government, supported by the Congress, took over for a few months, it was clear that elections were not far away. The Congress withdrew its support to Chandra Shekhar on a flimsy excuse within a few months. The instability of these successive governments caused widespread concern in political circles.

Things were not going well for Mayawati and the BSP during this phase. She contested again in the 1991 Lok Sabha elections from both Bijnore and Hardwar but lost in both constituencies. Undaunted, she contested a by-election in November 1991 from Bulundshahr but lost once again. In 1992, Mayawati decided to change not just her constituency but also the state and contested from Hoshiarpur in Punjab, but she was unlucky yet again. The BSP's disappointing performance plunged her into deep depression. Except Kanshi Ram, no other BSP candidate could manage to win.

Things, however, began to look up when the SP and the BSP got back together to contest the Assembly polls in 1993. They also sealed a pact with the help of the industrialist Jayant Malhotra, who was promoting Kanshi Ram. This enabled Mulayam Singh to form the SP-BSP coalition government. In this new set-up, Mayawati kept a low profile on Kanshi Ram's advice, as Mulayam was wary of women politicians and Mayawati was blunt in her dealings with him.

SECOND TERM AS CHIEF MINISTER

The 1996 Assembly polls did not provide a majority to any party and a coalition could not be formed. President's rule seemed inevitable. The BSP broke its ties with the Congress and joined hands with the BJP to form a coalition. Both parties wanted to check the rise of Mulayam Singh and his party; finding common cause, they struck a power-sharing deal. Each realised the need for the other's support to come to power. Senior BJP leaders, despite the reservations expressed by state party chief Kalyan Singh, saw a winning combination. Learning from the previous experience during Mayawati's first term, Kanshi Ram was careful about the details of the alliance. In fact, his initial effort was to get unconditional BJP support but the BJP refused. Both parties agreed to have an equal share in the Council of Ministers. The Speaker's post went to the BJP. Senior leaders from both parties were to monitor the performance of the ministry. Each partner would have its own chief minister by rotation for six months.

Senior columnist T.V.R. Shenoy, who was close to Kanshi Ram, points out, 'Kanshi Ram was very fond of Mayawati. He did not want to become chief minister because of his failing health. Advani and Vajpayee did not trust Mayawati and wanted Kanshi Ram on the post.'* Shenoy also explains the reasons for the BJP-BSP combination; it was he who brought them together. 'Scheduled Caste is not a factor but Scheduled Tribe is a factor in national politics. Even while in alliance with Mulayam Singh, Kanshi Ram understood this. The top and the bottom do not go with the middle. Scheduled Castes had no options. So he thought the combination of upper castes—represented by the BJP—and the SCs, represented by the BSP, would work. By the time the alliance was finalised, he was unfortunately hospitalised. So he chose Mayawati as the chief minister for a second time.'*

Mayawati's star began to rise again when the BJP supported her as the chief minister to end President's rule in the state. Referring to this in her autobiography, she wrote, "Finally I became the chief minister for the second time. By accepting the proposal to form a coalition government in UP, the BSP scripted a new history of political developments in the state at a time when, even five months after the mid-term elections to the Assembly, no party was able to promise a stable government. The BSP, however, came out triumphant in its singular determination that 'if a government were to be formed in the state, it must be under the leadership of Mayawati and no one else.' The government may have been formed on the basis of power sharing, but people in the state, especially within the Bahujan Samaj Party, benefitted tremendously from the dispensation because by heading the government for the first six months, as per the coalition arrangement, the party piled up a series of enviable achievements as it had done in its first stint of government."[19] But top leaders of the BJP and the BSP, in their first press conference on March 19, 1997 in New Delhi, said their first priority would be to streamline the law and order situation and launch a crackdown on criminal elements.

Mayawati began her second term as chief minister on March 21, 1997. BJP leader Kalyan Singh was sulking at what he perceived as an unfair deal.

He was opposed to the two parties sharing an equal number of ministers, because the BJP had a hundred more seats than the BSP. A strong backward classes' leader, Kalyan Singh did not want to play second fiddle to Mayawati or the BSP. Mayawati realised the hard way that to find her place in UP, she had to fight the Yadav leader Mulayam Singh and the Lodh leader Kalyan Singh. This was tough because both had had long political innings.

Kanshi Ram had discussed the BSP's role with the two top BJP leaders Lal Krishna Advani and Atal Bihari Vajpayee and made it clear to them that his party had an agenda of social transformation and economic emancipation of the Bahujan Samaj. His wished that all energies during Mayawati's first six months should be spent towards that goal and the BSP would not allow any interference from the BJP. Kanshi Ram observed once, "I had told Mayawati that during her six months rule, she must achieve results suited to six years and execute the BSP agenda in a big way."[20]

Things, however, did not turn out the way the party leaders hoped. Hardliners from both parties did not want to lose their identity. As Professor Pai points out, "BSP leaders were particularly keen to implement programmes for Dalit upliftment, especially in the fields of education, social welfare, employment generation and health, which had been initiated in 1995 during the tenure of the previous government."[21] Mayawati explains, "We had an understanding that for six months the BSP will rule and the Speaker will be from the BJP, and then in the next six months, the BJP will rule and the Speaker would be from the BSP. But the BJP did not agree to the Speaker being from the BSP and that is why we parted ways. They said 'our Speaker is your Speaker', which was not acceptable to us."[22] The BJP had to, very soon, reap what they had sowed. The BSP opposed the Vajpayee government in 1999 even though it was an NDA partner. 'If we had told them beforehand, they would have applied pressure on us. That is why I kept the cards close to my chest. A betrayal has to be answered by a betrayal.'*

Dr. Swamy, who had worked towards the downfall of the Vajpayee government in 1999 along with Congress President Sonia Gandhi and Tamil Nadu Chief Minister Jayalalithaa, explains, 'Mayawati was part of the NDA and she had five MPs so I went to seek her support. She said, "Kanshi Ram has so much faith in you. So for his sake, I will do what you want but only on one condition: don't meet me until the voting is over. I am part of the NDA and these people may hold it against me if they come to know. I will speak on the voting day and say I have decided against voting for the NDA." She feared that the BJP might split her party if she did not vote for the NDA. So I did not meet her at all and she kept her promise.'* Thus, three women brought the Vajpayee government down: AIADMK chief Jayalalithaa, Congress President Sonia Gandhi and BSP supremo Mayawati. Had the five members of the BSP voted for the NDA, Vajpayee's government would have been saved, as it lost by just one vote.

Mayawati felt that six months were not enough for her agenda in the second term. But she considered it her duty to perpetuate the memory of the leaders who secured human dignity for the Dalits and went ahead with her distinctive plans for their empowerment. She installed as many as 15,000 Ambedkar statues all over the state. Renaming schools and libraries also figured high on her to-do list. These were meant as a symbolic challenge to the upper castes. Kanshi Ram thought that the BSP must do something to remember popular Dalit leaders. So, in 1997, Mayawati started the Ambedkar memorial. That should have been the end of it, but she continued installing more statues, including those of herself and Kanshi Ram. Punia recalls her fixation: 'She was so obsessed with it that she did not have time for other things. She left all the developmental work to me. She knew that once the statues were installed, they would not be demolished. She wants to be remembered as an iconic leader of the Dalits, even bigger than Kanshi Ram. She once said, "Babasaheb Ambedkar created the ideas but I implemented them."'*

When the six month period was over, as per the agreement, the BJP took over. Mayawati resigned as chief minister on September 20, 1997, and was replaced by Kalyan Singh. While on the one hand, the new CM tried to lure the legislators of other parties to stabilise his government, on the other, he withdrew the order against Harijan atrocities issued by the Mayawati government. Ugly scenes were witnessed in the Assembly. Contrary to expectations, when the BSP pulled out, the Kalyan Singh government did not fall, much to the surprise of Kanshi Ram and Mayawati. Singh hit back by engineering defections from the BSP (which was the soft target), the Congress and the Janata Dal by offering ministerial berths and other inducements. Governor Romesh Bhandari, a Congress nominee, upset Kalyan Singh's designs and recommended President's rule. However, President K.R. Narayanan did not agree and the Kalyan Singh government continued. Five months later, when the governor installed Congress leader Jagdambika Pal as a one-day chief minister, the court held that the Kalyan

Singh government's dismissal was unlawful and restored him. By then, much to Mayawati's annoyance, the BSP had lost as many as 17 legislators due to Kalyan Singh's manipulations.

The 1998 Lok Sabha elections brought no cheers either to Kanshi Ram or the BSP, as the party did not fare well. The BSP had decided to go it alone and not align with any party. The Congress was wiped out and the BSP got just four seats. While Mayawati won her seat, Kanshi Ram lost the contest. The BSP's only consolation was that it managed to retain the 20% vote share it had in the state. The BJP led the vote tally and was followed by the SP.

The 1999 Lok Sabha elections saw the BJP come back with a bang. Vajpayee secured sympathy votes because his government had lost the confidence vote by a one-vote margin. The Congress, which was responsible for bringing the government down, lost miserably getting only 114 seats—its lowest ever. The BJP-led NDA found itself in a comfortable position. The BSP too did well by going it alone, securing 14 seats, a huge increase from its 1998 tally.

AS KANSHI RAM'S POLITICAL HEIR

The highlight of the next two years was the shot in the arm that Mayawati got when Kanshi Ram, whose health was failing, announced at a public rally in Lucknow that he was handing over complete control of the party to his protégée. By this time, Mayawati was already taking most of the decisions for the BSP and UP was her fiefdom. Kanshi Ram's declaration gave official sanction to what was known informally. He told a cheering crowd on December 15, 2002, "I am not immortal. I also have to leave this world one day. But this work, this movement ought to continue. Therefore before I depart I need to make Mayawati my heir. This work should go on after me."[23]

The relationship between Mayawati and her mentor was often discussed in political circles as being more than one of a *shishya* (disciple) and guru. The fact that the two lived together and that he went out of the way to promote Mayawati, earning displeasure from other leaders in the party, gave credence to such rumours. But Mayawati claimed, "I have no hesitation in saying that since I have also kept my life free from family ties under a missionary objective, I respect Manyawar Kanshi Ramji more than my own father. A father or the head of the family is confined to his family members alone and thinks of their welfare and makes efforts for their happiness, whereas the Bahujan Samaj, with a population of 85 crore, is our entire family and our interest lies in its interest, its happiness is our happiness and its well-being is our well-being. As a disciple, it is my duty to take care of Manyawar Kanshi Ramji and I am happy that I am discharging this duty well. Although in a male dominated society, I have to put up with a lot of things, but I have not been put off because my goal has a higher purpose and is humanistic."[24]

Armed with this public endorsement from Kanshi Ram, Mayawati began to plan for the 2002 Assembly elections. She toured every district and village tirelessly, establishing contact with the local workers. All her hard work resulted in spectacular results in the next Assembly elections.

MAYAWATI'S THIRD TERM

By the time she became the chief minister for the third time in 2002, Mayawati had travelled a long way from riding a bicycle and campaigning on foot. Besides her own personal affluence, her party also mobilised funds and she could now afford to travel by helicopter. By virtue of being an ex-chief minister, she was provided personal security and a convoy of cars. She also set up the Bahujan Volunteer Force (BVF) in every district, a BSP outfit whose members don blue uniforms with brass stars and belts, caps and lapels. This unit assisted the police in controlling the crowds during political rallies. It also kept an eye on the activities in the air-conditioned, carpeted tent that Mayawati used to meet visitors at campaign venues.

By 2002, the BSP was looking for an opportunity to form a coalition government again. The elections resulted in a hung Assembly. Sudha Pai observes that rather than taking the difficult path of Dalit mobilisation and upliftment based upon a distinct identity, the BSP once again decided to seize power by collaborating with the BJP, an avowedly *Manuvadi* (upper caste) party. The move was justified, like it was on the two earlier occasions in 1995 and 1997, as a shortcut to gain power in order to help the downtrodden sections of the state. "The coalition had been formed precisely at that point when the BSP had performed impressively in the 2002 Assembly elections, emerging as the second largest party and overtaking the BJP. The coalition, once again, was clearly an opportunistic step by the BSP to grab power by taking advantage of the political situation."[25] Kanshi Ram and Mayawati preferred to go with the BJP because the BSP would be a senior partner and therefore in a position to assert itself, quite different from its 1995 experiment.

Several BSP Muslim legislators were apprehensive of the alliance with the BJP; some MPs even resigned in protest. This was also soon after the Godhra riots in Gujarat where the Muslim community was affected and the country was shocked by the carnage. Mayawati, however, claims that she went in for the coalition with the support of the Muslim legislators. "I had asked them if they had any objection to our forming the government with the BJP and its allies. They said that they would certainly object to a government under the leadership of the BJP, but that they would be fine with a dispensation under me. In fact, they said that they would be quite happy with that arrangement since they were confident that with me, the life, property and faith of the Muslims would be fully protected."[26]

After the Godhra riots in 2002, when the entire Opposition demanded the banning of the Vishwa Hindu Parishad (VHP) and the Bajrang Dal, two constituents of the parent organisation, the Rashtriya Swayamsevak Sangh (RSS), Mayawati chose to keep mum. There was even a call for the dismissal of Gujarat Chief Minister Narendra Modi and the then Home Minister L.K. Advani. The NDA was in trouble after the allies had expressed their unhappiness over Godhra. It was then that Kanshi Ram assured the BJP top brass that if they supported Mayawati as the UP chief minister, the BSP would prevent the NDA government's collapse. The BSP's position as the senior partner in the government gave Mayawati and Kanshi Ram an upper hand. The deal was struck directly with Vajpayee and Advani; both were soft on Mayawati for their own reasons. They needed to consolidate the BJP in UP, and for that they wanted to share power. Kalyan Singh had, by then, rebelled and was thrown out of the party but other strong state leaders like Rajnath Singh, Kalraj Mishra and Vinay Katiyar opposed the deal. Vajpayee and Advani ignored them and forged the alliance.

After learning her lessons in the previous terms, Mayawati was careful this time around. Besides the crucial portfolios, she also kept the all-important post of the Speaker with the BSP, since the Speaker had played a crucial role at the time of the vote of confidence in the Assembly during her second term. The Rashtriya Lok Dal, another regional party, also joined the coalition to strengthen it. The alliance partners thought that the coalition should work within the parameters of a common minimum programme and the BSP should not follow its own agenda.

When she became chief minister on May 3, 2002, Mayawati took on her adversaries, particularly those from the SP. Raja Bhaiya, an upper caste legislator and rich local bully belonging to the Samajwadi Party, challenged her party's slim majority. Mayawati outsmarted him and put him in jail using the Prevention of Terrorism Act, 2002 (POTA), a law passed by the BJP-led NDA regime. By arresting Raja Bhaiya, she showed that a gutsy lower caste woman could take on powerful upper caste enemies.

Mayawati, however, adopted a conciliatory attitude towards the BJP. While she had the blessings of Prime Minister Vajpayee, she also cultivated Home Minister Advani. She tried to appease the Sangh Parivar by hinting at a national alliance with the BJP in the 2004 Lok Sabha polls. She allayed fears of the upper castes that she might oppose them. On the whole, she was more accommodative, looking at a long-term agenda. Talking about her difficult relationship with the BJP, Mayawati elaborates, "in order to pander to the BJP's ego, I shelved my image of the 'Iron Lady' for some time and put up with insults, which was not in my nature. For the honour of those great men, let alone my bearing with insults, I can even sacrifice my life."[27]

The so-called "insults" are a reference to the Taj corridor corruption case. Under the Taj Heritage Corridor Project, an expanse of land was developed to promote tourism on the Yamuna riverbed behind the World Heritage Site of the Taj Mahal. The then Urban Development Minister Jagmohan asked the Uttar Pradesh government to stop construction due to its detrimental effect on the Taj Mahal. Although she obliged him initially, a month later she challenged him claiming that he was needlessly blaming her government and insisted on the upright minister being dismissed from the ministry. It's likely that she knew about the upcoming Supreme Court order asking the Central Bureau of Investigation (CBI) to inquire into the issue. Mayawati thought Prime Minister Vajpayee would oblige her because of her rapport with the NDA leadership but he rejected her demand. The Chief Vigilance Commissioner also said in his report that Mayawati was directly involved in the irregular commencement of the work and the releasing of the funds to the contractors and that she should be booked for being party to the conspiracy under the Prevention of Corruption Act and the Indian Penal code.

Mulayam Singh did not spare Mayawati and went after her, exposing scandal after scandal. Corruption was rampant during her third term; she was capricious and ruled like a dictator. To counter Mulayam Singh, she filed a number of lawsuits against him and his associates, indulged in mass transfers and played vendetta politics against her opponents. She, however, continued with her Dalit agenda and the Ambedkar Park project. Law and order was one of her main concerns and she ordered a crackdown on criminal elements.

Eventually, the RSS began to realize that the tie-up with Mayawati was a big mistake and before long tensions began to surface between the BJP and the BSP. When the Taj corridor scandal broke out, Vajpayee and Advani could no longer support Mayawati. She even offered to support a BJP-led government but the BJP had already made a secret pact with Mulayam. When she heard that her government might be brought down by the BJP on August 25, 2003, Mayawati had the Cabinet pass a resolution for the dissolution of the State Assembly. In her letter to Governor Vishnu Kant Shastri (a BJP appointee), she complained, "The government led by me enjoys absolute majority but the Opposition, by indulging in manipulation, inducements, coercion and baseless propaganda through the media, is playing mean politics devoid of decorum and has created an atmosphere of instability in the state [...] Nobody can say how many legislators of both sides will go which way out of their greed. Therefore, in order to end the present instability, it is imperative to dissolve the Legislative Assembly for a fresh mandate."[28]

But Mulayam Singh had other plans up his sleeve. The BJP was feeling awkward with the mudslinging between Mayawati and Mulayam and chose to back the SP chief. Mulayam planned to form an alternative government with the BJP once the BSP government fell. As a counter move, Rashtriya Kranti Party leader and former Chief Minister Kalyan Singh, Congress state leader Jagdambika Pal and Rashtriya Lok Dal leader Ajit Singh met the governor and gave their letters of support for an alternative government led by Mulayam Singh. The SP leader sowed dissent within the BSP and, together with all these groups, gave a list of 210 supporters by the late evening of August 26 to the governor, showing he had the numbers. Later, the SP influenced more BSP MLAs, outmanoeuvring Mayawati.

Mayawati felt isolated and betrayed. Her party had broken up, no other party was supporting her and above all, she had to face the wrath of the new chief minister, Mulayam Singh. The Taj corridor case was, and still is, like the sword of Damocles hanging over her head, with the CBI raiding her residences on a court order. Kanshi Ram was ailing and bedridden. Mayawati had to prepare the party for the approaching Assembly elections in Rajasthan, Madhya Pradesh, Delhi and Chhattisgarh. She observes, "I was being attacked from every side because the movement depended on me due to the ill health of Manyawar Kanshi Ramji. *Manuwadi* (upper caste) forces had not only been harming the Bahujan Samaj movement, but in fact conspiring to finish it off. But I continued to struggle against them and they had to finally bite the dust."[29] The governor, however, installed the SP-led coalition government and Mulayam Singh became the chief minister, thus temporarily ending her dream of ruling the state for a fourth time.

The 2004 Lok Sabha elections came even as the BSP was struggling to put its house in order. This was the first time Mayawati led the party without Kanshi Ram's guidance. All the same, the results proved satisfactory for her: as the BSP got more seats than the two national parties. It also got support from the Muslims; four Muslim candidates even won their seats. At the national level, the BSP performed remarkably well in Rajasthan, Punjab, Bihar, Madhya Pradesh, Chhattisgarh and Maharashtra. Its success was ascribed to Mayawati's micromanagement in building up committed cadres and enthusing them. In her public speeches, she not only raised local issues but also had customised pamphlets printed for each constituency.

The BJP-led NDA was confident of winning a second term with its "India shining" propaganda launched to tom-tom its achievements. The party was so confident that it even advanced the polls by six months. Most opinion polls predicted the return of the NDA. The Congress, nervous about the BJP's newfound confidence, started looking for coalition partners. Congress chief Sonia Gandhi personally approached each of the potential allies, including the BSP. As a prelude, she attended Mayawati's birthday party on January 15, 2004. Despite the Congress supporting Mulayam Singh in UP, Sonia gave enough hints that the Congress would like an alliance with the BSP.

The 2004 results were a huge disaster for the BJP and its partners. The Congress formed the UPA government with Manmohan Singh as the prime minister. The BSP did well in UP and elsewhere. It had gone to the polls on its own, spurning the advances of other parties, including the Congress. The BSP won 17 seats while the SP excelled by winning 36 seats. The

Congress emerged as the single largest party winning 141 Lok Sabha seats and formed the United Progressive Alliance (UPA) government. The BJP was the second largest party, winning 137 seats. For the first time, the two UP regional parties—the SP and the BSP—had no role as kingmakers and remained outside the UPA providing need-based support.

MAYAWATI'S FOURTH TERM

Undaunted by the 2004 Lok Sabha results, Mayawati began to chalk out a strategy for social engineering. Her first move was to enlist the support of the upper castes. So in 2002, when she became the chief minister, she appointed Satish Chandra Mishra, a Brahmin lawyer, as the state's advocate-general. Recalling his first meeting with her, Mishra admits that he was surprised that Mayawati chose him for the post, as he did not know her at all. 'Behenji reasoned that if a person is sick, he would go to the best doctor. You are one of best lawyers and that is why I am coming to you'* To assure him of cooperation from the government, she kept the Law Ministry with herself. He later became her lawyer and represented her in the Taj corridor case. In 2003, she made him the All India BSP General Secretary and brought him to the Rajya Sabha in 2004. Mishra played a crucial role in the new policy of social engineering. Within three months in 2005, he covered 21,000 miles, preparing the ground for the Brahmin *mahasabhas* (meetings). As the Brahmins in UP were disappointed with the BJP, they were willing to support the BSP.

Working closely with Mishra, she set aside her narrow caste-based ideology and appealed to the Brahmins. She also showed her commitment to secularism and wooed the Muslims. Her new slogan invited everyone, including the high castes, to "come ride the elephant", the BSP party symbol. It was Mishra who advocated the rainbow coalition and convinced her of its need.

The original BSP mantra, *"Tilak, tarazu aur talwar, inko maaro jutey chaar"* (throw your shoes at anyone from the Brahmin, trader and warrior castes), turned into: *"Tilak, tarazu aur talwar, inko pujo baarambaar"* (worship the Brahmin, trader and warrior castes). With the help of Satish Mishra, Mayawati organised a Brahmin conference in June, 2005, which was a great success. At the end of the conference, which boasted an attendance of half a million participants, Mayawati declared, *"Haathi nahin Ganesh* hain, Brahma, Vishnu, Mahesh hain" (It is not just an elephant but it is Lord Brahma, Lord Vishnu and Lord Shiva), marking a transition from an ideological high ground to a tactical one. Although Mayawati's designs to expand her constituency were executed in 2002, it was the timing in 2005, two years before the next Assembly polls, which brought her tremendous success. She became flexible, realising that Dalit votes alone would not get her power. Taking a leaf from the Congress's book, which had long ruled the state through its winning combination of Dalits, Brahmins and Muslims, she changed her poll strategy.

A US embassy telegram from New Delhi puts Mayawati's strategy in context: "Many dismissed Mayawati's strategy as naive wishful thinking, but she has stubbornly pursued it, and it now appears to be bearing fruit. In the run-up to the elections, Mayawati has organized Brahmin conferences all over UP, which have been well-attended by both Brahmins and Dalits. At the rallies, Brahmin speakers pledging loyalty to Mayawati and the BSP have been cheered on by Dalits. Mayawati currently enjoys the ironclad loyalty of the Dalits, who constitute 21 percent of the state's population. Brahmins, who are 10 percent of the state's voters, have been politically adrift. Formerly with the Congress and the BJP, many could be attracted to vote BSP in this contest, especially if the party sponsors large numbers of Brahmin candidates."[30]

Meanwhile, Mayawati's mentor Kanshi Ram passed away, leaving a vacuum in the party. Mayawati, who nursed him until the end, much to the annoyance of his family, quickly claimed his political legacy at his funeral attended by thousands of Dalits. On October 18, 2006, she declared to a mourning crowd, "I will fulfil Manyawar Kanshi Ram's dream." Her entire one-hour speech justified how she deserved to don the mantle. "'It was on August 23, 2003 in this very city (Lucknow) that Kanshi Ram had declared that he was entrusting the reins of his party to me and that he expected me to take his unfulfilled mission to its logical conclusion,' she told a mammoth gathering outside the Bahujan Prerna Bhavan (Inspiration Centre), the resting place for her mentor's ashes."[31]

Wearing a cream-colored *salwar kameez* and holding the urn containing Kanshi Ram's ashes, Mayawati appealed to the crowds to ensure an "absolute majority" for the BSP. "'You would fulfill the last wish of the party founder by striving hard to see that the BSP rides on to the power pedestal in Uttar Pradesh entirely on its own, so that we can stay a full term and let people find the difference between a lawless Mulayam-ruled state and one where only the rule of law would prevail,' Mayawati told the gathering amidst repeated applause."[32] Fortunately for her, the dream was fulfilled in the 2007 Assembly polls when the BSP secured 206 seats, paving the way for the party to form the government on its own.

Mayawati stunned the country by becoming the chief minister for the fourth time in 2007 and forming the government, ending 14 years of coalition rule. Her party won, achieving a two-thirds majority, comprising of 62 Dalits, 51 Brahmins, 24 Muslims and 18 upper caste Rajputs. This was the first time she came to power without the support of any other party, a feat achieved because of her novel experiment: developing a broad multi-class and multi-caste electorate, thereby inverting the voting pyramid, which until then had been formed with the upper caste at the top but held together by the lower castes at the grassroots, as they make the numbers. Mayawati offered political representation to the upper castes, incorporating them into the Dalit agenda set by the BSP. In 2007, the BSP fielded as many as 139 upper caste candidates, including 86 Brahmins. She also gave tickets to 61 Muslims and 110 Other Backward Classes (OBCs). Only 93 candidates were Dalits. This rainbow coalition, built assiduously by her political astuteness, gave her the unprecedented victory. Responding to her appeal, even Muslims dumped Mulayam Singh, whom they called the "Maulana" (Muslim priest).

As usual, the media did not take her seriously and most opinion polls gave the BSP a lower number of seats; no one could predict that the party would win a majority. All media pundits were completely off the mark. It was Mayawati's moment of pride when the Cabinet was sworn in and the Brahmin and other upper caste ministers chosen by her touched her feet, showing their gratitude in front of the cameras.

When this stunning victory was announced, the international media sat up and noticed. *Newsweek* ran a cover story on her. *The Guardian* (UK) headlined: "Surprise landslide in Indian state elections: Untouchable leader uses caste-cross appeal to win"; elaborating, "Mayawati, 51, remains an enigma in the country's politics. She rarely gives interviews and was best remembered for her lavish birthday celebrations."[33] The *International Herald Tribune* stated: "Low-caste party defies expectations in Indian state vote"; further adding, "The ascendance of the caste-based parties has transformed Indian politics in recent decades, but Ms. Mayawati's victory is the first time a Dalit-led party has won a state election single-handedly. It is also the first time a Dalit party has so deliberately embraced Brahmins into its political fold."[34] *The New York Times* wrote, "Brahmin vote helps party of low caste win in India"; going on to explain: "Ms. Mayawati's triumph lay not only in rallying the state's Dalits around her party, but also in astutely fusing its traditional low-caste base with people from the other end of the social ladder—upper-caste Brahmins, whom she aggressively wooed."[35] While the Dalits accepted her decision to include the Brahmins in her *sarvajan* (all castes) concept, the upper caste too accepted her leadership.

A US embassy telegram from New Delhi predicted serious implications for the UPA government in Delhi and for Indo-US relations as a result of her election. "We can now expect Mayawati to take her winning combination to other states, where she will try to undercut Congress by tapping into lower caste resentment over unequal economic growth."[36] It added, "Congress projected Rahul Gandhi as the 'savior' of UP and his failure to deliver victory is a stunning setback and embarrassment for the Gandhi family. Party loyalists remain reluctant to criticise Rahul Gandhi, whose 'road shows' had no apparent impact on the election, but we can expect a storm of media criticism in the weeks ahead. We expect party President Sonia Gandhi to act quickly to save her son's chances for political advancement."[36]

Analysing her success, another US embassy telegram pointed out: "Despite her three previous stints as Chief Minister, she never made much progress in reviving the economy and providing governance and social services. With an absolute majority and freed from coalition politics, she now has another opportunity to deliver. On the national level, she has hastened the decline of *Hindutva* [Hindu nationalism] and put a badly divided BJP back on the defensive. Mayawati has also caused real worries to Congress. By reviving the old Congress combination of Dalits, Brahmins and Muslims, she is set to extend her appeal to other Hindi belt states and Gujarat in the months and years ahead, making it difficult for Congress to extend its political base."[37] Even before the poll results were announced, she had told her close circle that the party would get 200-plus seats. She also began to nurse prime ministerial ambitions, with the media predicting that her party would become the kingmaker, if not the king, in the 2009 Lok Sabha elections.

Mayawati began her fourth term with a wealth of goodwill but the expectations were not met. While her earlier terms were shaky, the stability of this fourth term provided her with an opportunity to deliver, which she did not seize. In the first 100 days of her fourth term, she made progress in checking mafia politics and the criminal-politician nexus. She, however, did not develop a coherent agenda to address the deep-rooted problems of poverty, lack of education, unemployment and poor governance. Instead, she remained preoccupied with undoing many of her predecessor's decisions.

Another US embassy telegram from New Delhi noted that a wide range of business, political, academic and media contacts generally agreed that Mayawati had done little to promote development since the May 2007 election. It also stated that Mayawati's vice-like grip on all levers of power was apparent. "All decisions must run through Mayawati or her very small coterie of advisers. One Lucknow journalist related a story in which a State Minister was forced to do sit-ups in front of her as penance for not first asking permission to call on UP's governor. Mayawati forced a civil servant to resign when she learned his daughter had joined the Congress Party in Delhi. Other than the BSP stalwarts, none expressed an even begrudging approval of Mayawati's rule."[38] Describing her newly amassed wealth, the *Newsweek* noted: "She is among India's richest politicians, with a taste for diamond jewelry and glittering silk saris and kurtas (she is especially partial to pink). Her 2007 filings put her cash and assets at 525 million rupees ($10.4 million). In 2003, India's Central Bureau of Investigation, while probing allegations that she had embezzled money from an ill-conceived project to build a giant shopping mall next to the Taj Mahal, found that Mayawati and her family owned 72 houses, including several mansions in Lucknow and New Delhi. She claims all this wealth has come as gifts from her admirers, and in 2003 said that the CBI 'has found nothing, and they do not have any case against me.' But CBI investigators uncovered evidence of poor Dalit sweepers, rickshaw pullers and hawkers being paid in front bank accounts through which large sums of cash flowed to Mayawati. "[39]

Two years later, during the Lok Sabha elections in 2009, the BSP's rainbow coalition disintegrated. This was due to all those who were part of her coalition—the Brahmins, the Rajputs and the minorities—getting disenchanted with her. The *sarvajan* concept did not do the trick. As journalist Vidya Subrahmaniam observes, "If anything, the empathy has been replaced by a hostility that expresses itself in malicious, intemperate language towards the BSP boss."[40] During her campaign trail she found that, "From impoverished rickshaw pullers and pavement shopkeepers in Lucknow in Awadh to entire Brahmin villages in Gonda in the east to Muslim clusters in Moradabad in the west, hardly anyone has a nice word to say about the BSP or its supremo. And many of these are the same people who had enthusiastically lined up behind the party in 2007."[40]

While Mayawati did restore law and order and contained criminals, she had no concrete vision to tackle the deep-rooted problems endemic to UP. Obsessed that she was with her predecessor, she spent the first few days undoing many of his decisions, doling out symbolic gestures towards Dalit empowerment and frittering away the goodwill. The voters wanted development and good governance, which she could not provide.

MAYAWATI LOSES THE 2012 ASSEMBLY POLLS

By the time the 2012 Assembly elections were held, Mayawati was on the back foot. The accumulated disappointment of her five-year rule stared her in the face. Her bête noire Mulayam Singh was making a last ditch attempt to revive his party. He toured all the districts relentlessly with his son Akhilesh Yadav, projecting him as the new face of the SP. Akhilesh, a young man with a clean slate, was able to catch the imagination of the voters who were fed up with Mayawati's corrupt rule.

A US embassy telegram from New Delhi notes that Mayawati had done little to promote development since she took over in 2007: "She has become a virtual dictator replete with food tasters and a security entourage to rival a head of state.... Civil servants will not speak to the press for fear of losing their positions. Journalists admitted they feared retribution should they print anything negative about Mayawati."[41] It also pointed out that her absolute majority victory in the May 2007 Assembly polls left her beholden to no one and had allowed her to act on eccentricities, whims and insecurities.

Mayawati developed her own methods of securing finance for the elections. One of them was the donations she accumulated by way of birthday bashes. She usually celebrates her January 15 birthday parties both in Lucknow and Delhi. Another US embassy telegram from New Delhi explains how "Ranking party officials vied for a chance to feed Mayawati a piece of her birthday cake. The BSP terms the day 'fundraising day' and party members make donations to Mayawati directly, often tens of thousands of dollars apiece. With the BSP enjoying a full majority in the UP Assembly, party legislators can rely on generous donations from cowering civil servants, fearful of demotion or transfer, and local business people, who must deal with the state government on a daily basis."[42] In May 2012, while filing her nomination for the Rajya Sabha, she declared that her wealth has doubled to Rs 111.26 crore, as compared to Rs 52 crore in 2007. She also ranks among the top 200 taxpayers in the country.

Vidya Subrahmaniam remarks that the stone statues of Mayawati and acres of parks have become eyesores and are seen as symbols of an obsessively self-centred regime. What the people wanted was governance and not statues. Farmers and Muslims were particularly aggrieved by their construction. The Muslims also rued the lack of warmth towards them. Mayawati did not get the message during the 2009 Lok Sabha polls when her party's vote share had reduced. She has now learnt the lesson that courting communities is not going to keep her in power forever and voters will not support her on the basis of caste alone; development plays an important role too.

In contrast to the state of affairs in the BSP, the SP's mellowed campaign brought the party closer to the people. The voters were still willing to give Maulana Mulayam a chance; the Muslims went back to him, whereas most forward castes returned to the BJP and some to the Congress. The emergence of Mulayam Singh's son, Akhilesh Yadav, was a master stroke. Above all, Mayawati had lost touch with the people.

Radhika Ramaseshan opines that Mayawati lost the 2012 elections perhaps because she was at the mercy of the bureaucrats. She was surrounded by a coterie who had completely taken over; they were allowed to establish a rapport with the MLAs and other party functionaries. It was they who actually ruled. Secondly, at the party level, she had mediocre officials who were given free rein to make money. This further led to her alienation from the party cadre. 'She was locked up within the four walls, not being able to meet people due to her insecurities, not communicating with the media and deprived of a *janata darbar*. During her coalition days, she was meeting people. She had to prove herself, so she was on her toes. She was careful and clued in. But when she got the full mandate, she became lax and somehow got alienated from the people.'*

The BSP's "plus votes" had fragmented over the five years of Mayawati's rule. Vidya Subrahmaniam, who had covered Mayawati's 2011 Assembly polls campaign, elaborates that the "Dalits, who worshipped their Behenji, had begun to complain. In the Ambedkar villages, spruced up for the big match (the Assembly polls), villagers showered praise on Ms. Mayawati, but were bitterly critical of officials who 'defied Behenji's orders'.... Yet through the whining, there was no doubt that their votes would go only to "our Behenji."[43] Her core supporters continue to back her.

The electoral defeat was a big shock for Mayawati, who could not believe that her strategy had failed. She did not waste a day in moving to Delhi and becoming a Rajya Sabha member. She continues to support the UPA at the centre and tries to be in its good books. Even in the presidential and vice-presidential elections, she backed the UPA. For now, Mayawati is waiting for her opportunity as she continues to tour the state.

In the final analysis, it is clear that Mayawati is a loner in politics and wants to work on her own terms. She believes in hard work and has the courage to take on powerful enemies. This leader has survived by her wits and fine-tuned poll strategies. She has no advisers and keeps changing her coterie. She does not trust anyone and is completely insecure. She seeks absolute faith from her followers and believes in her identity politics. Her only weakness appears to be the lack of a pan-India following. While she has been able to make some inroads in states like Maharashtra, Delhi and Punjab, her party has not been able to expand in these states, although this has given the BSP some kind of a national status. Despite repeated attempts, she is unable to spread her wings to the South because she has not able to win caste votes. Mayawati clearly has no vision and lacks administrative skills, but she has the ambition to become the prime minister some day; even if she manages that, thanks to a lopsided support from Uttar Pradesh, she would not be able to rule because she does not understand the aspirations of the other states. She has no vision on a foreign, security or even economic policy pertaining to the whole country, as she does not have the requisite background.

A US embassy telegram from New Delhi corroborates this fact: "... Mayawati had not made many statements on foreign policy issues, save her opposition to the Civil Nuclear Initiative. During the debate over the Civil Nuclear Initiative in July 2008, Mayawati termed the deal 'anti-Muslim' in a blatant effort to appeal to Muslim voters unhappy with U.S. policies in the Middle East and Afghanistan."[44] In essence, she has no broad worldview. However, one thing is certain. Mayawati is down but not out.

She may come back to rule UP after five years or whenever the Assembly elections take place, and she may even do better in the 2014 Lok Sabha polls, but she will have to work hard if she wants to be in the prime minister's chair. Though an astute politician, she has been hampered by a lack of political sophistication, a mercurial nature and a strong autocratic streak. Her approach to politics is suffused with strong emotionalism that could prevent her from playing a greater political role in national politics. In the rough and tumble of UP politics, she has acquired a lot of enemies and is bent on taking revenge. She runs the party as her personal fiefdom. According to a US embassy telegram, "At the head of a 'one woman party', her rule has taken on quasi-fascist trappings including a cult of personality, replete with garlanding of her statues and the construction of large public monuments to her and other Dalit heroes at public expense. She is also fond of staging large public rallies that rival anything seen in Nazi Germany during Hitler's regime."[45]

Another interesting feature of present-day politics appears to be that there are too many regional satraps to compete with Mayawati. There is Nitish Kumar of the Janata Dal United (JD(U)) in Bihar, Mamata Banerjee of the Trinamool Congress, Naveen Patnaik of the Biju Janata Dal (BJD), Jayalalithaa of the All India Anna Dravida Munnetra Kazhagam (AIADMK) and Mulayam Singh of the Samajwadi Party (SP)—all having prime ministerial ambitions in an era of coalition politics. These regional leaders are convinced that their chance will come in 2014 as the two national parties—the BJP and the Congress—are on the decline. Mayawati may have an edge only if she manages to get about 35 or 40 seats from UP and a few more from other states.

Mayawati has to introspect on whether her brand of identity politics would work at the national level. Also, she has to figure out why the BSP is not able to expand in other states, particularly in the South. She would have to give up her dreams of presiding over a pan-national party if she continues to be undependable. While the BSP has grown in UP, in other states, it has made negligible progress in the 25 years of its existence. It has made no penetration in the South, where caste plays out in a different manner. Also there are too many caste parties fragmenting the South Indian polity. This shows that caste politics alone will not get her the top job. The electorate today wants performance, development and progress and this is what the political parties have to think of providing.

Mayawati may have to change her tactics if she wants to make a mark at the national level.

NOTES

1. http://www.thedailybeast.com/newsweek/2009/04/17/india-s-anti-obama.html.
2. Mayawati, *A Travelogue of My Struggle-ridden Life and of Bahujan Samaj*, Vol. 1, p. 77, Prakash Packagers, Lucknow, 2008.
3. Mayawati, *A Travelogue of My Struggle-ridden Life and of Bahujan Samaj*, Vol. 2, p. 18.
4. Sudha Pai, *Dalit Assertion and the Unfinished Democratic Revolution*, p. 110, Sage Publications, 2009.
5. Kalyani Shankar, *Gods of Power: Personality Cult and Indian Democracy*, pp. 279–280, Macmillan India, Updated Edition 2005.
6. Pai, *Dalit Assertion and the Unfinished Democratic Revolution*, p. 174.
7. *The Times of India*, New Delhi, August 21, 1997.
8. *A Travelogue of My Struggle-ridden Life and of Bahujan Samaj*, Vol. 1, p. 63.
9. *A Travelogue of My Struggle-ridden Life and of Bahujan Samaj*, Vol. 2, p. 5.
10. Ibid.
11. Shankar, *Gods of Power: Personality Cult and Indian Democracy*, p. 280.
12. Ajoy Bose, *Behenji: A Political Biography of Mayawati*, p. 110, Penguin, 2009.
13. *Gods of Power: Personality Cult and Indian Democracy*, p. 284.
14. *A Travelogue of My Struggle-ridden Life and of Bahujan Samaj*, Vol. 1, p. 36.
15. Ibid., p. 19.
16. Ibid., p. 16.
17. Ibid., p. 56.
18. Ibid.
19. *A Travelogue of My Struggle-ridden Life and of Bahujan Samaj*, Vol. 2, p. 108.
20. *A Travelogue of My Struggle-ridden Life and of Bahujan Samaj*, Vol. 1, p. 58.
21. *Dalit Assertion and the Unfinished Democratic Revolution*, p. 178.
22. *Gods of Power: Personality Cult and Indian Democracy*, p. 278.
23. *A Travelogue of My Struggle-ridden Life and of Bahujan Samaj*, Vol. 2, p. 438.
24. Ibid., p. 679.
25. *Dalit Assertion and the Unfinished Democratic Revolution*, p. 237.
26. *A Travelogue of My Struggle-ridden Life and of Bahujan Samaj*, Vol. 2, p. 672.
27. Ibid., p. 761.
28. Ibid., p. 740.
29. Ibid., p. 863.
30. http://wikileaks.org/cable/2007/03/07NEWDELHI1508.html.
31. http://www.rediff.com/news/2006/oct/18maya.htm.

32. Ibid.
33. Randeep Ramesh, "Surprise landslide in Indian state election", *The Guardian*, UK, May 12, 2007; *28 Custom 150 Online Journals*, July 18, 2012.
34. Somini Sengupta, "Low-caste party defies expectations in Indian state vote", *International Herald Tribune*, May 14, 2007; *3 Custom 150 Online Journals*, July 18, 2012.
35. Somini Sengupta, "Brahmin vote helps party of low caste win in India", *New York Times*, May 12, 2007; *Custom 150 Online Journals*, July 18, 2012.
36. http://wikileaks.org/cable/2007/05/07NEWDELHI2268.html.
37. http://wikileaks.org/cable/2007/05/07NEWDELHI2313.html.
38. http://wikileaks.org/cable/2008/10/08NEWDELHI2783.html.
39. http://www.thedailybeast.com/newsweek/2009/04/17/india-s-anti-obama.html.
40. Vidya Subrahmaniam, "There is an elephant in the room", *The Hindu*, March 2, 2012.
41. http://www.ndtv.com/article/wikileaks-revelations/wikileaks-cable-on-mayawati-131441.
42. http://wikileaks.org/cable/2009/01/09NEWDELHI108.html.
43. Vidya Subrahmaniam, "Booted up and ready to go", *The Hindu*, November 26, 2011.
44. http://wikileaks.org/cable/2009/05/09NEWDELHI960.html.
45. http://wikileaks.org/cable/2007/05/07NEWDELHI2433.html.

Mamata Banerjee

MAMATA BANERJEE IS A Kolkatan who became chief minister through sheer hard work and determination. It is amazing how a middle-class unmarried woman has been able to capture the imagination of the people, exploding the myth that only those with a political family background, mentor, money or glamour can succeed in public life. It is said that in politics you need a godfather; Mamata never had one, but she achieved great heights on her own and has now become a phenomenon. If the quintessential qualities of a personality cult could be summed up as the ability to attract crowds, deliver results and retain mass base, Mamata seems to possess all.

What is it about her that appeals to the common man? Her support base is the youth, particularly those between the age group of 18 to 35, who are riveted by her fiery speeches. They see her fighting their battles. Mamata claims she does not worry about organising meetings or rallies. "My boys come, work day and night and make it a success,"[1] she acknowledges. It is common knowledge Mamata can assemble a massive crowd within minutes. "People come and help because I don't collect money. For elections some money comes. Membership *chanda* (fee) is there but it is very little."[2]

Those who see her on television in her simple white cotton saree with a blue border (some say she is trying to copy Mother Teresa), a cloth *jhola* (bag) over her shoulder, Hawai *chappals* on her feet, speaking incoherently in her shrieking voice, cannot connect with the phenomenon that she is. She is short, a little on the plump side, shabbily dressed and would not merit a second glance if they did not recognise her. She outmarxed the

Marxists on the streets and as chief minister, she has emerged as a populist woman of action. She explains: "I have never been fond of dressing up or wearing make-up. At home I sometimes amuse myself by styling or cutting hair and my victims are ladies of my household."[3] Krishna Bose, a former Trinamool Congress MP and a close associate, admits that it is difficult to shop for Mamata. 'I go to a shop and ask them to show me the ugliest saree!'* To her credit, Mamata does not put on airs. She is arrogant within her party but her doors are open to all. What really steals the show is her girl next-door image, which she has assiduously cultivated. After her historic win in the 2011 Assembly elections, the *TIME* magazine rated Mamata among the "100 Most Influential Women in the World" on April 18, 2012. A poor schoolteacher's daughter, Mamata believes in simple living and still puts up in a single 8 by 8 feet room in a south Kolkata neighbourhood in Kalighat. She is also old fashioned and believes in the joint family system; she lived with her mother until she died last year, and now lives with her brothers and their families.

No one would think of this middle-aged woman as a maker of history. But she is all this and more because of her determination to fight the Communist Party of India (Marxist) and ultimately oust them from the Writers' Building (the chief minister's office and secretariat). Her ideology is simple and rigid: get rid of the Marxists. As the famous poet Mahasweta Devi said, it is nothing more than being anti-CPI(M).

A US embassy telegram from New Delhi described Mamata as "Mamata Mia" and went on to add that she is fearless and aggressive, likening her to a tigress. "Due to her unpredictable and high-strung nature, she has succeeded in occupying the political limelight in West Bengal as no other politician has. She has taken on the Left, when no other leader was willing, and has capitalised on Nandigram and Singur anger to mount what analysts view as the most credible challenge to Left Front rule in West Bengal since they came to power in 1977."[4]

HER CROWNING GLORY

Although she has been in politics since the late seventies, Mamata's crowning glory came when she threw out the Left and marched into the Writers' Building as the new chief minister. The whole world watched the first woman chief minister of West Bengal being sworn in on May 20, 2011, ending the 34-year communist rule. *The Times of India* described her metamorphosis as that of "... a street fighter to a change agent. And now an icon. Mamata Banerjee's single-handed demolition of the Left Front in Bengal is the stuff legends are made of."[5] This by itself was a feat but Mamata came to power with a massive majority, leaving the mauled Left with a humiliating defeat and her junior partner, the Congress party, irrelevant. It was indeed a sweet revenge when Chief Minister Buddhadeb Bhattacharjee also lost the election along with several other prominent Left leaders. She came to power in West Bengal 13 years after launching her party, the Trinamool Congress (TMC). This success has made her somewhat of a super woman. "This is a victory for *Maa, Mati, Manush* (the mother, the land, the people). This is a verdict against years of exploitation, agony and oppression," said Banerjee, emerging from her modest home in south Kolkata amid a sea of frenzied supporters. "People of Bengal got independence for a second time."[6] Even the international media sat up and took note of the woman who wears crumpled sarees and Hawai *chappals*. Bill and Melinda Gates have approached her for help in polio eradication. US Secretary of State Hillary Clinton was stunned by her achievement and quite impressed after meeting her.

MAMATA'S STRATEGY

What are the reasons behind her unprecedented victory? Although she had been working against the Left for a long time, its decline began as early as the 2009 Lok Sabha polls when the Left parties lost a large number of seats in its strongholds in West Bengal and Kerala, winning only 15 seats. This was a poor show as compared to their tally of 60 plus in the 2004 Lok Sabha election. The Trinamool Congress fared extremely well, bagging 18 seats, while the Congress won only 7 seats. Mamata became the railway minister in the UPA-2 government, while four of her colleagues became Ministers of State. The Left now had no influence either at the Centre or in the state after losing the polls. Some claim that Mamata got the crown because people were fed up of Left rule, and she was the only alternative.

A US embassy telegram from New Delhi pointed out, "Trinamool supremo and new Railway Minister Mamata Banerjee has achieved what no other political leader in West Bengal has been able to do so in 32 years—shatter the illusion of the CPI(M)'s invincibility—and is riding an increasing wave of momentum.... The 2009 parliamentary elections may have been the first tolling of the CPI(M)'s death bell, internally prompting considerable soul-searching and perhaps its transition into more of a social democratic party."[7]

While the state CPI(M) leaders blamed the national leadership for reasons like the withdrawal of Left support to the UPA-1 on the Indo-US nuclear deal in 2008, or failure of marketing the idea of a Third Front as an alternative to the Congress and the BJP, others blame the state leaders for their mistakes such as forcible land acquisition and departure from the party's pro-poor agenda. The CPI(M) had also alienated its traditional supporters—Muslims and farmers—through aggressive industrialisation policies.

Mamata had been in hibernation for some time and she chose this moment to lead a mass movement. In fact, after her party's miserable performance in the 2004 Lok Sabha polls, Mamata was disheartened over having won only one seat (her own), as against the credible victory of the Left. She was cooling her heels waiting for an opportunity, and that opportunity came when Singur and Nandigram happened. The West Bengal government's disastrous attempt to forcibly acquire agricultural land for industry in Nandigram in 2007 and Singur in 2008 had resulted in a backlash from the farmers and tribes. Singur is about 40 kilometres away from Kolkata. The Tatas, one of the most well-known industrialists in India, decided to set up a factory in Singur, which would produce the world's cheapest car, the Nano. Mamata grabbed this opportunity to hit back at the government. She led the agitation against the factory, claiming that the government had acquired the land at a very low cost and given it to the Tatas. She and her party demanded that the land be given back to the farmers. Keeping the elections in mind, she also promised to give back some of the land to the farmers if she came back to power, thus positioning herself as their saviour, someone who stood up for them and resisted the government's moves to acquire their land forcibly both in Singur and Nandigram villages. A US embassy telegram from New Delhi concluded, "In short, she projected herself as more left than "Left" and forced a humbling retreat by the CPI(M) government in Nandigram and Singur while simultaneously striking a devastating blow to the economic activity in the state."[8]

Mamata undertook a 25-day fast from December 3–28 in 2006 to protest against the Tata's project in Singur. She received wide publicity thanks to the media camping with her. Responding to the requests of former Prime Minister V.P. Singh, former Prime Minister Atal Bihari Vajpayee and President Kalam, she ended her fast. She got the support of civil society leader Medha Patkar, Booker Prize winner Arundhati Roy, ultra-Left activist Kanu Sanyal and even some BJP supporters. On December 4, ultra-Left activists even attacked a Tata showroom.

Chief Minister Buddhadeb Bhattacharjee remained firm, stating that the Tata's project would continue. He had written four letters to Mamata offering to discuss the matter. It was a difficult month for him; there were at least three strikes over the Singur land issue. What made it even more difficult was the fact that the civil society leaders' support lent the agitation credibility and it offered an alternative pro-farmer and anti-corporate voice in the country. A US embassy telegram from New Delhi to Washington pointed out, "The fact that this battle is being waged in a Communist-run state is ironic as the Left has been actively blocking efforts by the GOI to implement necessary reforms in the agricultural sector."[9] Mamata ran a successful campaign against the "so called" misdeeds of the Left. Her tactical pre-poll alliance with the Congress helped both the parties to secure more seats. The Left Front had no leader of stature after Chief Minister Jyoti Basu retired in 2000.

The national CPI(M) leaders did not support Chief Minister Buddhadeb Bhattacharjee's policies and felt embarrassed by the Singur and Nandigram agitations, which they felt were not handled well. Former Lok Sabha Speaker Somnath Chatterjee observes that the Left leaders did not heed the warning of the 2008 Panchayat elections. 'The impression was created that the CPI(M) has not served any of its constituents. Two events—one was Nandigram and the other Singur—were so badly handled that there was an administrative collapse. Mamata was talking of change, and people thought, why not give her a chance.'* The Left lost its hold not only in urban areas but also in rural regions. The base of the party was rural, not urban. To lose that was the party's and its leadership's failure, Chatterjee notes.

There was indiscipline and factionalism in West Bengal and Kerala, which hurt the CPI(M)'s prospects. Several youth who had come with aspirations soon left the party after getting disenchanted. Bitter quarrels between the camp led by Kerala Chief Minister Achuthanandan and his rival, state unit president Pinarayi Vijayan, confused the cadres. Another important reason could be that several people who had joined the Left in their youth were from powerful and influential families who had lost touch with the common man.

Mamata was lucky because she emerged stronger than the Congress. The Trinamool Congress (TMC) was more aggressive and took up the issues concerning the common man. She was more alert to the situation and certainly more active. Moreover, for two years after becoming the railway minister in 2009, she and her ministers worked overtime in Bengal, using their ministerial power and influence to throw out the Buddhadeb government. She gave a bonanza to West Bengal when she was the railway minister in 2010 and effectively won over the poor with her simple image and slogan for *paribartan* (change), just as Barack Obama did during his 2008 presidential campaign with his slogan "yes, we can", offering change for the better. She had the support of the regional language and English media before the 2011 Assembly polls. The TMC focused on the rural voters, establishing a special cell for winning over poorer sections and minorities. The Left alleged that she also got support from the Maoists, who were running a parallel government in the state with a secret understanding.

Mamata attempted a makeover to appear like a chief minister-in-waiting. According to a US embassy telegram from New Delhi: "Skepticism remains whether Banerjee's makeover truly represents a new product—cooler, more level-headed, and willing to accept outside advice—or simply the season's new political makeup. Consensus exists that she is conscientiously trying to transform her image from political maverick and firebrand into a woman ready, able and willing to lead India's fourth most populous state.... Since the May 2009 parliamentary elections elevated West Bengal's regional party, All India Trinamool Congress, from obscurity to the second largest constituent party in the United Progressive Alliance, it leader, Mamata Banerjee, conscientiously sought to rebrand herself as West Bengal's chief minister-in-waiting. She is using the considerable administrative resources at her disposal as railway minister, political resources as leader of the state opposition party, and personal resources to initiate this transformation. Supporters and critics acknowledge the new image, but question whether it is indeed a new product, or simply new packaging."[10] The culmination was the *paribartan* she sought, and the change came when people threw out the communists and brought her Trinamool Congress to power in West Bengal.

WEST BENGAL POLITICS

Before one goes further, one should understand West Bengal politics in order to appreciate Mamata's achievement. It is the fourth most populous state in India, with 70% Hindus, 25% Muslims and a small percentage of Buddhists, Christians and Jains. There are 18 million Scheduled Castes and 4 million Scheduled Tribes. The majority, almost two thirds, is engaged in the agricultural sector, with a small percentage working in industries. The Left parties had been ruling the state uninterruptedly since 1977.

Earlier, the *Bhadralok* (elite Bengali) leadership of the Congress came primarily from the Hindus. As Atul Kohli, professor at Princeton University, observes: "A significant proportion of the Bengali *Bhadralok* shunned the Congress. They experimented instead with radical nationalism and militant politics, both rightists and leftists. A minority of them were attracted to communism.... Over time, however, a faction of the communist leadership broke away from Moscow's counsel, utilised Bengali nationalism and reformism as mobilising themes, and made significant inroads in the Bengali countryside. It was those reform-oriented communists who eventually filled the power vacuum created by Congress's weakness."[11] Bengal has its own peculiar caste and class system, which helped these non-Congress political forces. The problem for the West Bengal CPI(M) unit was that a strong leader like Jyoti Basu, who had a place in national and state politics until his death, had a hold on the party; he was a cult figure. After his exit, Mamata had more than adequate space for building up her own personality cult.

Also before independence, West Bengal was one of the few states where the Congress did not share power. After partition and the Muslim League's departure to Pakistan, the Congress filled up the vacuum. Throughout the years of Congress dominance, there were several Left parties, including the CPI and later also the CPI(M), but there was no united opposition; therefore the Congress exploited this and continued to rule. In the sixties, some of the political developments hurt the Congress and helped these Left parties. Corruption and factional fights within the Congress also helped them. Ultimately, when Ajoy Mukherjee left the Congress to form his own Bangla Congress, things came to a head. As a result, the Congress did not get a majority in the 1967 Lok Sabha elections. Those polls—the first held after the death of Nehru—proved to be equally disastrous for the Congress in other states as well. Ajoy Mukherjee's efforts were of no benefit since his coalition was not cohesive. After Indira Gandhi won the Bangladesh War, the prospects of the Congress soared. Meanwhile, different parties in Ajoy's coalition were becoming wary of each other and started looking to the CPI(M). That was how the CPI(M) came to power in 1977, after which no one could displace it until 2011.

When Mamata entered the scene there were several senior Congress leaders hailing from the state like former Chief Minister Siddhartha Shankar Ray, Subrata Mukherjee, Pranab Mukherjee, Priya Ranjan Das Munshi and others. She was junior to them and knew she had a long way to go. But she chose one issue which the others did not—the anti-CPI(M) plank—and stuck to it, which earned her dividends. Mamata had been fighting them since the seventies, right from her college days. The Congress was concentrating more on national level politics and Mamata's grouse was that it was not fighting the Left. When the time came for a change, she was the only anti-CPI(M) face. Since Mamata Banerjee founded the Trinamool Congress in 1998, it has become the main opposition party to the Left.

THE KOLKATA GIRL'S DREAM

Who is Mamata and how has she has become the superwoman that she is today? Mamata claims, "I never imagined that I would enter such a large arena of politics, become an MP, find a place in the Union cabinet or address a historic rally at the Brigade (Parade) Grounds in Kolkata."[12] Just as most people start their life with a dream, Mamata too had a dream. "Mine was to do something different—to look at politics from a humanitarian angle."[13]

There is a story behind her visceral hatred towards the comrades. She claims out of 365 days, 300 were spent fighting for their lives on the streets of Calcutta. There was always some kind of agitation happening in the state of West Bengal and this time it was a protest against a rise in public transport fares. Mamata got word from someone in the administration that there was a conspiracy to get her killed. She immediately went to the press with it. The Congress had called for a *bandh* (state-wide shutdown) on August 16, 1990, to protest against the death of Raghunandan Tiwari, Manas Banerjee and Bimala, who were killed in police firing. Just the previous day her mother had forbidden her to go out, fearing an attack on her. Mamata was not only close to her mother, she would not do anything without her blessing as long as she lived. But she convinced her mother that she was going to sit in her office. When she and her colleagues reached Hazra crossing, suddenly some CPI(M) goons attacked them with iron rods in broad daylight. Just before the attack, four or five taxis carrying CPI(M) activists virtually took over the area and sanitised it so that no one could come to the rescue and there would be no eyewitness. Thereafter, they attacked the rally from the front. She saw Lalu Alam and a couple of others approaching from the other side. Mamata narrates the story of the brutal attack on her, calling it one of the most tumultuous periods in her life. "I still remember two thick rods hitting my skull, and then blood everywhere. Yet, even in that moment of madness I did not lose my nerve. Almost in slow motion, I saw the third rod descending towards me and, in a split-second reflex motion, covered my head with my arms. The red rod hit my arms but if it had hit the skull, I would have died on the spot."[14] Mamata had to go through extensive plastic surgery for her skull injuries and even today, the area operated on the skull swells and gives pain. She still cannot sleep at night and goes to bed very late and wakes up late. This was not the only brutal attack on her. There was the 1996 assault near Garden Reach. "It was yet another of those miraculous escapes for me," she reminisces.[15] Mamata is quite superstitious and believes a guardian angel is protecting her.

THE TURNING POINT

Mamata's defining moment came when she fought her first election in 1984. Her rise in politics was phenomenal. Saugata Roy, veteran Trinamool Congress leader who later became a minister in the Manmohan Singh government, recalls that Mamata's rise began when the Congress split in 1978. He has seen her as a young girl in college where he was teaching. She was a challenge for the Socialist Unity Centre of India (Communist) and soon became popular. Roy was also the general secretary of the Congress party in the state—that was how he came to know her. She even campaigned for him in the 1977 Lok Sabha polls. 'But her real recognition in the party came after the Congress (Indira) was formed. She was working with Congress leader Subrata Mukherjee and taking part in many militant agitations. By 1983, she was known in Kolkata.'* The young shrieking woman became a national hero and a "giant killer" when she defeated CPI(M) veteran Somnath Chatterjee in the 1984 Lok Sabha elections. Had she not entered Parliament, she would not have become a national leader. Jadavpur, the constituency from where she won, had been considered a red citadel for long, and Somnath Chatterjee, a veteran lawyer, had represented it many times. Congress leaders were always hesitant to contest from this seat. Rajiv Gandhi, who became the prime minister after the brutal assassination of Indira Gandhi, chose to go for polls in December 1984. Mamata's critics say tongue-in-cheek that she was chosen because no one else was willing to contest from Jadavpur. "I was in a quandary. Our colleague Rashid Ghazi from Bishnupur said, 'We don't want anyone else from Jadavpur... It has to be you.'"[16] And finally, Mamata decided to contest; it took a lot of courage to make that decision. She campaigned from door to door, ultimately demolishing communist leader Somnath Chatterjee. Saugata Roy observes that she campaigned in her strident style. 'Somnath Chatterjee did not take her seriously and he was complacent. He thought he could defeat her easily.'*

Mamata makes no bones when she says, 'I did not enter the fray with the confidence that I would win, but I was determined not to give up without a fight. Finally I won.'* Attributing her victory to the common man, she claims with modesty, "If I deny this, I will be telling a lie about what is a historical fact. The common man's affection carved out my victory to national level politics; there was also the selfless love and affection of the people of Jadavpur."[17] There was another important factor in her victory: the elections were held in the aftermath of Indira Gandhi's assassination. Congress leader Mani Shankar Aiyar explains, 'Even a lamppost would have won at that time because of the circumstances.'*

But Somnath Chatterjee, the man who was defeated by her, claims that it was not her charisma but the media which propelled her to such success. 'She has shown tremendous guts and initiative and has had favourable media exposure right from the beginning.'* Chatterjee also thinks that where there is confrontational politics, where people's expectations are not fulfilled easily, and where anti-incumbency is a factor, it is very easy to adopt an attitude of confrontation. 'Therefore if somebody is projected as a mouthpiece of this feeling of protest, articulating the case of the common people as a denial of their rights, that takes some shape. Simply put, it is based on negative politics.'*

Having started her career with an image of a giant killer, it was not difficult for Mamata to move forward, screaming in incomprehensible English as she went along. 'She used to screech and move towards the well of the house, as was her standard practice. One could see that this was sheer antipathy but her loyalty to Rajiv Gandhi was unquestionable,' remarks Mani Shankar.* He was then an official in the Prime Minister's Office (PMO), and his term coincided with Mamata's first five-year term.

Once Mamata entered Parliament her life changed. She developed a style of her own. She would challenge the CPI(M) on any pretext. But she had to fight not only the CPI(M) but also her own colleagues who were jealous of her instant rise in popularity. Her critics not only thought that she would fade away but also started a personal vilification campaign against her. They alleged that in her biodata she had written that she has a doctorate degree from a foreign university, which did not exist. "The way it was talked about, it made me seem like an illiterate person who could not even sign her name.... Indeed the idea was to escalate the issue so much that I would lose my seat in Parliament."[18] It was Prime Minister Rajiv Gandhi who restored her spirit by standing by her.

Mamata took up issues connected with atrocities on women as well as those pertaining to West Bengal. When she raised the issue of the alleged murder of former Deputy Prime Minister Chaudhary Devi Lal's daughter-in-law in Parliament, demanding a CBI inquiry, she was not allowed to speak by the Left members. Enraged, she walked up to the Janata Dal leader Madhu Dandavate and placed her bangle in front of him, declaring, "If none of you has the guts to do anything about this, please wear this bangle and sit at home."[19] A bewildered Dandavate just looked on helplessly. This provoked a Telugu Desam member to take his shoes off and place them on her table amidst uproar in the House, resulting in a phone call from Rajiv Gandhi late at night, congratulating her for her courage. He continued to promote her as long as he lived. Mani Shankar Aiyar remarks that Rajiv Gandhi was then fully involved in the election campaign as was Mamata, although she was low in the pecking order. 'Rajiv Gandhi was trying to see whether people of his generation could be brought into positions in the party. Mamata was there wherever we went for the campaign.'*

GHASTLY ATTACK

Mamata lost in the 1989 Lok Sabha polls and kept a low profile but she continued to be active in West Bengal. The Congress party also lost and Rajiv Gandhi decided to sit in the Opposition; V.P. Singh had become prime minister, followed by Chandra Shekhar for a few months. The next big milestone in Mamata's life was when CPI(M) goons attacked her on August 16, 1990. Having passed out due to the violent attack, she woke up to find herself in hospital and had to undergo surgery. Rajiv Gandhi paid for the entire hospitalisation charges and even offered to send her abroad for treatment. She was quite happy when Rajiv Gandhi appointed her the West Bengal Youth Congress president while she was still in hospital. Saugata Roy points out that when she came out of the hospital she was already a heroine. 'People began to feel that here is a girl who is willing to sacrifice her life and fight with courage.'* The conspiracies against her continued even after that. "Never, never in my life will I forget how many times Rajiv saved me from these party conspiracies," acknowledges Mamata.[20]

AS JUNIOR MINISTER

Mamata contested the 1991 Lok Sabha polls from South Kolkata and won. She was shattered when Rajiv Gandhi was assassinated by the Liberation Tigers of Tamil Eelam (LTTE) in May 1991 while he was campaigning in Chennai. When Rajiv Gandhi came to address a meeting at Deshapriya Park prior to his assassination, Mamata had a premonition that something might happen to him. "I instinctively felt something terrible was about to happen. I kept thinking I hope this is not the last time I am seeing him… Please god doesn't let it be so," she thought to herself.[21]

The next important milestone in her life was when Mamata joined the Narasimha Rao government in May 1991. Shocked by the assassination of Rajiv Gandhi, Mamata was sitting with Vincent George, Rajiv Gandhi's secretary, and watching the cabinet swearing-in. Unable to concentrate, she returned to the house of a colleague with whom she was staying. There she learnt that she was being appointed a minister. She was hesitant but rushed to Rashtrapati Bhavan (Presidential Palace) immediately, where she took oath as a junior minister.

She took up her post in Shastri Bhavan where her ministry was located and started assembling her team. She had no experience whatsoever in running a ministry but was enthusiastic to make a difference. Youth Affairs and Sports was a fitting ministry for her because she knew how to deal with young people. She was impatient to do things and brought into focus areas like rural sports. However, Mamata was not enamoured of power and was itching to return to West Bengal to do party work. She remained a minister for 17 months only. Former Prime Minister P.V. Narasimha Rao explained that "in order to click one has to have the innate ability to sustain the popularity. It needs other talents too. You have to make yourself understood and your sincerity acknowledged. If people think that you are doing all this with some ulterior motive, then immediately, or in the course of time, it becomes counterproductive, so one has to maintain that image of sincerity. The image is not important but the perception is more important. But in

Mamata's case I think she has succeeded by demonstrating that she is with the people and genuinely cares for them. She is also fearless; people know that she would go to any extent to help them. She has done things which takes tremendous courage and imagination—all these traits are combined in one person."[22]

MAMATA RESIGNS AS MINISTER

In her inimitable style Mamata decided to resign while she was addressing a huge rally at the Brigade Grounds on 25 November 1992. It was easy to become a minister but difficult to give it all up, and Mamata chose this moment to sacrifice her ministerial berth. She also wanted to test how many of those who flocked around her would remain with her when she was not a minister. The rally was a great success, as the grounds were packed with people. As Mamata puts it, "I thought this was the moment to unfetter myself from my responsibilities as a minister. A lot has been said about my decision but it was an intensely personal call… a voice was telling me from inside, before you dedicate yourself to the people, give something back."[23]

Confirming her ability to attract crowds, former minister Sontosh Mohan Dev said, 'At the rally people stood on the roofs. By the time I arrived from Delhi, she had already announced that she was going to resign as Youth Affairs and Sports minister. I tried to dissuade her but she would not listen.'* Narasimha Rao later observed, "I could see that she was one of the few rare politicians who was not comfortable with power and soon she gave up her position as a minister to find her place in the West Bengal Congress."[24]

CONTESTING FOR STATE CONGRESS PRESIDENT

Mamata continued to work for the party and soon there were changes in the West Bengal Congress. The then state Congress chief Siddhartha Shankar Ray decided to step down. This triggered a power struggle. Mamata saw her opportunity and threw her hat in the ring. She was the president of the Youth Congress for barely a year. She realised that by becoming the state chief, she could intensify the fight against the CPI(M). Senior Congress leader Pranab Mukherjee was the candidate and this was the beginning of the troubles between them. Mamata decided to contest although she had only 37 of the 400 Pradesh Congress Committee (PCC) delegates with her. She knew the odds were against her. "I became a discarded rag doll in the puppet show where money, power and a cosy arrangement between the Right and the Left were the strings attached. So I lost."[25] That was the time when she realised how much the Left was interested in the Congress's internal elections. Saugata Roy recalls how since 1992 she was trying to create an anti-CPI(M) space for herself; she wanted to be the anti-CPI(M) face.

Mamata Banerjee continued to fight the Jyoti Basu government. An incident on 7 January 1993 made her resolve that she would never enter the Secretariat as long as Basu remained chief minister. Felani Basak, a woman from Nadia, had complained to Mamata that a CPI(M) goon had raped her fourteen-year-old daughter and she had become pregnant. The young girl was deaf and mute and therefore could not tell anyone what happened. By the time the mother came to know about it, it was too late. Still Mamata wanted to bring this to the notice of the chief minister, who had just come back from a holiday. She sought an appointment at the Writers' Building, the secretariat of the West Bengal government. She and another MLA reached the chief minister's office at 3 pm. Mamata asked the MLA to sit on *dharna* (protest) in front of the chief minister's office. Suddenly she found a police contingent arriving and taking them away. Mamata, who was waiting near the corridor, rushed to the mother and daughter and told the policemen they should not be inhuman towards a differently-abled girl. Meanwhile the chief minister arrived but he did not stop to talk them. After the commotion, the police was ordered to forcibly remove all of them from the premises. The police kicked them and took them to a nearby police station against their will. It was midnight by the time Mamata and her colleagues were allowed to leave. She vividly recalls that "on reaching the foot of the Gandhi statue at Mayo Road that cold winter night, I took an oath that as long this arrogant chief minister remains in power, I will neither see his face nor set foot inside the Writers' Building."[26]

The bitterness continued even after Mamata got elected to the Lok Sabha from the South Kolkata constituency in 1996. The Congress had lost the elections and decided to support the United Front (UF) coalition government—first headed by H.D. Deve Gowda, and succeeded by I.K. Gujral. There was despondency in the party when Sitaram Kesri took over as Congress president. The party ignored Mamata and, much to her chagrin, did not even give her a chance to speak in Parliament. When the

Deve Gowda government fell after Kesri pulled out Congress's support, Mamata confronted her party men asking why they had withdrawn support. There was confusion as to who would form the next government. A large number of MPs were ready to support the BJP. Mamata was given a proposal that if she, Ajit Panja and Krishna Bose supported the BJP with one third of the Congress, an alternative government could be formed. "I refused outright because I was clear in my mind that we had won on a Congress symbol and if we betrayed the party, we would be betraying the people who elected us."[27] Soon Gujral was sworn in.

Meanwhile the BJP, which had won just two seats in the 1984 elections, was growing fast and tried to lure some disgruntled Congressmen to join its ranks. Some leaders, fed up with the Kesri regime, decided to defect to other parties. It was a suffocating period for Mamata, who was upset over her humiliation by the coterie around Kesri. The hardliners who were against the CPI(M) were completely ignored. This led to their revolting against Kesri's leadership.

During the All India Congress Committee (AICC) session held in Kolkata the revolt in the Congress became clear. As a *Hindustan Times* representative, I had gone to cover the event and got a firsthand report of what happened during the August 9, 1997 AICC session. The Congress also had its Working Committee's elections, which was creating a lot of interest. Kesri presided over the meeting, but the main news was about a rally organised by Mamata outside the stadium where the AICC session was being held. The "indoor versus outdoor" became a huge controversy. The other big news was the presence of Rajiv Gandhi's widow Sonia Gandhi, who had remained outside the political domain all along. Speculation was rife that she might enter politics soon, although she refused to even be seated on the dais during the session. She did however agree to make a short seven-minute speech when the delegates insisted. She was also supposed to address Mamata's rally, but that did not happen. Kesri tried his best to dissuade Mamata from holding the rally and sent several Congress leaders openly as well as secretly to strike a bargain. But Mamata was adamant. The AICC session showed the amount of money, power and muscle that went into the Congress Working Committee (CWC) elections; on the other hand, there were thousands of people flocking to attend Mamata's rally without any inducement. Congress officials even tried dissuading the delegates from attending the outdoor meeting. Her rally was a great success and the AICC delegates were impressed with the show of strength.

Mani Shankar recalls, "She wanted Kesri to come for the rally. But his advisers vetoed it and he did not go. Soon after I went to meet *Ananda Bazaar Patrika's* proprietor, Aveek Sarkar, who felt that Kesri should have gone. Sarkar told me nobody else could have revived the party or given a fight to the CPI(M).* Encouraged by the rally's success, Mamata thought that "in terms of trust and rights, August 9 was a turning point, a crucial new beginning… This meeting gave birth to a new-found emotion and 'can-do' spirit."[28]

By the end of 1997, it was becoming clear that Mamata would not remain in the party; it was equally clear to Mani Shankar Aiyar. One day he went to the Central Hall of Parliament in a bleak mood and was not sure if he was going to get a ticket. Mamata was sitting in a far right hand corner of the hall. When Mani sat next to her, she asked him about his future plans. Pointing to senior Congress leader G.K. Moopanar, who was sitting at the far left corner, he said it all depended on his ticket. She surprised him by suggesting he contest from West Bengal. Taken aback, Mani told her that he belonged to Tamil Nadu and did not even know the language. Mamata stated that everybody knew him as Rajiv Gandhi's shadow and then offered him to contest from Barrackpore on her quota of seats. Since she was in the Congress, Mani thought it was a bizarre idea and did not accept the offer, little knowing that she was planning to launch her own party. When he went to plead with Sonia Gandhi in December to take over the party, he did not get a positive response. As a result, he was exploring other avenues with the Samajwadi Party, which his close friends advised him against. Hence, he decided to join Mamata in her rally to launch the party on December 29 in Darjeeling. That was where the news arrived that Sonia was taking on a bigger role in the Congress. In January, when he met Sonia Gandhi again, she asked him to request Mamata to return to the party fold but Mamata refused, saying it was too late.

Meanwhile, there were several developments at the national level in the Congress. Sitaram Kesri suddenly developed prime ministerial ambitions and decided to pull down the Gujral government, which he had supported wholeheartedly until now. The Jain Commission's interim report, which delved into Rajiv Gandhi's assassination, had come out by this time and it hinted at the DMK's involvement. Kesri used it as an excuse and demanded that the United Front (UF) should drop the DMK ministers from the Cabinet. Gujral refused to oblige and his government fell shortly thereafter, resulting in the 1998 Lok Sabha polls. Many first-term MPs were upset that their terms were curtailed to just a few months. With his dream shattered, Kesri tried to bring some order to the party, but to no avail. The crisis was at its peak; people were looking for better prospects. Like Mamata, some of them rushed to 10 Janpath (Sonia Gandhi's residence) and pleaded with her to take over. Although Sonia heard them out, she refused to reveal her mind.

FLOATING THE TRINAMOOL CONGRESS

Totally disenchanted with the Congress, Mamata and her colleagues busied themselves in forming their own party, as elections were nearing. West Bengal was to go to the polls on February 22 and 28. Just before that she received a phone call from Sonia Gandhi, asking her to come to Delhi. Accompanied by her close associates Ajit Panja and Sudip Bandyopadhyay, a wary Mamata met her on December 14. She had continued to be in touch with Sonia after the rally and had been visiting her after Rajiv Gandhi's assassination often; she had come to know her well. Over a long meeting they thrashed out their issues and Sonia agreed with their grievances. Once again Mamata tried to persuade her to come forward and lead the party. According to Mamata, Sonia Gandhi said, "I can't. I am a foreigner. Not everyone will accept me."[29] On her part, Sonia dissuaded Mamata from launching her own party. Mamata was caught between her loyalty towards the Gandhi family and her own political compulsions. Meanwhile Sonia told Oscar Fernandes, the general secretary of the AICC, to sit with them and prepare a note. But even after this meeting, when nothing happened, Mamata realised that it was a ruse to keep her from filing the papers with the Election Commission on December 17, the last date for registering a new party. She was well prepared for all eventualities. Cautiously, she had already worked out the details for the new party: its symbol, constitution and the paper work. Since Mamata and her associates considered themselves the "real congress", the constitution was on the lines of the Congress's constitution.

December 17 turned out to be a rather eventful day. Pressure was coming from Sonia Gandhi not to file the papers. Even Mamata's brother from Kolkata was used to persuade her not to launch the party. So she took a decision that she would not go but would file the papers in the name of the Trinamool and the documents would be dropped in the Election Commission box. This was to safeguard any mischief from the Congress. Mamata still continued to wait for a settlement with the Congress but none came. On December 19, at 10.30 am they were called to Sonia Gandhi's house and in her presence another draft was finalised. "The announcement never came. Instead, Congress president Kesri went to Hyderabad and said exactly the opposite—that Mamataji has been chosen as the convener of the campaign committee."[30]

This was the last straw; Mamata and her colleagues decided to announce the new party on December 22, which she named Trinamool (grassroots) Congress. While she was holding the press conference she received the news that she and her party men had been expelled from the Congress. That was the end of her stint in the Grand Old Party. The Trinamool Congress was inaugurated on January 1, 1998. This was also the beginning of the new personality cult, which she consciously developed. She kept her party under a tight leash from the outset. Ajit Panja used to say, 'Mamata is worshiped not because of her character but because of her personality. The problem with Mamata is she expects everybody to be like her.'*

TRINAMOOL CONGRESS WINS SEVEN SEATS

Though the Trinamool Congress had been formed, there was no money, cadre or party office. It was an uphill task to fight the elections; to the surprise of everyone the TMC won seven seats in the 1998 Lok Sabha polls. Mamata decided to ally with the BJP, as it was no longer considered anathema. It had 24 partners in the government, some secular and others not so secular. She felt that what was good for the leaders of various parties like George Fernandes, Ram Vilas Paswan, Jayalalithaa, Karunanidhi and Chandrababu Naidu, should also be beneficial for her. After all, her aim was to get rid of the CPI(M), and her joining the BJP-led National Democratic Alliance (NDA) might further her goal. Moreover, she wanted to mobilise all anti-CPI(M) forces, and however weak it was, the BJP was certainly one. The TMC joined the 24-member NDA government headed by Prime Minister Vajpayee, even though she had initially resisted to do so when her senior colleagues had suggested this.

MAMATA AS RAILWAY MINISTER

When the All India Anna Dravida Munnetra Kazhagam (AIADMK) pulled down the Vajpayee government in 1999 and Vajpayee lost by one vote, Mamata continued to support the NDA. The results of the Lok Sabha polls that year proved beneficial to her party, as she was able to increase her strength by winning eight seats—one more than what she had in the previous elections. She was given the much-coveted railway ministry and became the first woman Cabinet minister for railways. Ajit Panja also became a Minister of State. True to her character, Mamata did not allow him to become a Cabinet minister for the simple reason that she did not want any other power centre in the party, even though he was much senior to her in age and experience. She resigned after a year when the magazine *Tehelka* exposed corruption in the government during a sting operation, much to the embarrassment of the NDA. *Tehelka* publicised secret videotapes of top politicians and military officials accepting bribes from two of its reporters, who had posed as arms agents trying to swing "deals". Mamata demanded the dismissal of Fernandes, and she quit on that ground. Samata Party leader George Fernandes, who was the defence minister, and party chief Jaya Jaitly, had to resign in the wake of this exposé. During this rather short stint, she could not do much for the Indian railways, as she was busy concentrating on West Bengal's problems.

TRINAMOOL CONGRESS'S POOR SHOW

In the next Assembly elections Mamata had to pay the price for being a former partner of the NDA. Her party won about 60 seats along with the Congress, and she drew much criticism. There were quite a few reasons for this poor performance. The anti-incumbency factor did not work for the CPI(M) after Jyoti Basu stepped down as chief minister. Plus, his successor Buddhadeb Bhattacharjee enjoyed a good reputation. What was seen as a weakness had become a strength. Basu was Mamata's main target; with him gone, she had no one to attack. Basu also brought in some sympathy votes because he had stepped down on grounds of age and health. The long track record of the CPI(M) stood in its favour in rural areas, although it lost favour in urban regions. Last but not least, the absence of a strong countervailing force like the Congress made it easy for the state to become a Marxist monopoly.

TMC WIPED OUT IN THE 2004 POLLS

The 2004 Lok Sabha polls brought no cheer to either the TMC or Mamata. She was the only member who was elected on her party's ticket. The

Trinamool Congress was almost wiped out from the state. The only consolation was that most of her candidates lost with a very narrow margin, and her party continued to have a 30% vote share. Like Jayalalithaa in Tamil Nadu, Mamata also blamed the election system, claiming that they may have lost seats but not votes. She was quite upset because the Left parties did exceedingly well and won nearly 64 seats, becoming the biggest ally of the Congress-led UPA government. Mamata had nowhere to go since the Congress was not willing to associate with her, and she did not want to strike an alliance with the BJP.

There were quite a few reasons for her rout. Firstly, she lost credibility because she miscalculated her alliances. She had fought the elections as the NDA's partner and was not able to woo the Muslim voters, who were apprehensive of the BJP, which was leading the alliance. The Left parties made a tactical shift by allying with the Congress, thereby blocking her entry into the UPA. By the 2004 polls, Mamata had come full circle. She had left the Congress after the 2001 Assembly polls and went back to the NDA. The other big worry was money. With election expenses rising by the day, she was not able to collect enough funds. Neither would she allow her party leaders to collect money because she did not trust them. She was ambitious and fielded 28 candidates out of 42 in the state, hoping to get more numbers than previously. The candidates complained about the lack of money; her popularity alone was not enough. The Left parties had their cadres, institutionalised donations around the year and were ruling the state. Mamata's flip-flop was also responsible for her party's defeat. She first walked out of the NDA, protesting against the petrol price hike. Then she left the NDA in the wake of the *Tehelka* exposé on the alleged corrupt deals of the then Defence Minister George Fernandes. She returned to the NDA within six months and after a short wait became a minister in the Vajpayee government. She was not happy with the coal ministry portfolio and in any case there was hardly any time to prepare for the polls. Another problem was the lack of coordination between the TMC and the BJP at the ground level. Mamata had changed alliances so often that it had dented her reputation. She first left the Congress, joined the NDA, went back to the Congress, and once again joined the NDA.

One more reason for her defeat could well be her behaviour towards her party members. When Ajit Panja, a senior colleague, moved closer to the BJP, she suspended him. He had to wait a long time to get back into her good books. Another close aide, Sudip Bandyopadhyay, too suffered the same fate when the BJP tried to prop him up. He was also removed, only to be permitted back later; today he is once again in favour. This proves that she was not able to retain her colleagues' trust. The workers were confused as to what was going on in the party. The TMC became a poaching ground for others and Panja almost returned to the Congress fold. All these factors made it clear that having charisma alone was not enough to win elections, organisational efforts were equally important. Having said that, Mamata is without doubt a crowd puller and has the capacity to retain their attention.

MAMATA LOSES THE 2006 ASSEMBLY POLLS

The bad run continued; the 2006 Assembly elections did not prove to be beneficial for Mamata. This losing trend continued to plunge her into depression. The Left Front came back to power, but she strove on and did not lose heart. The 2001 and 2006 Assembly reversals as well as the 2004 Lok Sabha poll results had given her time to reflect and she chose the correct path after these setbacks. She made a conscious effort to change her habit of throwing tantrums and issuing threats. She admitted those who had left into the party, including CPI(M) members and even former Naxalite leaders, thus expressing sympathy towards the Maoists by asking them to join the mainstream. While the CPI(M) claimed that she was only taking those who were dismissed by the party, she made the TMC a broader-based party with various types of people. When the Left parties withdrew support to the Congress-led UPA in 2008 over the Indo-US nuclear deal, Mamata got an opening into the Congress and forged an alliance with the UPA.

The Congress-TMC alliance won 19 Lok Sabha seats in 2004 polls and Mamata became the railway minister for a second time. But in order to concentrate more on West Bengal, she began her first day in office in Kolkata and it soon became evident that she functioned more as a railway minister of the state, and not as a Union minister. Even the 2010 Railway budget was full of sops for West Bengal, ahead of the Assembly elections.

Despite a love-hate relation with the Congress and the breakdown of seat-sharing arrangements in the municipal elections in 2010, she did not leave the UPA. By this time she realised that the TMC-Congress combination would work in the Assembly polls. She was careful not to split the Opposition's votes. She realized that it would also help immensely if she remained on the right side of the Centre in the run-up to the elections as well as retain Muslim support, so she rejected all overtures by the BJP. Her strategy paid rich dividends. She also modified her strategy by talking about "change" (*badlaav*) and not revenge (*badla*). She organised her party and believed in reaching out to every nook and corner of the state. She undertook *padayatras* (journeys by foot) and walked miles and miles before the elections, when other leaders were busy helicopter-hopping.

STINT AS CHIEF MINISTER

Power was not new to Mamata. She had been a junior minister, a cabinet minister thrice and understood what was involved in running a government. Her stint as chief minister began with a lot of expectations and optimism that she would deliver the change she had promised during the campaign.

Like US President Barack Obama, who used the slogan "yes, we can" with reference to change in the US administration, Mamata too captured the imagination of the people by promising *"paribartan"*. All those who supported her—and there were many—were full of hope and expectations. It was an immense task to fulfil their dreams. She had the luxury of a "honeymoon period" with the people; the Opposition was mauled and dispirited. There was no good CPI(M) leader who could raise issues in the Assembly. The Congress was a junior partner and therefore not in a position to ruffle feathers. Plus, there was no leader of stature in the Congress who could take her on. Her own party was subservient to her after the huge victory.

In such an atmosphere it should have been easy to deliver, but there were also problems. Soon after she took over, the cartoon controversy arose, which put off even her staunch supporters like Mahasweta Devi. Ambikesh Mahapatra, a Jadavpur University professor, was assaulted, arrested and forced to spend a night in jail for allegedly circulating defamatory cartoons of Mamata Banerjee. To everyone's surprise, Mamata defended the professor's arrest, yet again showing her intolerance to criticism.

She was so suspicious of her own party men that she would not decentralise power. She held on to more than nine portfolios and took every decision herself. Her ministers were not allowed to speak to the media and she held Delhi hostage to her whims and fancies. Since the Communist regime had left her with a whopping $39.8 billion debt, she inherited a bankrupt treasury. Public transport workers went for months without pay and coal companies restricted credit to the state-owned companies. There were enormous deficits and the state required money urgently, but she refused to introduce any new taxes in the state to raise money or even to collect existing levies. Hence, she began squabbling with the Centre for not providing a relief package. She fought with the Union finance ministry on a daily basis. The Centre was not willing to give her a bonanza because it would mean the other states would also ask for more money. So she started using her support to the UPA as a bargaining chip on every issue in Parliament. She opposed several second generation reforms which were necessary for economic growth. She became the voice of the Opposition in the UPA and resisted reforms even more vocally than the Left parties. Moreover, Mamata also held up various bills relating to land acquisition, pension and labour and opposed the entry of foreign direct investment in retail. She had the power to stall things because her party was the second largest contingent in the UPA.

Being a woman chief minister, it was expected that she would be concerned about crimes against women but her opinion on cases reported from cities like New Delhi, Chennai and Kolkata was that they were essentially political tools used by her Opposition—primarily the Left parties—and that the truth of these were exaggerated. Even recently, her response to reported crimes of rape and sexual assault remain extremely apathetic and ineffective. In her statement on October 17, 2012, she attributed the increasing incidence of rapes to freer interaction between men and women.

A year after her stupendous victory, there was a mixed response to her one-year rule, even from abroad. After 12 months into her rule, West Bengal saw a sharp division among the intellectuals who once staunchly backed her. There was some censure that she was autocratic and resistant to criticism. Educationist Sunanda Sanyal, litterateur Mahasweta Devi, actor Kaushik Sen and Bengali poet Sankha Ghosh have been critical of her rule.

The Americans who were praising Mamata for throwing out the Left rule were disappointed over her opposition to reforms. *The Washington Post* commented, "She spent her life fighting communists but is the biggest obstacle to economic liberalisation in India today."[31] The *International Herald Tribune* observed, "One year after Banerjee's landslide, however, the new boss is looking a lot like the old one—maybe even worse. The woman who fashioned herself as West Bengal's saviour has turned out to be a disaster.

Even Banerjee's common-woman credentials appear to be eroding."[32] It added that the question is whether Banerjee can learn from that year's worst mistakes; the signs are not good.

She was continuously taking on the Manmohan Singh government and the Congress leaders did not know how to deal with her. She could get provoked on any issue and pick up a fight, complaining that the TMC was not consulted on those issues. She would not agree to petrol, diesel or railway fare price hikes. She refused to go to Bangladesh when the prime minister wanted her to accompany his delegation during his visit, embarrassing him on foreign soil.

If these were the problems with the Centre, within the state she started making several changes—good and bad. The first thing she did was to paint the city blue. When she was in the Opposition, she could get away with blaming the CPI(M) government for everything wrong. But she continued the blame game even after coming to power, forgetting it was her duty to set things right. Having said that, she did introduce various reforms in the education and health sectors. Some of the education reforms included the release of monthly pay of the teachers on the first of every month and quicker pensions for retiring teachers. She also attempted a three-phase developmental system to improve the health sector. In order to better the law and order situation in the state, police commissionerates were created at Howrah, Barrackpore, Durgapur-Asansol and Bidhannagar and the total area of the Municipal Corporation of Kolkata was brought under the control of the Kolkata police. To remind the people of the rich history of the state, she renamed several metro stations after freedom fighters.

As for Mamata's intolerance to criticism, she sees the hand of CPI(M) everywhere and puts the blame on the party for everything. When a girl was alleged to have been raped in the city, she claimed the incident had been cooked up to defame her government. She took on the doctors and ill-functioning hospitals with surprise visits. As for the media, which was critical of her, she barred all but 13 newspapers from the 2400 government-approved libraries. All these factors turned several well-known intellectuals who had supported her in her campaign against her. She even wanted to remove the word Marxism from history books! On March 12, 2012, when Dinesh Trivedi presented the Railway Budget and suggested an overall hike in passenger fares ranging from two paise to 30 paise per kilometre for reasons of safety, network expansion and modernisation, Mamata fiercely opposed this hike and asked the prime minister to sack him. Trivedi was ultimately forced to resign. Somnath Chatterjee observes, 'I don't know if it is democracy or dictatorship. Today only one person is deciding on every issue. She says "I have not decided" or "I will decide". These are her exact words.'*

But many, including her detractors, agree that she took steps to deal with the Maoists. She pumped in money in the Jangalmahal area for development and created jobs for them. But the Maoists had long been demanding the release of their colleagues; they also wanted the withdrawal of security forces. However, Mamata stood her ground and retained the security forces. She also set up a committee to review the cases of these prisoners. Hence, the Maoists were ready for a dialogue. Additionally, she signed the Darjeeling tripartite agreement as was promised before the elections. As for land reforms, she claimed that most cases were still in the court and she could not do anything in a hurry.

Mamata had been giving pin-pricks to the Congress—both at the state and the central level. She came across as someone who wanted to be with the Congress yet was also fighting against the party all the time, confusing her cadres as well as the Congress. Now that her party had won a majority of the seats on its own, she regarded the Congress as excess baggage which she could dump. The Congress leaders were never sure of her cooperation. Her aim was to finish the Congress at the state level and emerge as the strongest party; in other words, she developed ambitions to play a pivotal role in national politics. She took a lead in the selection of the presidential and vice-presidential candidates in July 2012 and insisted on choosing former President Abdul Kalam, but the Congress was averse to his candidature. Samajwadi Party chief Mulayam Singh, with whom Mamata had teamed up, ditched her at the last minute and went ahead with the UPA to vote for its nominee, Pranab Mukherjee. Finding herself isolated, Mamata fell in line and voted for him. She was trying to form a front of regional satraps with other powerful chief ministers.

Two years are too soon to judge Mamata's governance capacity but so far the signals have been disappointing. Her gaffes and conspiracy theories are a great source of embarrassment to her party and the government. As senior bureaucrats point out, she is in a tearing hurry to do things but they do not move fast enough for her. She behaves as if she were a headmistress with her officials. She is looking to announce new projects, programmes and ideas without doing any homework. And she makes it more than clear that she hasn't reached the top just to listen to others.

The problem is that she is still searching for enemies, for people who she thinks are against her and with whom she can pick up a fight. Now that she has the government machinery at her command, she can take on those who criticise her. What better way than to put them behind bars and foist cases against them?

MAMATA PULLS OUT OF THE UPA

Mamata continued her ongoing battle with the Centre and threatened to quit the UPA many times. She withdrew support to the UPA on September 18, 2012, and her ministers submitted their resignations much against their will on September 21. After a discussion with her colleagues she made the decision to withdraw support by railing against the diesel price hike and the restriction on the number of cooking gas cylinders—issues that were connected directly to the common man. These issues, Mamata felt, also appeared to be firmly rooted on the ground, compared to the theoretical and intellectually-based Indo-US nuclear deal, over which the Left had withdrawn support from the Congress-led UPA-1 in 2008. It also provided her the much-needed opportunity to distance her party from the scam-plagued Congress. With the crucial rural polls knocking at the door and the West Bengal Congress always up in arms against the state government, she hoped that the break-up would help the Trinamool stretch its wings even in Congress bastions, which it had been eyeing, and her party would emerge as the only formidable force against the Left.

The Congress leadership was vexed with her opposition to economic reforms, including those concerning pension and banking reforms, and had reached the end of its tether. The Congress party was no longer willing to humour her; as a result, the Trinamool Congress left the UPA midway. If Mamata expected the UPA government to fall, she was disappointed, as it managed to retain the support of the Samajwadi Party and the Bahujan Samajwadi Party, which were supporting the government from outside. While her ministers at the Centre were upset, they could do nothing to change the decision of the party supremo. Within one year of her excellent performance in the Assembly elections, Mamata chose to remain isolated in the national scene after withdrawing from the government. There are questions whether it was a wise decision to move away from the UPA. What had she achieved by doing so? The UPA government went ahead and pushed the bill on foreign direct investment (FDI) in retail through in the Parliament during the winter session in 2012, while it also increased railway fares in January 2013. Mamata is now isolated in her state. If she had plans to mobilise support from other regional satraps, so far there is no evidence of a pressure group being formed.

Mamata has to wait to see how her party fares in the 2014 elections and this year's Panchayat elections in West Bengal. They will give her an indication of her capacity to deliver. But she has the chance of making a mid-course correction before the 2016 Assembly polls. Unless Mamata gives up her whimsical decisions and mercurial temper, she may end up as a one-time chief minister, despite the huge amount of goodwill she had received in the 2012 Assembly polls. Her ambitions of becoming prime minister may remain a pipe dream.

NOTES

1. Kalyani Shankar, *Gods of Power: Personality Cult and Indian Democracy*, p. 249, Macmillan India, Updated Edition 2005.
2. Ibid., p. 252.
3. Mamata Banerjee, *My Unforgettable Memories*, p. 53, Lotus Roli, 2012.
4. http://wikileaks.org/cable/2009/03/09KOLKATA79.html.
5. Mamata Banerjee: "Hysterics to History", *The Times of India*, May 14, 2011.
6. Rajiv Bagchi, "Mamata uproots world's longest-elected Red rule", *Hindustan Times*, (New Delhi, India), May 13, 2011; *Custom 150 Online Journals*, June 26, 2012.
7. http://wikileaks.org/cable/2009/05/09KOLKATA144.html.
8. http://wikileaks.org/cable/2009/03/09KOLKATA79.html.
9. http://wikileaks.org/cable/2006/12/06CALCUTTA578.html.
10. "Trinamool's Mamata Banerjee: From oppositional street fighter to West Bengal chief minister-in-waiting", *The Hindu*, April 21, 2011; *Custom 150 Online Journals*, June 26, 2012.
11. Atul Kohli, *Democracy and Discontent: India's Growing Crisis of Governability*, pp. 270-271, Cambridge University Press, 1999.
12. Mamata Banerjee, *Struggle for Existence*, p. 2, Cosmo Publications, 1998.
13. Mamata Banerjee, *My Unforgettable Memories*, p. 55.
14. Ibid., p. 39.
15. Ibid., p. 40.

16. Ibid., p. 67.
17. Ibid.
18. Ibid., p. 70.
19. Ibid., p. 72.
20. Ibid., p. 77.
21. Ibid., p. 78.
22. Shankar, *Gods of Power*, p. 246.
23. Mamata Banerjee, *My Unforgettable Memories*, p. 91.
24. Shankar, *Gods of Power*, p. 251.
25. Mamata Banerjee, *My Unforgettable Memories*, p. 88.
26. Bannerjee, *Struggle for Existence*, p. 81.
27. Ibid., p. 100.
28. Banerjee, *My Unforgettable Memories*, p. 109.
29. Ibid., p. 112.
30. Ibid., p. 121.
31. Simon Denyer, "Mamata Banerjee personifies populist force in Indian politics", *The Washington Post*, May 20, 2012.
32. Dan Morrison, "An Ineffectual Start for Elder Sister", *International Herald Tribune* (the global edition of *The New York Times;* Latitude Blogs), April 13, 2012.

Jayalalithaa

TAMIL NADU CHIEF MINISTER Jayalalithaa Jayaram is mercurial, unpredictable and an enigma to many. Like Ronald Reagan, Schwarzenegger, N.T. Rama Rao and her mentor M.G. Ramachandran, she is a successful film actor turned politician. Some people regard her as a megalomaniac, while others describe her as arrogant. A telegram from the US embassy in New Delhi to Washington sums her up succinctly: "A man brought her into politics but she rose to the height of power on her own, breaking new ground for women as she went along."[1] It adds that she has succeeded in Tamil Nadu's male-dominated political environment by literally reversing traditional stereotypes. She is considered the toughest, most muscular political figure in the state and has leveraged this image of strength into political power. She behaves like an empress of the South on her way to conquer the rest of India.

Jayalalithaa claims that she is much misunderstood. "I have been portrayed as a tough and formidable character. Some would call me *veerangana* (a warrior woman). To tell the truth, I am a very soft and kind-hearted person but life has placed me in very difficult situations. I have been surrounded by a whole set of adversaries, all coming at me with various kinds of weapons. I could not lie back and allow myself to be annihilated. The feeling I got then was: Why should I allow myself to be eliminated just because some people don't like me?"[2]

A film star turned politician, Jayalalithaa is often criticised for her lavish lifestyle and her habit of travelling with an entourage along with 40 to 50 suitcases. But she has given up her erstwhile glamorous clothes for plain silk sarees in pastel shades to cover her plump figure and, of course, a bullet-proof vest. She has even set up her own security system. She does not wear jewellery as a result of the 1996 episode when her ornaments were seized by the income tax department due to a case of disproportionate assets. Despite her abstinence, she still remains beautiful, majestic and imperious, and has aged gracefully from the film-goers' heart-throb to a respected chief minister. The highs and lows in her political life have not deterred her fighting spirit. A telegram from the US embassy in New Delhi to Washington describes her as the only man in her party, the All India Anna Dravida Munnetra Kazhagam (AIADMK), much like Indira Gandhi, who was regarded as the only man in her Cabinet. "Her ruthlessness—including her willingness to sanction violence in pursuit of her goals—eventually reversed the traditional view of gender roles, leading the public to see Jayalalithaa as the toughest person in Tamil Nadu politics."[3]

Jayalalithaa's life seems like a movie script, full of action, suspense and drama. Born on February 24, 1948, in Mysore, she excelled at studies at Church Park Presentation Convent School in Chennai. Her mother Vedavalli, also an actress (known as Sandhya on screen), wanted her to act in films. The good-looking teenage girl never wanted to be an actress. As a child, she often accompanied her actress mother to studios during the holidays. Her father Jayaram passed away when she was barely two years old and her mother struggled to bring up her two children, Jaya and her older brother Jayakumar. Jayalalithaa became a child actress by sheer chance. She recalls that when she was just seven years old, she was in Bangalore during the summer vacation. Her mother was acting in the Kannada film *Srisaila Mahatyam* (Glory of Sri Sailam). Jayalalithaa had tagged along with her to the studio. The child artiste who was to play Goddess Parvathi fell ill. "The producer and director saw me with my mother and asked her whether she would allow me to play that role; my mother agreed. That was the first time I used make-up and appeared before the camera."[4]

Jayalalithaa, whose pet name was Ammu, had a strict training regimen. "I was carefree only until the age of four. From then on, I had to rise at five in the morning. There would be a teacher to teach me classical vocal Carnatic music. After that I would leave for school, which used to last until 4 pm. I was given instructions not to stay back and play with other children. I was expected to come straight home, and even before I could enter the door, there would be two dance teachers waiting for me. Of course, I would glare at them but they would remain unmoved," she explained in a television interview.[5]

Jayalalithaa grew into a stunning teenager and had dreams of going to college. "If I had been allowed to study and have my way I'd have been a star on the legal firmament like Nani Palkhivala, Ram Jethmalani and Fali Nariman," she told Rajat Sharma during the talk show "Aap ki Adalat".[6] Jayalalithaa obtained good marks in her matriculation examination. "But fate willed otherwise. Subsequently, I thought it was time for me to take on the responsibility of supporting my family. That is how I gave up my dream of becoming a lawyer and entered the film industry at the age of 16."[7] Former minister Mani Shankar Aiyar observes, 'Jaya cannot help being outstanding. Her very first movie was a box office hit. So however reluctant she was, she excelled.'* He adds that she had a sense of destiny which only people with a kind of madness can have.

Jayalalithaa became a big hit in her first film *Vennira Aadai* (White Dress) in which she acted as a young widow. But her pairing with M.G. Ramachandran in *Aayirathil Oruvan* (One in a Thousand) gave her celebrity status. MGR, who later went on to become the chief minister of Tamil Nadu and also Jayalalithaa's mentor, was the undisputed ruler of the film world and the Tamil Nadu political scene. The MGR-Jaya pair clicked so well that they went on to act in more films and each one became a bigger hit. Soon she started acting in Telugu and Hindi films.

But things did not continue to be rosy; her mother suddenly died in 1971, which was a great shock for the young actress. She described her situation in a television interview: "After my mother's death I began to distance myself from the film industry and at one stage I stopped acting in films. This gave me considerable free time to reflect on the state of affairs in the country. I felt that there was much that could be done to rectify things that were going wrong. Around 1989, MGR invited me to join the AIADMK. I was not too keen in the beginning. I took nearly one and a half years to make my decision. Finally in 1982, he appealed to me saying he needed someone he could depend on 100 per cent."[8]

MGR, who formed his own party, the All India Anna Dravida Munnetra Kazhagam (AIADMK), by breaking away from the Dravida Munnetra Kazhagam (DMK), built up his base with the support of his tremendous fan following, who treated him like a god. In 1977, he became the chief minister of Tamil Nadu. Interestingly, both the DMK and the AIADMK shared the same Dravidian ideology. Dravidian politics strongly repudiates the Congress party; historically, it has always been anti-Brahmin and staunchly supports the Tamil language while opposing Hindi. These two Dravidian parties revolve around strong personalities and offer few policy differences. Both have alternately been in power in the state, making the national parties irrelevant. The Congress lost power in 1967 and has been riding piggyback on one Dravidian party or the other ever since.

Films have a strong influence on state politics. In addition to Jayalalithaa and MGR, M. Karunanidhi, a five-time chief minister of Tamil Nadu, was a successful scriptwriter. Sivaji Ganesan of the Congress was also a big star; he went on to become a member of the Rajya Sabha (House of Elders). The DMK made superstar Sarath Kumar a Rajya Sabha MP. Recently, another superstar, Vijaykanth, floated his own party and won seats in the Assembly. In Tamil Nadu, the gap between the top leaders and the masses is so pronounced, the common man feels they almost possess superhuman qualities.

MGR was not new to politics but he was new to administration. Changes in the national scene also affected him and his party. Indira Gandhi, who was thrown out of power after the Emergency in 1977, was coming back slowly. Her successor Morarji Desai's Janata government, which was a hotchpotch coalition, soon fell and Charan Singh took over with the support of the Congress. But his government also fell without even facing the Parliament, leading to the 1980 Lok Sabha polls. In the interim, there was a split in the Congress in 1978 and it became the Congress (I).

Indira Gandhi joined hands with the DMK as an electoral ally in Tamil Nadu. The combination swept the polls in 1980. The AIADMK got only two seats, which depressed MGR to no end. With the Congress (I) capturing power at the Centre and the DMK posing a challenge in the state, MGR became nervous. The Congress-DMK victory in the 1980 Parliamentary elections emboldened the latter, which claimed that people had lost faith in the MGR government. DMK chief Karunanidhi chose this moment to settle scores with MGR, who had dared to cross him; he pressed the Central government to dismiss the Tamil Nadu government, using similar allegations made by MGR to dismiss his government in 1976. The Assembly was dissolved and fresh elections were held in 1980 in which MGR came back to power. He realized that he was losing touch with the people; he knew a strong connection with the masses was important to keep his party afloat. He needed someone who could go around the state on his behalf and connect with the masses. He looked around and found no one to whom he could entrust this important task.

JAYALALITHAA'S DEFINING MOMENT

That was when he thought of Jayalalithaa. He knew that she was charismatic and intelligent; she had a magnetic appeal and could attract crowds, and more importantly, he could trust her implicitly. He knew that he could depend on her to share his burden. So MGR brought her back into the limelight and initiated her into politics, making her the propaganda secretary of the party in 1982. She soon acquired enormous clout due to her proximity to MGR and the importance of her new job.

Mohan Das, a police officer who was close to MGR, notes that Jayalalithaa is one of the few leaders in the country who possesses good fighting spirit. "Anyway she had MGR's ears. She was studious and personally supervised the mid-day meal scheme. MGR was very keen on the scheme and is basically responsible for the kudos it got from the World Bank."[9] She also undertook tours within the state where she drew huge crowds. Her well-prepared speeches supported by facts and figures impressed the crowd. Jayalalithaa soon became the vital link between the government and the party, invoking jealousy among AIADMK senior leaders like S.D. Somasundaram and MGR's close friend R.M. Veerappan. There were complaints that she had overreached herself and had even started summoning ministers to her office. A crisis was brewing in the party, with the senior leaders revolting against Jayalalithaa's larger-than-life image.

AS RAJYA SABHA MP

MGR decided that the best way to resolve this issue was to move her to the national scene; he made her a Rajya Sabha member in 1984. N. Ravi, former editor of *The Hindu*, points out that MGR wanted her to get experience at the national level. 'This proved to be a launch pad for her. But initially, she was MGR's shadow. She would not have thought at that stage that she would take over the party. After 1986, she proved to be very popular and the party obviously had no strong leadership. She was probably the best-known and popular figure after MGR. This, as well as her exposure to Delhi, proved to be to her advantage.*

Mani Shankar observes that after she was sent to Delhi as an MP, she discovered that she had far greater potential as a politician. 'She realized that she was not just a high-class film star but also a high-class politician.'*

Along the way Jayalalithaa imbibed MGR's style of functioning. When she was made a Rajya Sabha member, she took Parliament by storm with her good looks and articulation. The then minister Margaret Alva recalls, 'I used to urge her to come to the House because whenever she was present, the attendance also improved.'* Delhi Chief Minister Sheila Dikshit, who was then the Minister of State for Parliamentary Affairs, also had good relations with Jayalalithaa. 'I would say that I find her a private person. She knows exactly what to do and when. She is not given to bullying and is a mature politician. She is a contrast to Mamata and Mayawati.'*

In the meantime, the Congress-DMK relationship became strained; as a result, MGR drew closer to Indira Gandhi. He believed in being on the right side of the Central government. Jaya became the face of the AIADMK in national politics after she moved to Parliament. Mrs. Gandhi took a fancy to her and even invited her for dinner. They shared a good rapport right until Indira Gandhi's assassination. But Jayalalithaa's detractors did not remain quiet. Taking advantage of her absence from state politics, they tried to create a wedge between her and MGR. Senior AIADMK leader S.D. Somasundaram led the revolt against her. This continued unabated even until the last days of MGR's rule.

The author Mohandas explains that the advent of a newcomer like Jayalalithaa as the powerful propaganda secretary and almost number two, hurt S.D. Somasundaram (as it did other leaders and ministers), who by his seniority and simple living had endeared himself to the party workers. "Jayalalithaa had charisma no doubt, next only to MGR, but S.D.S. (Somasundaram) felt she was raised to a very high position in the party because of her proximity to MGR. Others took it silently but S.D.S. was of a different mettle and took advantage of the slight demoralisation in the party after the loss in four by-elections."[10]

Indira Gandhi was assassinated on October 30, 1984. The country was shocked when two of her Sikh security guards shot her dead. Her son Rajiv succeeded her and within two months he called for general elections. In Tamil Nadu, the Congress and the AIADMK fought together, and the latter came to power. Rajiv Gandhi won a massive majority in the Lok Sabha in 1984 and became the prime minister.

Meanwhile MGR fell ill on October 5, 1985, and was later shifted to a hospital in New York. Jayalalithaa lost access to her mentor, as the coterie around him would not allow her to talk to him. There was a bitter fight between Jayalalithaa and Veerappan (an important minister in the MGR Cabinet) during the Assembly elections, even as MGR's nomination papers were brought from New York. His video message from his hospital bed made the AIADMK win the elections hands down.

Ravi observes that Jaya wanted to visit him in New York but was denied permission. 'The coterie refused to let her meet him in Apollo Hospital when he came back to India. She was very angry and even issued a public statement virtually saying that a clique was controlling MGR. Some of the AIADMK leaders like Thirunavukkarasu (a minister in the MGR Cabinet) were solidly supporting her. They were shrewd, as they knew she had popular support and the votes would easily transfer from MGR to her. This was a period of darkness in her political life.'*

Thirunavukkarasu notes that MGR did not meet her when he returned from New York in February 1985. He called Thirunavukkarasu immediately and wanted to know what had happened in his absence. While they were talking, those waiting outside the room thought that Thirunavukkarasu was pleading on Jayalalithaa's behalf and sent the American doctors inside. 'They told me I should not disturb him. MGR said it was he who called me. His wife Janaki also came inside in the meantime. I felt embarrassed and left, requesting him to rest. He called me again later and I took the entire press clippings along. He went through all of them patiently. He knew I was supporting Jaya.'*

MGR realised that the internal feud had reached its height. Thirunavukkarasu remarks that Jaya was not allowed to meet him for almost three months after his return. Finally, MGR gave her an appointment at the Secretariat when she persisted. 'He probably felt that she was overambitious and wanted to be the chief minister and party general secretary,' Thirunavukkarasu explains while remembering how Jaya fought with MGR that day.* 'She bluntly told him, "In your absence I toured the state; I was one of the people responsible for the party returning to power. You have included such useless people in your ministry, but you have not included me. I must be made the deputy chief minister." MGR promptly called me; Panruti Ramachandran (one of the ministers) was also present. Panruti told me what had transpired and that MGR was very angry. I told MGR, "It's not fair on her part to ask for deputy chief ministership; it may send the wrong signals. If you want to give anything to her, make her a minister since she was one of those who campaigned. She also attracted more crowds. In appreciation of all this, you may consider it."'* But MGR's reaction was negative. He did not like the advice. Thirunavukkarasu adds, 'As far as I know, MGR never hinted or thought she would become his successor. She was even dismissed as the party's propaganda secretary and kept away from active politics because he got many complaints from senior party leaders… After returning from the US, he gave oral instructions to all ministers, including myself, not to go to Jaya's house, or talk to her personally, or on the phone. All the office bearers of the party were also similarly instructed. He was also aware of the letter she had written to Rajiv Gandhi asking to be made the deputy CM, since she had developed a rapport with Rajiv Gandhi, Buta Singh and others. Before his death, MGR was very angry with her. Nobody could influence his decisions.'*

MGR had created a personal suite for Jayalalithaa in Tamil Nadu House in Delhi, but she was not allowed to occupy it when she was removed from her post as propaganda secretary and leader in the Rajya Sabha. She knew her political struggles had only just begun. She was in disgrace and biding her time.

Kondath Mohandas, a police officer close to MGR and the author of his biography *MGR, the Man and the Myth*, observes that it was Veerappan who was most vociferous in his opposition to Jayalalithaa being given any position in the party or the government. "He took me aside one night at Apollo Hospital in Madras and told me that unfortunately it was he who was responsible for the reconciliation between Jaya and MGR in 1981 by giving her a chance to present a dance-drama before the delegates at the World Tamil Conference in Madurai. The two were estranged before and he rued the day he brought them together. He said it seemed Jaya was not satisfied with being a lady companion and that she fancied herself, with her convent education and charisma, to be a cut above the rest and to be the only eligible successor to MGR in the party as well as the government."[11]

Later, MGR relented and once again made Jayalalithaa the propaganda secretary on September 6, 1985. Concerned about the mediocre performance of the party in the local body elections, he decided to revive his fan clubs and organised a huge meeting. Jayalalithaa insisted on being made the president of the MGR fan club at the party conference in Madurai; when he did not agree, she left in a huff. 'MGR showed me the newspapers and the publicity she got in the conference. Before his death he was very angry with her,' recalls Thirunavukkarasu.*

MGR died on December 24, 1987. Although he was ill, his death was sudden. It shocked the whole state and his fans were grief-stricken. Jayalalithaa, who was in disgrace, also rushed to MGR's Ramavaram Garden residence and tried to get a glimpse of her mentor. But her detractors turned her away.

Mohandas distinctly remembers a scene when he went to see MGR's body. He came out of the room and saw Jaya screaming and shouting, making her way upstairs, taking more than one step at a time. She was fury personified. "I made a quiet exit because I had no role to play, being no longer the intelligence chief. Later I came to understand she was not allowed to see MGR's body, as it was taken outside from the backdoor to Rajaji Hall, where it lay in state for mourners to have a last look."[12]

Prime Minister Rajiv Gandhi deputed three central ministers to attend MGR's funeral. Being journalists, R. Rangarajan and I managed to hitch a ride to Chennai in a special plane designated for the ministers. On reaching Rajaji Hall, we found Jayalalithaa standing like a statue near MGR's head while his wife Janaki was sitting on a stool at his feet. Mourners streamed past continuously. Jayalalithaa did not leave her post throughout and stood there for two days without food or sleep.

ANOTHER DEFINING MOMENT

This was the next defining moment in Jayalalithaa's career: she decided to claim the political legacy of her mentor. In the afternoon, she went to place a wreath on his body and quickly sat on the gun carriage that was carrying MGR's body to the cremation at Marina beach. She wanted to send a signal that she was the political heir of the departed leader, which her detractors saw through immediately. MGR's nephew Deepan rushed forward and pushed her down. Insulted and humiliated, she was forced to leave the place with a police escort. The whole world saw the beautiful heroine being pushed away from the gun carriage on television; this marred the solemn occasion. She immediately sent out telegrams to the governor, chief secretary and other officials about the way she was manhandled, while the media ran the incident as front-page news. The public assault on her elicited great public sympathy, which helped her in times to come. This was certainly the turning point in her political career. Jayalalithaa admits, "Yes, I will say that my real growth and development started in 1984 when MGR fell ill. My adversaries in the party started to marginalize me. That was when I really had to fend for myself and it was totally so after his death."[13]

Ravi notes, 'In a sense two things helped her. First was MGR's death, and the second was Rajiv Gandhi's assassination. MGR would never have allowed anyone to be his second-in-command while he was alive. He was the sole leader and everybody else was below him.'*

As expected, after MGR's demise there was a power struggle. His wife Janaki ultimately saved the situation by offering to become the chief minister. She was propped up by Veerappan and was sworn in as the first woman chief minister of Tamil Nadu on January 7, 1988. She had to prove her strength soon enough. Factional fighting was rampant and ugly scenes were witnessed in the House. Former Chief Minister M. Karunanidhi recollects that on January 28 there was a massive fight in the Assembly. Shoes and soda bottles were thrown at the MLAs. The Speaker P.H. Pandian and other members were attacked. At the last minute, the Congress decided not to vote for MGR's widow, leaving her and Jayalalithaa's groups to fight it out. The Congress, which had given its full support to MGR, changed its stance after Jayalalithaa's visit to New Delhi in the interim. Karunanidhi further explains the situation: "When Janaki was deserted at the last minute she suddenly remembered the DMK. Her faction leaders K. Rajaram and others came to my house and requested me to support her. She also spoke to me over the phone and requested me. I told them we had already taken a decision not to support either group. The IUML (Indian Union Muslim League) leader Samad also asked me to back him. I expressed my inability to change the executive decision. The Speaker dismissed 33 MLAs and announced that Janaki had won. The Centre dismissed the Janaki-led government on January 30 and imposed President's rule."[14] Mani Shankar Aiyar recalls that the public felt that the Congress was going to support Janaki Ramachandran, but that was not the case. 'I remember Arjun Singh travelling with us to Jorhat in Rajiv Gandhi's plane; they were discussing the Congress's support. Rajiv was not going to stand for any interference by the Congress Party in the fight between the two factions. So we did not support Janaki.'* With no party in a position to form the government, ultimately President's rule was imposed. In the absence of a personality of MGR's calibre, the AIADMK began to crumble with infighting; it broke into two factions, one led by Janaki and the other under Jayalalithaa.

Jayalalithaa struggled for three years for the control of the party, finally prevailing in 1990. The DMK captured power and Karunanidhi, who was in political wilderness, became the chief minister after a lapse of 13 years. The Jayalalithaa faction won 27 seats in the 1989 Assembly elections and she became the Leader of the Opposition in the Tamil Nadu Assembly. The Congress, by contesting alone, got only 26 seats. The election results showed that Jayalalithaa was a popular leader in her own right and Janaki, who realised she was no match, decided to quit politics and move to the United States.

The first budget session was a black mark in the history of the Tamil Nadu Assembly after Karunanidhi took over. When it began on March 25, 1989, Karunanidhi, who held the Finance and Home portfolios, stood up to present his budget. Jayalalithaa rose, alleging that at the instance of Karunanidhi the police were harassing her; she wanted to move a breach of privilege motion against him. Pandemonium broke out and in the melee, when Jaya attempted to leave the House, DMK minister Durai Murugan pulled her saree and humiliated her. Jaya stormed out infuriated and announced she would never enter the Assembly until conditions improved. She never did until she became the chief minister in 1991.

Meanwhile things were happening on the national front. Rajiv Gandhi was embroiled in the Rs. 64-crore Bofors kickback controversy. The allegation was that the Gandhi's family friend, Ottavio Quattrocchi, was given kickbacks for the gun deal, which was stashed away in Swiss banks. The Opposition was belligerent and demanded a joint parliamentary committee to probe into the scam. V.P. Singh, a minister in Rajiv Gandhi's Cabinet, who exposed the corruption, revolted against Gandhi and formed his own outfit. The Opposition resigned en masse over the Bofors issue. Rajiv Gandhi called for general elections a few months ahead and lost. V.P. Singh, with the support of the Left and the BJP, formed the National Front government along with small and regional parties. Soon after, pandering to vote-bank politics, he announced reservations for the backward classes as recommended by the Mandal Commission. The others opposed the reservation. The BJP too simultaneously started an agitation for building a Ram temple in Ayodhya, and ultimately withdrew its support to Singh. Chandra Shekhar, propped up by the Congress, became the prime minister for a brief period. In the meantime, with thousands of refugees from Sri Lanka pouring into Tamil Nadu, the Liberation Tigers of Tamil Eelam (LTTE) had become active in the state. Prime Minister Chandra Shekhar was concerned about its activities. The Centre's repeated efforts to persuade the state government to check the LTTE did not yield any results. Suspecting foul play, Chandra Shekhar sacked the DMK government and imposed President's rule.

By the time the 1991 Lok Sabha and Assembly elections took place, the Congress and the AIADMK realised their mistake of not joining hands. Rajiv Gandhi found that going it alone in the state had not paid electoral dividends. This brought the two parties together. When Rajiv Gandhi was assassinated, Jayalalithaa won sympathy votes; as a result, the AIADMK secured 169 of the 223 seats. Jayalalithaa put up 25 women candidates to show her commitment to her gender; all of them won. The AIADMK got the 11 seats it had contested and the Congress won 27 of the 28 seats in the Lok Sabha.

Thirunavukkarasu mentions that at the time Jaya did not have her personal vote bank. 'It was still MGR's vote bank, as his name sells even today. People did not know that MGR did not want Jaya as his successor. The perception was that he brought her into politics to succeed him. The "two leaves" election symbol was also important because it was associated with MGR.'* Although the AIADMK split and there were other smaller parties, she was the only one leading the anti-DMK sentiment. The supporters of the DMK would not vote for the AIADMK and vice versa.

AS CHIEF MINISTER

Jayalalithaa came to power at a crucial time in the history of Tamil Nadu. The state as well as the whole country was shocked by Rajiv Gandhi assassination's; law and order needed improvement; the LTTE had to be checked; and Jayalalithaa was new to administration. Tamil Nadu Governor Bhishma Narain Singh recalls how she was keen to be a good administrator. 'I administered the oath to her on June 21. When she came to see me the next day, it was not a long meeting. I gave her a list of things that needed to be looked into: law and order, the LTTE and the economic situation. She was glad that my list was short. This was her first stint as chief minister. My meetings with her were fruitful. We discussed important issues: how to prevent militancy and how to speed up development.'* Throughout his governorship, Jayalalithaa met him regularly after every ten days. Singh remembers she was quick on the uptake and intelligent. 'If you explained anything to her she understood. I told her that she should have good relations with the Centre but I don't know what happened later when she fell out with Narasimha Rao.'*

A US embassy telegram from New Delhi notes that Chief Minister Jayalalithaa ruled with an iron hand. The first thing she did after assuming office was to order a crackdown on the LTTE, which had been openly operating in the state for a long time. This was a reversal of her mentor MGR's pro-LTTE stand. "A bureaucrat who held a key security portfolio at the time said that Jayalalithaa ordered him to do 'whatever it takes to finish off the LTTE' in Tamil Nadu, even if it required extrajudicial killings of LTTE associates in the state."[15]

Tamil Nadu is separated from neighbouring Sri Lanka by a narrow 20 kilometre strip of sea known as the Palk Strait. The LTTE militants often crossed it illegally and maintained an extensive network. According to an estimate, there were nearly 2,00,000 Sri Lankan Tamils, including about 1,000 suspected rebels, in the state. The LTTE was alleged to have been involved in the assassination of Rajiv Gandhi. Initially, MGR supported the rebels and even provided them with funds. Rajiv Gandhi utilised MGR's services to deal with LTTE chief Velupillai Prabhakaran, even before the Indo-Sri Lankan accord was signed. But when the Indian Peace Keeping Force (IPKF) was sent to Sri Lanka later, Prabhakaran's forces opposed it. Ravi points out, 'MGR had the choice of continuing his support to the LTTE, but he distanced himself. Then the LTTE made a critical move; they rushed to Karunanidhi for support. Had they waited, MGR would have softened. The break with the LTTE happened during MGR's time. The 1991 polls, when the state voted silently, were post-LTTE elections. An opinion poll conducted by *The Hindu* at the time revealed that the DMK supported the LTTE.'*

Soon Governor Bhishma Narain Singh's term was completed and despite Jayalalithaa's plea to the prime minister, he was not granted an extension.

Prime Minister Rao brought in Rajasthan Governor Dr. M. Chenna Reddy as his successor. This proved to be a disaster, as the governor and the chief minister did not see eye to eye on many issues. There were ego clashes as Chenna Reddy too had a strong personality. On one occasion, when Prime Minister Rao visited Chennai, Reddy and Jayalalithaa held separate receptions at the airport, since they were not on talking terms. The bonhomie between the Congress and the AIADMK was also shortlived. Two groups in the Tamil Nadu Congress led by G.K. Moopanar and Vazhapadi Ramamurthy were fighting, and Jayalalithaa felt that the prime minister was supporting Moopanar.

The Rao–Jaya relationship also had its ups and downs. She thought Chenna Reddy was sent to spy on her. Rao describes their peculiar relationship: "I had no idea whether she was annoyed with me and why. Regarding the appointment of Dr. Chenna Reddy, the reasons for his shift, at his own request, lay entirely in Rajasthan and had nothing to do with Tamil Nadu. Indeed I did the customary consultation with Jayalalithaa and she agreed. There was not the slightest intention on my part to cause any difficulty to her."[16]

Ravi notes that initially Jayalalithaa was learning the ropes. 'Soon she found that some people were trying to exploit her; she even named President R. Venkataraman, Chief Election Commissioner T.N. Seshan, political analyst Cho Ramaswamy, among others. She was very bitter. Then she wriggled out of their control and believed that she could do no wrong. Even bureaucrats were afraid of her and became "yes men". Even if she did the most outrageous things, they would simply go along.'*

Jayalalithaa was in a confrontational mood and resorted to theatrics. This was in contrast to MGR's strategy of teaming up with the Centre so that the state received ample benefits. His election formula was also well defined. In the Assembly, the AIADMK would contest only 60 per cent of the seats, leaving the rest for the Congress; in the Lok Sabha, the figure was reversed. This suited both the Congress and the AIADMK, and it worked well.

Jayalalithaa began to take on the Central government on all issues. She asserted that the poll victory was due to her charisma, while the Congress felt it was the sympathy votes. One fine morning, she decided to sit on a fast near the Marina Beach over the Cauvery water sharing dispute between Tamil Nadu and the neighbouring state of Karnataka. Even today this issue remains a thorn in ties between the two states. The rift between the chief minister and the governor reached its peak when Jayalalithaa felt that Reddy was using the Raj Bhavan to promote the opposition parties.

The relationship with the Congress soured so rapidly that by March 1993, Jayalalithaa severed all ties unilaterally. The next two years witnessed constant squabbling between the Raj Bhavan and Fort St. George (where the Secretariat is located).

Jayalalithaa began to function in a dictatorial way. Sycophancy and subservience became the norm. Her MPs and ministers were not allowed to speak to the media. Dr. Subramanian Swamy recalls, 'Once when I was sitting with Jayalalithaa, one of her ministers walked into the room to consult her on some urgent matter. He prostrated before her. I waited for him to get up but he would not. Finally, I asked her, "Why can't you make this man get up and leave?" She said in Tamil that they deserve such treatment and sent him away. I asked her what the problem was. She said women were treated badly in the cinema, so what do I care for these men; I have come up in spite of them.'*

Jayalalithaa's first term began well and she was full of enthusiasm to do things and raised expectations. But she could not maintain the tempo and soon ran into controversies. Ravi observes that in her first term she depended on a few ministers to organise the party at the district level, but largely left the administration to bureaucrats. 'She posted good secretaries in critical departments and worked through them, even bypassing her ministers. The minister was just a dummy. The real power lay with the secretary who could directly interact with the chief minister.'*

The last two years of Jayalalithaa's first term have not been all smooth sailing, as corruption charges piled up against her and her ministers. She was criticised for her style of functioning and her inaccessibility. Dr. Swamy, who had a love-hate relationship with her, appealed to Governor Chenna Reddy, seeking permission for her prosecution. She enjoyed the good will of the media in the beginning but could not maintain it. In addition, she did nothing to improve this relationship. Instead, she foisted lawsuits on many newspapers. "By and large I have been given a bad press. Those who really got to know me always felt that I am a likeable and friendly person.... I was not inaccessible as the chief minister. I took my work seriously and really did my work conscientiously, which left me very little time for the media and to meet people. This was probably being considered as inaccessible," she told talk show host Rajat Sharma on "Aap ki Adalat".[17]

By the time she finished her term, Jaya was embroiled in a number of scams. Her popularity took a nosedive in five years. She lost her urban base gradually consequent to these corruption charges. Her charisma was waning as a result of maladministration. The sympathy wave, which swept her to power, had disappeared. There was a controversy over her close aide Sasikala Natarajan, who once used to supply video films to her. She had developed a close relationship with Jayalalithaa and began living in her house. There were allegations that Sasikala was interfering in the administration and also making money. To add to the controversy, Jayalalithaa suddenly decided to make arrangements for her foster son's marriage (Sasikala's nephew) on a grand scale. The bride was the granddaughter of matinee idol Sivaji Ganesan. Neither the bride nor the bridegroom was related to Jaya. While she never admitted her mistake, some believe its opulence proved to be her undoing. At least 12,000 guests sat down for a meal cooked by 3,500 cooks! The *New York Times* described the wedding: "One of India's leading film-set designers was summoned to make whole avenues in central Madras into a tableau of Tamil mythology. For miles between Jayalalithaa's official residence and the wedding site, streets were decorated with pillared castles decorated with Grecian statues and gilded lions. Shrines were erected, with icon-like images of Jayalalithaa in place of Hindu gods. Fountains played, and the turmoil of daily street life was hidden from view by walls of banana leaves."[18] It goes on to speculate why she staged such an extravaganza. While some said it was done to boost her sagging popularity, others said the wedding, like the personality cult, grew from a craving for respect.

Ravi points out that she seemed to have lost all sense of proportion and even political instinct. Nobody in their senses would have thrown such an opulent wedding. 'That marked her decline from a well-meaning person, eager to learn and do good, to what she had now become. In fact, half of her first term was spent controlling law and order.'*

As her first term was coming to an end, Jayalalithaa realised the need for a Congress alliance and telephoned Rao in 1996 just before the polls. The local Congress leaders, including Moopanar and P. Chidambaram, were against an alliance, arguing that it might mar the Congress's chances. Even Dr. Chenna Reddy advised the prime minister to stay away from her and go in for an alliance with the DMK instead. Karunanidhi's representative sat in Delhi for a week, but Rao was hesitant to back the DMK since he was apprehensive of Sonia Gandhi's reaction. Ultimately, he decided to continue the alliance with the AIADMK. Rao said, "The Congress Working Committee's decision to go with the AIADMK was unanimous and final."[19]

The Congress party split over the alliance issue. Moopanar and P. Chidambaram and a few others quit the Congress and formed a regional party, the Tamil Maanila Congress. This new party forged an alliance with the DMK and between them they won a good number of seats. After the 1996 polls, the BJP came to power for 13 days at the Centre, emerging as the single largest party, but collapsed when no other party supported it. The Congress propped up a United Front government consisting of many smaller regional and Left parties, and supported it from outside. Karnataka Chief Minister Deve Gowda became the prime minister.

The 1996 election results were a blow to Jayalalithaa, although she was the first chief minister to complete a full term in the state. Both Rao and Jayalalithaa got embroiled in several court cases and spent time fighting them. She was isolated without support in the state or the Centre. Karunanidhi, who had succeeded her, was bent on harassing her by foisting cases on her.

Why did Jayalalithaa lose? Political analysts reflect that generally the Tamil Nadu voters alternate between the DMK and the AIADMK governments. Both parties had 30 per cent votes each; whichever one had a better arithmetic, won the state. Moopanar, whose party successfully won seats in the Assembly and the Lok Sabha, attributed it to the fact that "Jaya had a very bad image."[20] Dr. Swamy adds that "again her politics was only vis-à-vis DMK and she had no role to play elsewhere. Still she could not digest the fact the people of Tamil Nadu could throw her out just like that. She was terribly upset and blamed them for letting her down. She felt she had wasted her life."[21]

The DMK came to power in Tamil Nadu and the next two years were extremely difficult for Jayalalithaa. She and Sasikala were even sent to jail for a few days in connection with a court case. While fighting the many court cases against her—which she claimed were politically motivated—with the aid of a battery of lawyers, she decided to lie low and bide her time in Hyderabad and Ooty.

JAYALALITHAA'S REVIVAL

Within two years, Jayalalithaa managed to get back to centre stage when the 1998 Lok Sabha elections were nearing. The United Front government led by Deve Gowda, and later I.K. Gujral, did not last long. Jayalalithaa broke her alliance with the Congress once again and joined hands with the BJP. It was described as a natural alliance. She thought it was better to join hands with a national party and hoped that the BJP would come to power in view of the disarray in the Congress, with several Congressmen leaving for greener pastures. The AIADMK won 28 of the 39 seats and was the biggest contingent in the BJP-led National Democratic Alliance (NDA) coalition government under Vajpayee. Right from the beginning, Jayalalithaa was unpredictable, demanding her pound of flesh, including several portfolio allocations. As she had done with Narasimha Rao, she began to show disrespect towards Prime Minister Vajpayee, refusing to receive him when he visited Chennai. The relationship between the BJP and the AIADMK soured within a year. Jayalalithaa decided to pull down the government by allying with the Congress. The Vajpayee government fell in 1999. Dr. Swamy played a role in the swift operation. He brought Sonia Gandhi and Jayalalithaa together. 'Their relationship was cordial but there was a certain animosity stemming from the time of Rajiv Gandhi. Sonia avoided talking to Jaya. It took a lot of persuasion to bring them together,' reveals Swamy.*

Vajpayee was reaching the end of his patience due to constant demands from Jayalalithaa. The then BJP president Jana Krishnamurthy observed, "The BJP-AIADMK relationship had never been deep-rooted. We also knew the difficulties we may face when we went into the tie-up with Jayalalithaa. She too must have felt that she may not be able to get along with the BJP for long and that its leadership will not be pliable. We were also ready from the beginning to break off the relationship but we would not have done so on our own."[22]

The break was inevitable. It came in the form of a tea party on March 29, 1999. Jayalalithaa was itching to exhibit her power—what better way than to pull down the government of which she was a partner? Dr. Swamy says that it was Jaya's idea from the beginning. 'I had been telling her from day one not to go with the BJP but she went with them. Later, she admitted I was right and declared that she wanted to pull out. I told her to first build bridges with the Congress and the other parties, but she expressed apprehensions that Sonia would not go along with her. This was in July

1998. I made them talk to each other on my cellular phone. Then in the first week of March 1999, Jaya called and told me, "I am coming to Delhi; you have to throw a tea party." The BJP was already hosting a party for her, so I told her she was already invited, to which she responded, "You arrange for a tea party and if Sonia comes for that, we will work out the fall of the Vajpayee government." Even then I told her, "This is your ace of trumps. Don't use it unless you have something else as an alternative." She came for the tea party and described it as a political earthquake. She got carried away.'*

The *New York Times* notes, "The two women spent less than 10 minutes together, drinking tea. But the mere fact of their public chat made the front pages. 'We are old friends,' Mrs. Gandhi said, which was news in itself. Conjecture began about a budding alliance."[23]

Dr. Swamy claims that Jaya miscalculated her strategy. 'I told her to wait for some time and she went back to Chennai. This was on March 29, and on April 12 she announced at the Chennai airport that she was going to Delhi and would not come back until a new government was formed. Nobody was willing to talk to her in Delhi because she was still with the BJP and they thought she was only bargaining.'* To prove them wrong she withdrew her support.

It was a free-for-all as each party had its own interests and agenda. The Opposition had one thing in common: the aim to pull down the government. Several parties were involved in this scheme but, being the largest party in the Opposition, the Congress was in the forefront. Jayalalithaa was sidelined after the government fell and the Congress took over. The Congress was keen to form an alternative government when Vajpayee lost by one vote in the House. Sonia Gandhi went to the President of India, claiming she had 272 seats in the Lok Sabha (the magic number to form the government) but found that Samajwadi Party chief Mulayam Singh was not willing to support her. Jayalalithaa had ambitions to become the prime minister; she broached the subject with Mulayam Singh but ultimately it was her loss, as she had no bargaining power. In the 1999 Lok Sabha polls, to her horror, she found that the DMK had joined the NDA as a partner and had also won a good number of seats. Swamy, who was one of the main players in the whole drama, claims, 'For me it was a great adventure. I had only one thing to do—pull down the government. But for Jaya it was sad. Once the government fell, she said she would handle the situation herself and the whole thing became a mess.'*

CHIEF MINISTER ONCE MORE

Jayalalithaa did not have to wait long; the 2001 Assembly elections brought her back to power. She shrewdly cobbled together an alliance with a number of smaller parties, including the Left and regional parties in Tamil Nadu, which worked like magic. In these polls, an alliance consisting of the Congress, the Left Front and the Pattali Makkal Katchi (PMK), regained power, winning 197 seats, of which 132 belonged to the AIADMK.

The DMK was trounced and Karunanidhi was sidelined once again. The alliance arithmetic worked. Public memory being short, Jayalalithaa came back with a massive majority, despite corruption charges and other allegations. The electorate seemed to have forgotten or forgiven her corruption. Columnist T.V.R. Shenoy points out that there are two aspects to this win. The first was that in India there was a perception that women cannot be corrupt. 'What will they do with money? Maybe buy jewellery and clothes? But for a man it is different; he may spend it on other things. They had defeated Jayalalithaa but they may not have accepted the legal side. It was not a permanent punishment. Politics is not an element of legality; it is an element of morality. In Indira Gandhi's case also they tried to fix her with the Shah Commission but she bounced back.'* Secondly, there was the anti-incumbency factor. People thought Jayalalithaa was wearing MGR's mantle and her vote bank remained intact. She cleverly forged a formidable alliance and, above all, luck was on her side. Through the 1998 and 1999 Assembly elections, she was able to prove that the public was ready to ignore the corruption charges levelled against her.

The *New York Times* describes her victory thus: "Jayalalithaa Jayaram, a flamboyant politician convicted six months ago on corruption charges, led an alliance of parties to a landslide victory in elections this week in Tamil Nadu, taking the state with the heavy support from women and the rural poor."[24]

LEADING FROM BEHIND THE SCENES

In the beginning of her second term a legal problem arose. Jayalalithaa did not contest the 2001 Assembly elections due to her entanglement in corruption cases. She knew that when it came to the eligibility criteria for being chief minister, there was a provision through which, without being a legislator, one could be appointed by the governor on stipulation that he or she should become a member within six months. When the AIADMK won a landslide victory, Governor Fathima Beevi appointed her chief minister. Three months after Jayalalithaa assumed charge, the Supreme Court ruled her appointment as chief minister null and void on September 21, 2001, in response to a Public Interest Litigation (PIL), which challenged how a convicted person could be sworn in as chief minister. Jaya was not worried. She chose her successor, O. Panneerselvam, a first-time MLA, and installed him as chief minister that very evening. He was to function as a puppet chief minister and was well aware of that. In a way, Jaya showed the way to Sonia Gandhi, who later chose Manmohan Singh as prime minister in the UPA government.

Panneerselvam was so much in awe of *Amma* (Jayalalithaa) that he would not even sit in the chief minister's chair or allow his official car to be parked in the portico of the Secretariat. Jayalalithaa practically decided every single issue, as the seat of power was not Fort St. George, but Jaya's Poes Garden residence. The new CM prostrated at her feet in public view before taking charge.

Relief came within a few weeks when the Tamil Nadu High Court cleared her in the TANSI and Pleasant Stay Hotel cases on December 4, 2001. It was alleged that Jaya Publications and Sasi Enterprises, in which Jayalalithaa and her close associate Sasikala were partners, had bought properties belonging to the Tamil Nadu Small Industries Corporation (TANSI) in the industrial estate at Guindy (Chennai) at less than the guideline/market value. This was said to have led to a wrongful loss of Rs. 3.5 crore and Rs. 66 lakhs respectively to the government. Since Jayalalithaa bought these properties while she was the chief minister, she was charged under the Prevention of Corruption Act (PCA), which applies to public servants. She and her partners were also charged under sections of the Indian Penal Code (IPC). In the Pleasant Stay Hotel case, Jayalalithaa, former Local Administration Minister T.M. Selvaganapathy and three others, were charged with illegally granting exemption from building and hill area development control rules for regularising the illegal construction of five additional storeys of the hotel in the hill station of Kodaikanal. On February 2, 2000, Special Judge V. Radhakrishnan convicted and sentenced Jayalalithaa to one year's rigorous imprisonment under the PCA. The others were sentenced to one year in prison. All the accused in the three cases appealed in the High Court against their conviction and sentence.

After the court cleared her, a beaming Jayalalithaa said, "There is no legal hurdle now. All legal hurdles have been crossed." She claimed that her legal victory was purely due to god's grace. Thousands thronged to greet her at her residence. In the afternoon, the AIADMK legislators met; there were only two items on the agenda. One was the resignation of Panneerselvam, the other was to elect Jayalalithaa as the chief minister. At 4 p.m. Panneerselvam went to the Raj Bhavan and submitted his resignation.

In February 2002, Jayalalithaa contested the by-election from Andipatti, 500 kilometres south of Chennai, and won by a 40,000 vote margin over her DMK rival Vaigai Sekar. After her victory she declared, "My case is a lesson for anyone who is on the brink of hopelessness, that courage and confidence will win in the end."[25] She took over as chief minister on March 2, 2002.

HER SECOND TERM

Jayalalithaa, who inherited empty coffers when she took over in 2001, tried her best to revive the state's economy through some tough, unpopular measures. As expected, her main target of attack was the DMK, particularly its chief Karunanidhi. The whole country witnessed the crackdown on June 30, 2001, at about 2 a.m., when policemen barged into the former chief minister's house and dragged him out of bed while the old man agonised and screamed, "They are killing me!" Two DMK central ministers— Murasoli Maran and T.R. Balu—who intervened were beaten up and not allowed to accompany their leader in the police van. A magistrate remanded Karunanidhi to judicial custody and he was taken to the central jail. The two ministers were charged for obstructing the police from discharging their duties. When Prime Minister Vajpayee learnt of this, he telephoned the chief minister, but Jayalalithaa refused to come on the line. She further irked the prime minister by demanding the dismissal of the two DMK ministers.

The shock waves were felt in Delhi, with Prime Minister Vajpayee sending a team of ministers to console Karunanidhi in his prison cell. Amidst demands for the dismissal of Jayalalithaa's government, Vajpayee, to make his annoyance felt, recalled Governor Fathima Beevi, who had sworn in Jayalalithaa. The chief minister got the message loud and clear;

Karunanidhi was released on what she called "humanitarian grounds in view of his age".

Her next act of revenge was the arrest of Marumalarchi Dravida Munnetra Kazhagam (MDMK) leader Vaiko under the draconian Prevention of Terrorism Act, 2002 (POTA), which enabled the authorities to arrest anyone on mere suspicion and keep him or her in jail without trial for days together on grounds of terrorism. Vaiko was her one time ally but had fallen out with her soon. He was allegedly involved with the Sri Lankan terrorist group LTTE; he was kept in jail for 19 months.

Within the party, she continued to show her dictatorial tendencies. The ministers in her Cabinet were perpetually apprehensive of how long they would remain in power since she would drop them at her whim and fancy.

Jayalalithaa lived up to her "iron lady" image once again when in 2004 she ordered the police to go after the dreaded forest bandit Veerappan and had him killed. Veerappan had defied the authorities time and again, killing many people, including policemen and rangers, while reigning over vast stretches of forest land in Karnataka, Tamil Nadu and Kerala with the connivance of the authorities.

Jayalalithaa was also tough on bureaucrats. She regularly punished those who displeased her by transferring them to unpleasant assignments. In the first two years of her term, she changed as many as four chief secretaries. Yet other reason for her unpopularity could be the anti-conversion law she introduced in 2002 to check religious conversions. After the disastrous results in the 2004 Lok Sabha polls, Jayalalithaa repealed the law but religious leaders were so incensed, they took revenge by asking their followers to vote her out of power. In addition, the 200,000 state government employees whom she fired in 2004, and who consequently went on strike, were only reinstated by a court order later; they too did not forget her ruthlessness.

Yet another controversy was the arrest of godman Kanchi Shankaracharya, who was charged by Tamil Nadu state prosecutors with being a conspirator in the murder of a temple manager in Kanchipuram. On January 10, 2005, the godman managed to get bail from the Supreme Court. On October 26, 2005, the case was transferred to the neighbouring Union Territory of

Pondicherry, and is still going on. Shankaracharya's arrest and subsequent prosecution hurt the religious sentiments of his devotees.

Come 2004, Jayalalithaa got a taste of the voters' anger when her party was humiliated in the Lok Sabha polls. The AIADMK did not win a single seat, while the DMK-led UPA coalition won all the seats. The DMK was on the upswing again, getting important ministries at the Centre. It had teamed up with the Congress as an alliance partner along with other smaller parties. Jayalalithaa was shocked once again and tried to restore her image in the public by resorting to populist measures. She knew that the Assembly elections were scheduled in 2006 and she did not want to taste defeat again.

DMK COMES TO POWER

As expected, the DMK came to power after the 2006 Assembly polls. Apart from the arithmetic of alliances forged, Karunanidhi also announced populist schemes like free colour TV sets, cheaper rice and gas connections.

By this time Jayalalithaa had developed an image of a consummate autocrat. Her dominance over her party extended beyond symbolism. She was the party's sole decision maker and even the most mundane matters required her permission. She accepted advice from a very limited circle and none of them are allowed to become powerful on their own.

A US embassy telegram from New Delhi describes her total domination of the AIADMK as legendary. "Jayalalithaa casts a huge and menacing shadow over her party. Even in private meetings with Consulate officers, AIADMK leaders never call her by her name; they call her 'Amma' (Tamil for mother), 'Madam,' or 'our Leader'. Their offices, vehicles, and homes are festooned with multiple pictures of Jayalalithaa. Senior AIADMK leaders, especially men, used to physically prostrate themselves before her to demonstrate their obeisance. Jayalalithaa has since started to discourage the practice after the English language media began to mock it."[26] It further noted the cut-out poster culture: "At a major intersection near the Consulate there is a three-story picture of Jayalalithaa with the words 'Amma is god' directly above the AIADMK leader's head. In the past her supporters have run into trouble with religious groups for depicting her variously as a Hindu goddess and the Virgin Mary."[27]

Mani Shankar Aiyar points out that 'Jaya has an extraordinary command of English, Tamil and Kannada and a good knowledge of Hindi. She has the ability to do anything and everything she wants to. And this fascist following she has acquired has made her believe she is a child of destiny and nothing and no one can stop her from becoming what she wants to, which is the prime minister of India, not just the chief minister of Tamil Nadu. She became a street fighter. After Swamy switched sides and supported her, she took advantage of him and then refused to give him a seat. So she is the Bourbon Queen. She never forgets and she never forgives.'*

Karunanidhi became the chief minister for the fifth time and formed a minority government in May 2006. The alliance won 163 seats and 45 per cent votes, while the AIADMK alliance won 40 per cent. The DMK was generous in its pre-poll allocation to its partners, offering them winnable seats while almost assuring them that it would be able to get the 118 seats required for a majority. The DMK put up a good show, winning 96 of the 122 seats it contested, but was just short of the majority of its own. The other parties—the Congress, the PMK, the CPI and the CPI(M)—supported the government from outside. The Congress wanted to join Karunanidhi's Cabinet but he was not willing to share power. The AIADMK won 61 seats but the consolation was that this was relatively better compared to a four-member AIADMK in 1996 and an even lesser two-member Opposition in 1989.

There were at least three primary reasons for the DMK's victory. The coalition Karunanidhi had forged was strong and had an edge right from the beginning. Tamil Nadu votes on traditional caste, religion and social group lines. The second was the aggressive and populist manifesto of the DMK, which promised free rice, free television sets and other bonanzas. The third was the traditional anti-incumbency factor. Tamil Nadu has a tradition of favouring the DMK and AIADMK rule alternately, and it was the DMK's turn to rule. Plus, there was a surprise element. A new party led by another film actor, Vijayakanth, emerged, which cut into the AIADMK's votes. The matinee idol's popularity also contributed to the higher voter turnout.

The AIADMK's loss was also partly of its own doing and due to Jayalalithaa's style of functioning as chief minister. Although she had repealed the anti-conversion law of 2002, the post-poll analysis showed that a large number of Muslims and Christians voted for the DMK. Just before the elections, MDMK chief Vaiko quit the DMK alliance to join the AIADMK. The voters viewed him as an unprincipled leader, since Jayalalithaa had thrown him in jail for 19 months three years back. His party won six seats of the 35 seats contested. The Congress found itself in the third position, behind the two Dravidian parties, winning 34 of the 48 seats contested.

The other big loser was the BJP, which never had much clout in the state anyway. It won none of the 225 seats it contested. Jayalalithaa's openly disclosing her inclination to forge a post-poll alliance with the BJP contributed to her defeat to some extent. She told the media that a good politician never rules out anything; in other words, there was a possibility of her party aligning with the BJP. This scared the religious minorities for whom the BJP is a red rag.

The voters were also wary of the DMK's family-dominated politics. Karunanidhi's sons, M.K. Stalin and M.K. Azhagiri, had entered the political arena; the latter was a minister in the UPA government. Karunanidhi's daughter Kanimozhi is an MP, while his grand nephew Dayanidhi Maran is also an MP as well as a former minister. Moreover, Jayalalithaa and the Pattali Makkal Katchi (PMK) also alleged tampering of the electronic voting machines to manipulate the outcome in favour of the ruling party.

JAYALALITHAA LOSES THE 2009 LOK SABHA POLLS

Jayalalithaa was biding her time until the 2009 parliamentary elections. Two successive losses in the 2004 and 2006 elections did not dampen her fighting spirit. The AIADMK was making every effort to win more seats. More than Jayalalithaa's role as the Opposition leader, it was the infighting within the DMK which damaged its chances. Jayalalithaa went ahead and forged a strong pre-poll alliance, which included the CPI, CPI(M) and the PMK. The DMK ousted the PMK at the state level. Karunanidhi managed to do some damage control by not asking the UPA to remove the PMK from the government. The next important aspect was the Indo-US nuclear deal and the Left parties parting ways with the Congress-led UPA. The Left could not digest the fact that the DMK supported the nuclear deal; hence it became difficult to continue with its alliance with the DMK. After weighing the pros and cons, the Left parties felt that aligning with the AIADMK would be beneficial at the national level. The CPI and the CPI(M) had won two seats each in the 2004 Lok Sabha elections and they wanted to at least retain these seats in the 2009 elections.

Southern Tamil Nadu has about ten traditional AIADMK seats in the districts of Madurai, Sivaganga, Ramanathapuram, Tuticorin and Virudhunagar. In 2004, because of the strong DMK-led front, this advantage was negated; therefore, the other parties shared the spoils: Congress (5), DMK (2), CPI(M) (2), CPI (1) and MDMK (1).

Many expected that the AIADMK and its allies would win hands down. However, due to the late surge of support for the DMK and the nationwide support for the UPA government, the DMK front won more seats than it thought it would. This helped the Congress-led UPA to form the government at the Centre, even without the Left parties. The DMK-Congress front won 27 seats, leaving only 12 for the other opposition parties.

The Opposition focused on the Sri Lankan issue, which had no impact on the public. As a telegram from the US embassy in New Delhi notes, "Jayalalithaa, for her part, had long taken a stern anti-LTTE line, which included often calling her rival Karunanidhi soft on terrorism. But sensing changing political winds in favor of a more "pro-Tamil" position, Jayalalithaa pulled in the PMK and made a full about face. She ratcheted up the rhetoric by calling for an independent homeland of Tamils in Sri Lanka, Tamil Eelam, as the only solution for the conflict, which is the LTTE's demand. In the final days before the voting, Jayalalithaa even declared that she would send the Indian army to Sri Lanka to carve out Tamil Eelam, drawing a parallel with Indira Gandhi's support of an independent Bangladesh."[28]

The DMK won 18 out of the 22 seats it contested, forming a large chunk of the UPA. The AIADMK won 9 out of 23 seats. A disappointed Jayalalithaa, who had planned to go to Delhi after the results for government formation, remained indoors, refusing to talk to anyone. The election results further cemented the Congress-DMK ties at both the state and central level.

Jayalalithaa had not only worked hard to forge a powerful coalition, but also toured the state by helicopter, covering every nook and corner. In comparison, the DMK campaign was weak, with its chief as the lone campaigner. But what mattered most was the successful election management of the DMK with the administration's help.

Another US embassy cable from New Delhi states that it was alleged that the DMK widely distributed cash to buy votes. "One of the more audacious distribution networks was reportedly in Madurai (in the central part of the state), where M.K. Azhagiri (son of Chief Minister Karunanidhi and now Union Minister for Chemicals and Fertilizers) scored an impressive win. Local media reported that the DMK was able to insert INR 500-notes (about USD 10, or two days' wages for a reasonably paid day laborer) into the daily newspaper, delivered directly to the voters' homes. Our own contacts, including Congress supporters perhaps jealous of their own party's inability to match the scale of the DMK's cash-handout machine, confirmed these accounts."[29]

The AIADMK also improved its tally from zero in 2004 to 9 seats. But its allies (the PMK, the MDMK and the Left Parties) significantly lost compared to the previous elections, when they had allied with the DMK. The PMK lost all 6 of its seats, emerging as the biggest loser. The MDMK was able to get more DMK votes than AIADMK votes in the 2006 Assembly polls, but in 2009 it cut into more Congress voters from 2004, than any another party.

JAYALALITHAA'S THIRD TERM

After facing defeat in the 2009 Lok Sabha elections, Jayalalithaa did not give up. She started preparing for the 2011 Assembly elections despite not faring well in three successive elections (2004, 2006 and 2009). She was hopeful that this time the people of Tamil Nadu would not ignore her claims. She not only built up the party but also tried to strengthen her alliances. Affected by the weakening of the party due to desertions, Jayalalithaa hit the road and toured the state in order to make contact with the masses once again. She launched a vigorous campaign against the DMK's dispensation. Luckily for her, the 2G telecom scam concerning spectrum allocation to some telecom companies in which DMK minister A. Raja and Karunanidhi's daughter Kanimozhi were alleged to have been involved, got exposed. They were arrested and put in Tihar jail. This adverse publicity helped Jayalalithaa. Karunanidhi fell out with the Congress, but did not withdraw support to the UPA government. It was in this atmosphere that the 2011 Assembly elections were held. Taking advantage of a silent anti-incumbency wave in the Assembly elections, the AIADMK stormed back to power in Tamil Nadu; Jayalalithaa became the chief minister on May 12, 2011. The AIADMK front won 203 out of 234 seats.

Those who know Jayalalithaa say that she has mellowed in her third term. She has become media friendly and has promised to meet journalists at least once a month. On the day of counting, Jayalalithaa surprised everyone by opening the gate to allow her party supporters, who were trying to get a glimpse of their leader, inside the premises.

However, she did not give up her habit of reversing the DMK government's orders. One of the first things she did as soon as she took over was to relocate the Assembly from the newly constructed building back to Fort St. George. Karunanidhi had the new building constructed at a cost of Rs. 1,000 crore.

Meanwhile she became ambitious and began looking for a national role, wanting to go beyond Tamil Nadu. As a prelude to her raised political profile, she had a successful meeting with US Secretary of State Hillary Clinton who visited the state soon after she took over. Jayalalithaa discussed the status of Sri Lankan Tamils, while Hillary voiced concern over the plight of Internally Displaced Persons in Sri Lanka and said the US was looking at some innovative and creative ideas to break the impasse over the Sri Lankan Tamils issue. The latter also appreciated the mid-day meal scheme introduced by MGR which is being implemented successfully.

The Economist magazine put Jayalalithaa's strong stance down to the need to position herself well for the 2014 Lok Sabha polls. It notes: "How then should leading Tamil politicians, such as the chief minister, who are trying to position themselves to be influential in 2014, go about building up support among voters in the coming months? One natural answer is to bash Sri Lanka's rulers and speak up for Tamils across the water, make a loud fuss when votes are expected on war crimes at the United Nations, criticise Delhi's ruling class as supine in the face of Sinhalese nationalists and keep alive tensions between the two countries. Indian Tamils care strongly about the issue, so there is an opportunity both to attack the ruling Congress party and just possibly to influence foreign policy. For Miss Jayalalitha, the closer the national election looms in India, the greater the reason to inveigh against the wicked Sinhalese in Colombo. If this analysis is right, India's internal politics will discourage warm ties with Sri Lanka until at least 2014 and probably beyond."[30]

Jayalalithaa played an active part in the Sri Lankan issue in 2013 by getting a resolution passed in the Assembly in favour of the Lankan Tamils; she also led the agitation in the state against the Sri Lankan government. She was delighted when the DMK decided to withdraw from the UPA government over the issue of the Lankan Tamils, as that rendered the DMK isolated both in the state and at the Centre.

Jayalalithaa has also teamed up with other regional satraps like Orissa CM Naveen Patnaik to sponsor the candidature of former Speaker P.A. Sangma as the presidential candidate, knowing fully well that he might lose. She invited Gujarat Chief Minister Narendra Modi for her swearing-in function. Moreover, she also became part of a pressure group to insist on the rights of the states when the Central government wanted to create a National Counter Terrorism Centre (NCTC), resulting in the Union government backing out.

Jayalalithaa has done a good balancing act in the past one year. It was a huge responsibility to fulfil her poll manifesto with not much money in hand. She began implementing her poll promises, starting a free rice scheme for about 1.85 crore poor people, enhancing old age pension, hiking maternity assistance for women and distributing free laptops to government higher secondary school students.

Jayalalithaa has made allocations for welfare schemes to the tune of Rs. 30,331 crore, setting rather high standards. In fact, the social sector outlays in Tamil Nadu, including the mid-day meal scheme for school children, has been one of the highest in India since the 1990s. She has also come up with a "Vision Tamil Nadu 2023" that outlines her plans for the state for the next ten years.

She has made her presence felt in the capital. During her frequent visits, she has met the press to explain her points of view, be it the Cauvery water sharing dispute, or the setting up of the NCTC, or the policies on Sri Lanka. In short, she is certainly preparing for a bigger role in national politics since she came back to power in 2011.

The options before her are attractive. She could join hands with the other anti-Congress chief ministers who are growing in numbers. She has already established contact with Gujarat Chief Minister Narendra Modi and Orissa Chief Minister Naveen Patnaik. Now that West Bengal Chief Minister Mamata Banerjee has left the UPA, there is a possibility of her joining the anti-Congress club. Jayalalithaa has her eyes set on the next Parliamentary elections and is working diligently towards it. All these chief ministers want to bag the maximum number of seats in their respective states so that they can play kingmakers in the next government.

This leader has come a long way since her celluloid days. From expanding MGR's constituency of women to identifying the weaker sections, she has developed an image of an "iron lady" and a cult of personality. Her future may be bright if she plays her cards well. The added advantage is the developments in the DMK. DMK chief Karunanidhi has announced that his younger son Stalin would be his political heir but he is not liked by his siblings—Azhagiri and Kanimozhi. The family has been fighting for its share of power for a long time. In the post-Karunanidhi era, if the DMK happens to split, it would benefit the AIDMK. Simultaneously, Jayalalithaa is working for her place in the national political scene. The future is wide open and she is playing her cards quite well.

NOTES

1. http://wikileaks.org/cable/2009/03/09CHENNAI81.html.
2. Kalyani Shankar, *Gods of Power: Personality Cult and Indian Democracy*, p. 84, Macmillan India, Updated Edition 2005.
3. http://wikileaks.org/cable/2009/03/09CHENNAI81.html.
4. Shankar, *Gods of Power*, p. 86.
5. Ibid., p. 87.
6. Interview with Rajat Sharma on "Aap ki Adalat" aired on India TV, January 1999.
7. Shankar, *Gods of Power*, p. 87.
8. Ibid., p. 91.
9. Kondath Mohandas, *MGR, the Man and the Myth*, Panther Publishers, 1992.
10. Ibid., p. 94
11. Ibid., p. 101
12. Ibid., p. 167
13. Interview with Rajat Sharma on "Aap ki Adalat" aired on India TV, January 1999.
14. M. Karunanidhi, *Nenjukku Needhi*, 1987.
15. http://wikileaks.org/cable/2009/03/09CHENNAI81.html.
16. Shankar, *Gods of Power*, p. 109.
17. Interview with Rajat Sharma on "Aap ki Adalat" aired on India TV, January 1999.
18. John F. Burns, "For Indian Politician, An Opulent Wedding means Political Bliss", *New York Times*, September 10, 1995.

19. Shankar, *Gods of Power*, p. 110.
20. Ibid.
21. Ibid.
22. Ibid., p. 112.
23. Barry Bearack, "India's Coalition is Teetering as Ex-Actress Pushes Demands", *New York Times*, April 5, 1999.
24. Celia W. Dugger, "Fiery Actress Helps Opposition Strengthen Role in India", *New York Times*, May 13, 2001.
25. E.R. Gopinath, "Jayalalithaa wins Andipatti by a landslide", *Gulf News*, February 25, 2002; *Custom 150 Online Journals*, July 2, 2012.
26. http://wikileaks.org/cable/2009/03/09CHENNAI81.html.
27. Ibid.
28. http://wikileaks.org/cable/2009/05/09chennai145.html.
29. http://wl.wikileaks-press.org/cable/2009/06/09CHENNAI185.html.
30. "Jayalalitha's Gambit", *The Economist*, September 6, 2012.

Sheila Dikshit

DELHI CHIEF MINISTER SHEILA DIKSHIT is a classic example of how personal popularity and good public relations combined with patronage of the leadership can keep a politician in power. She is one of the few Congress leaders who has scripted a success story for herself and her party. Her perceived able governance and work ethics have won her the voters' confidence. No wonder Dikshit won a third chief ministerial term, earning the sobriquet "the winning granny".

While the chief minister might claim to have changed the face of Delhi by giving it swanky metro rails and fabulous flyovers, many in the capital complain about lack of basic amenities like clean drinking water, a regular supply of electricity or sewage facilities. Sheila's detractors grumble that much more needs to be done, and draw attention to the irregular colonies, slums and the homeless living without shelters. In any case, it is not easy to remain in power for three consecutive terms, especially in a city which has alternated between the Congress and the Bharatiya Janata Party (BJP) governments for so long. Former minister K. Natwar Singh describes her as an extraordinary person. 'She is very low key, well educated and has a modern mind. She has an ideal political temperament.'*

Sheila is a suave politician who connects with people; she attends weddings and funerals in the capital and participates in local events. She does her own publicity effectively. With her hair tied in a neat bun and wearing handloom sarees, Sheila does not look glamorous but reminds one of a "granny next door", an image she has cultivated with great care since she first became the chief minister of Delhi in 1998.

FIRST STINT AS CHIEF MINISTER

Although she had been a minister in Prime Minister Rajiv Gandhi's Cabinet in the mid-eighties, the defining moment came when Congress President Sonia Gandhi chose her as the Pradesh Congress Committee (PCC) president of the Delhi unit in 1998. It was Sheila's luck and Sonia's support which got her that status. This was a tumultuous period for the Congress since it was facing a leadership crisis. Members were deserting the party in search of greener pastures after it did not fare well in the Lok Sabha elections held in February. It was also a difficult period personally for Sheila. The party she had joined—the Congress (Tiwari)—had almost disintegrated. She had lost four consecutive elections in 1989, 1991, 1996 and 1998 and was in political wilderness. Sonia Gandhi had taken over in March as the party president and was trying to stem the erosion in the Congress. The party had won just 140 seats in the elections, while the National Democratic Alliance (NDA) was able to form the government with 24 partners. It was a major setback for the Congress, which had been out of power for two years.

Within six months of Sonia Gandhi's taking over, the Delhi, Rajasthan and Madhya Pradesh Assembly elections were to take place. It was at this time that Sheila moved to Delhi state politics. The Congress leaders who had pitched for Sheila, including M.L. Fotedar, Natwar Singh and Arjun Singh, were all with her in the Congress (T) breakaway party. They wanted to rehabilitate Sheila from her political oblivion. A few weeks after Sonia took over, Sheila received a phone call from Sonia Gandhi's private secretary, Vincent George. 'He informed me that I had to contest the East Delhi Lok Sabha seat. I said, "What!" And he said that was Sonia Gandhi's decision. I told him I would have to decline the offer. Half an hour later, George called back and said I had to contest,' recalls Sheila.*

So while Sheila got a ticket for the election, she had a difficult seat to fight from. She went to file her nomination papers in her brother-in-law's old rickety car. East Delhi was a huge constituency; Sheila had to work hard during the campaign. She could not mobilise many votes because the campaign began late and she did not expect much because old-timers within the Delhi unit of the Congress resented her being imposed from above. Some party members did not work for her success, while others did not join her campaign. Many viewed her as an outsider. The result: she lost the elections, yet again.

The Delhi Assembly elections took place within a few months. Sonia was looking for a person to lead the Congress in the state. Sheila's luck held; despite losing four consecutive elections, she was made the PCC chief. Natwar Singh suggested Sheila Dikshit's name to Sonia Gandhi to lead the party. He persuaded her that Sheila was the right person because she was connected to different castes and communities. 'She was a Punjabi, her husband a Brahmin, and her daughter had married a Muslim.'* There were other Congress leaders like Fotedar and Arjun Singh who supported Sheila. Fotedar also stressed on Sheila's cosmopolitan background.

Sonia Gandhi was initially reluctant, but soon saw the merits of the argument and decided to give Sheila a chance. Even though the BJP-led NDA government was ruling at the Centre, it was not faring well in Delhi. There were internal squabbles within the party, which had now reached a peak. Sahib Singh Verma was the chief minister of Delhi and he was becoming unpopular. Verma was opposed to his rival Madan Lal Khurana staking his claim to lead the party. So the BJP chose its firebrand leader Sushma Swaraj as the first woman chief minister of Delhi. She now faced a difficult situation: she had not been given enough time to settle down in the Union Territory where the BJP was facing an anti-incumbency wave. The prices of essential commodities had been skyrocketing and people resented the scarcity of basic vegetables like onions. By and large, the voters were dissatisfied and in a mood to oust the BJP.

Lady Luck smiled on Sheila when the Congress won in Delhi. Sonia Gandhi was happy that she had made the right choice and appointed Sheila the chief minister against the wishes of the old timers of the party and the local Congress unit. Senior journalist Pankaj Vohra claims that the powerful people who helped her to become the PCC president also propped her up as the Delhi chief minister. He is of the view that it was not because of Sheila that the Congress came to power; the entry of Sonia, the anti-incumbency factor and BJP's internal squabbles created the right conditions for the Congress win in 1998. Natwar Singh observes, 'When Sheila was brought to Delhi politics, there was a lot of opposition, as she was seen as an outsider. Entrenched Delhi Congress leaders like Jagdish Tytler opposed her.'*

INTRODUCTION TO POLITICS

Sheila was born into a non-political family. She grew up like any other ordinary Delhi girl and had never dreamt of entering politics. 'Somehow politics seemed so far away, and at that age, I did not understand politics as I do today,' recalls Sheila.*

Sheila and Vinod Dikshit fell in love and had an inter-caste marriage, but there was no resistance from either side of the family, although Sheila's father was shocked that the young couple wanted to marry when Vinod did not even have a job. She recollects: 'I told him that he has graduated from the prestigious St Stephen's College and will surely find a job. My mother and father were absolutely astounded.'*

After marriage, Sheila found herself in the midst of a political family. Her father-in-law, Uma Shankar Dikshit, was a respected senior Congress leader from Uttar Pradesh. At the time of their marriage, he was the managing director of the *National Herald*, a newspaper owned by the Indian National Congress. Vinod went on to became an IAS (Indian Administrative Service) officer and was posted in Aligarh, a district headquarter in UP, and the two lived there happily. Sheila had had her children by then and spent her time looking after them. 'Even then, I did not have any idea of politics. I neither took an interest nor had any inclination towards it. All I knew was that my father-in-law was in politics and was close to the Nehrus,' claims Sheila.*

FORAYS INTO THE CONGRESS PARTY

Sheila's first involvement in political events was in 1969 when the Congress split took place. Congress, the country's Grand Old Party, faced its first major rift as the old guard, led by party president S. Nijalingappa, expelled Prime Minister Indira Gandhi for what they called "fostering a cult of personality". The syndicate, as the senior members were called, could not quite come to terms with the fact that Indira Gandhi, whom they called the *goongi gudiya* (dumb doll), had a mind of her own.

The rift between Indira and them was irrevocably sealed after the Bangalore Congress session in June 1969. The syndicate, which selected her as the prime minister after the untimely death of Lal Bahadur Shastri, thought that she would be a puppet in their hands, but Indira Gandhi turned out to be otherwise. The provocation for the split was the just-concluded presidential elections. While the Congress had fielded Neelam Sanjiva Reddy as the official candidate, Indira Gandhi favoured labour leader V.V. Giri, and quietly asked her supporters to vote for him under the pretence of a "conscience vote". Giri won and the official candidate lost. The syndicate criticised her action and a piqued Indira Gandhi stomped out of the session. The Congress split after this episode. Sanjiva Reddy, however, had his day when he later became the president once the Janata Party took over after the Emergency.

When the Congress split, Sheila and her husband had moved back to Delhi and were staying with Uma Shankar Dikshit, who was an MP by this time. They had just returned from Cambridge University after Vinod's study leave and had moved into Uma Shankar Dikshit's apartment at Ferozshah Road. Several Congress leaders came to meet him there and Sheila played host to them. Soon she started picking up political tips while interacting with them, especially when giving them company while they waited to meet her father-in-law. 'This was a great learning and a grooming which was truly unique,' she says, pointing out that her father-in-law had very little time to teach her politics.* Sometimes she used to sit with R.K. Dhawan, Indira Gandhi's private secretary, and see to the dispatch of party posters. 'The southern states had their own posters but in the north, we had to send them,' explains Sheila.*

Meanwhile, Indira Gandhi consolidated her hold on the Indian polity. The syndicate had misjudged her capabilities. She introduced several bold policies such as nationalisation of banks, abolition of privy purses and implemented several pro-poor measures like the 20-point programme. On the world stage, Indira Gandhi's grand achievement was the liberation of Bangladesh, after which her popularity soared. She had been preparing for the Bangladesh war months in advance. The hostilities which lasted for about 9 months, pitted East Pakistan and India against West Pakistan. War broke out when the West Pakistani army launched a military operation against East Pakistanis, who were demanding that the ruling *junta* honour the democratic results held in 1970. Several military officers defected and, along with the paramilitary forces as well as civilians, formed the Mukti

Bahini (Liberation Army) on March 26, 1971. They launched guerrilla tactics against the West Pakistani army with economic, military and diplomatic support from India. Pakistan retaliated by launching a pre-emptive strike on its south-eastern border with India, starting the Indo-Pak War of 1971. The allied forces of the Indian army and Mukhti Bahini defeated the West Pakistan army on December 16, 1971, leading to the birth of Bangladesh.

Indira Gandhi, who was singularly hailed for the birth of Bangladesh, came back to power with a massive majority in the 1972 Lok Sabha polls. All through this period, Uma Shankar Dikshit remained her trusted colleague and played an important role in the party and government affairs. Besides serving as the home minister in her Cabinet, he held several other portfolios. But things took a different turn in 1975 when the Allahabad High Court nullified Indira Gandhi's election to the Lok Sabha. Indira hit back by making the then president Fakhruddin Ali Ahmed declare an Emergency in the country. Uma Shankar Dikshit felt uncomfortable with the imposition and made this known to Indira. Although there were differences of opinion between them, it did not affect their family ties; Uma Shankar was made governor of Karnataka in 1976.

While living with her husband in Kanpur, Sheila used to shuttle between Bangalore and Kanpur. During her stay in Agra, Sheila found time to do social work. She did not have to worry about looking after her father-in-law since he had a retinue of servants to do the needful.

ENTRY INTO ELECTORAL POLITICS

Sheila joined active politics only in late 1984, after Prime Minister Indira Gandhi was assassinated. During that period, she was staying with her father-in-law who had moved to West Bengal as governor in October 1984. 'I remember very clearly that around ten o'clock in the morning on October 31, my father-in-law got a phone call from Delhi that Indira Gandhi had been shot. Rajiv Gandhi had been campaigning in the state, so he arranged for a plane on which we could all travel to Delhi. Speaker Balram Jakhar and Finance Minister Pranab Mukherjee were also on the plane. Jakhar was there to attend a Speaker's Conference which was being held in the state. During the flight, Rajiv thought that Indira Gandhi was already dead. So did I. Actually, it was his secretary Vincent George who called to inform him about her passing,' reminisces Sheila.* She had carried with her a copy of the Constitution because her father-in-law said they had to think of the next step: make Rajiv Gandhi the prime minister. 'The big wigs were in the plane and Uma Shankar Dikshit consulted them all, not really sure about what happens when such an emergency arises. Even Rajiv Gandhi was consulted.'*

As soon as they landed in Delhi, Arun Nehru and Arun Singh, two of Rajiv Gandhi's close friends, were at the airport to receive him and he was taken to the All India Institute of Medical Sciences, where Indira's body was kept. Sheila and Uma Shankar Dikshit also followed. The reality of what had happened dawned on Sheila on the way back from the hospital. There were horrible scenes on the roads where innocent Sikhs were being targeted, as Gandhi was shot dead by two of her Sikh bodyguards. Over the next several days, violence, arson and murders were witnessed across the capital as Hindu mobs preyed on the city's Sikh population.

President Zail Singh, who cut short his foreign trip on hearing the news of Indira Gandhi's assassination, quickly appointed Rajiv Gandhi as the prime minister to avoid any other claims. The Cabinet that was sworn in was very small and it took only emergency decisions, since Rajiv wanted to get legitimacy by winning elections on his own as soon as possible. As expected, the fast-track elections took place in December-January. The Congress party was not prepared, but the unprecedented sympathy wave in the wake of Indira Gandhi's assassination delivered a windfall for the party, which won an unprecedented 406 seats. The Opposition was decimated. The atmosphere was such that any Congress candidate would have won in the name of the Gandhi family and the party. There wasn't enough time to cherry-pick candidates. Sheila's turn to enter politics came under such conditions.

One day, on a trip to Delhi, Uma Shankar Dikshit told Sheila that Rajiv Gandhi wanted her to contest the Lok Sabha Polls. 'I was surprised since I did not even know what a polling booth was. But my husband and my father-in-law were very keen, so I said okay,' says Sheila.* Dikshit persuaded his daughter-in-law by pointing out that it was the right time for her to join politics. Sheila was offered three choices but she chose Kannauj in Uttar Pradesh. From then on, the whole family chipped in during the campaign and she won. She made no stirring speeches while campaigning but managed to convey her message to the public.

FIRST-TERM MP

When Sheila came to Parliament as a novice, she was overawed by its sheer grandeur and simply got lost in its history. 'Just to enter Parliament itself was awesome. I never dreamt that I would get into Parliament,' she exclaims.* For the first six to eight months she concentrated on learning the ropes. 'I was so tongue-tied that I could not even make speeches.'* In her first term, Sheila tried to learn the parliamentary procedures from her senior colleagues.

AS JUNIOR MINISTER

Soon, Sheila's family connections with the Gandhis worked to her advantage. One day, about 18 months after becoming an MP, Sheila got a call from Rajiv Gandhi around midnight. He said he wanted to make her a minister. She clearly remembers his words, 'My office will give you the details; I want you as the junior parliamentary affairs minister. I have a lot of faith in you, that you will do well.'* So Sheila joined Rajiv Gandhi's team as Minister of State for Parliamentary Affairs. Rajiv chose her because he was looking for a woman minister who could be tactful and pleasant to keep the members engaged. The job was not easy as she had to interact with all manner of leaders and MPs, but she handled it well.

STINT AT THE PMO

In 1987, Sheila lost her husband. Rajiv Gandhi came to pay his condolences and asked her if she needed anything. Sheila told him that all she wanted was more work. Perhaps keeping this in mind, Rajiv called her one evening and told her that he wanted her to move to the Prime Minister's Office as a minister. He reminded her how Nandini Satpathy, who later became the chief minister of Orissa, worked in Indira Gandhi's office as a minister. He wanted her to do the same. Sheila was hesitant because being in the PMO would create jealousies, which she wanted to avoid. She therefore sought some time. A week later, Home Minister Buta Singh told her she would have to join immediately.

The work was interesting but also very demanding. 'It was a powerful PMO. When you get so much power suddenly, you feel afraid of it. Also, it was a 24-hour job,' explains Sheila.* Rajiv Gandhi used to keep late hours and would often ring up past midnight. 'The problem was to keep a large number of Congress MPs happy. Although there was no Opposition since the Congress won a massive majority in the 1984 elections, everybody wanted to meet Rajiv Gandhi.'*

Then, the Bofors scandal broke out; allegations flew thick and fast that kickbacks had been paid to the Gandhi family friend Ottavio Quattrocchi for sealing the Rs. 64-crore Bofors gun deal. The allegations hit the government from the blue. Rajiv Gandhi, in a knee-jerk reaction, announced in Parliament that neither he nor anyone from his family was involved in the deal. The Opposition was belligerent and demanded a Joint Parliamentary Committee to probe the scandal. When the government reluctantly instituted the panel, the Opposition boycotted it on the grounds that it was dominated by Congress Party members.

For Sheila, this was a difficult period. Most of the burden of fending off the crisis came on her and others in the office. They had to spend late hours collecting information for questions raised in Parliament. The entire Opposition had ganged up against Rajiv Gandhi and his government. 'It was the toughest time. It really was. It was then that I realised that the PM can get a barrage of advice, yet ultimately he has to decide... But how does he decide? One secretary tells you one thing and another says something else. There are 30 voices speaking in different tones,' declares Sheila.*

She points out that, politically and personally, it was a difficult time for Rajiv Gandhi. 'Those whom he trusted like Arun Nehru and Arun Singh were out. His Finance Minister V.P. Singh rebelled against him, although the responsibility was as much his as Rajiv Gandhi's. When he became the prime minister, V.P. Singh claimed that he had the incriminating foreign bank account number in his pocket but never revealed it. He could prove nothing. It was a malicious attack of the combined Opposition on Rajiv Gandhi.'* Sheila had to balance her work in the PMO, the party as well as the ministry. She gradually became the buffer between the party and Rajiv Gandhi, often annoying members who could not get to meet him. They thought she was being arrogant because of her proximity to the Gandhi family.

Although Rajiv Gandhi seemed to have weathered the storm temporarily, Bofors proved to be his Waterloo, as the controversy refused to die down.

Rajiv called for early elections in October 1989. As expected, the mud stuck to him and his party lost the polls. V.P. Singh, who had gone on to form his own outfit, became the prime minister after garnering the support of the Left and the Right parties. Rajiv decided to sit in the Opposition despite the Congress emerging as the single largest party. Even though Congress functionaries were a disheartened lot after the elections, Sheila kept herself busy with party work.

SHEILA JOINS CONGRESS TIWARI

During the early nineties, Sheila did not have any major responsibility. Rajiv Gandhi's assassination just before the elections on May 21, 1991, was a colossal disaster both for the party and for Sheila personally. Within a year, she aligned with a group of Congress leaders who were disenchanted with Prime Minister P.V. Narasimha Rao. Senior Congress leaders like Arjun Singh, N.D. Tiwari, Natwar Singh and others, felt they were not being given the importance they deserved. A most unfortunate event occurred when the Babri mosque adjacent to the Ram temple in Ayodhya was demolished by a mob on December 6, 1992. The BJP had organised a large congregation at the temple, demanding that the mosque be replaced by a grand new temple, claiming it to be the birthplace of Lord Ram. Rao was blamed for not protecting the mosque. Sheila was one of the disgruntled leaders who left the Congress after the event. 'They kept pushing me to join them,' recalls Sheila.* Although it was rumoured that Sonia Gandhi had supported the split, Sheila was not sure. 'She did not say yes and she did not say no,' observes Sheila. 'I cannot say that she was the one who had given the signal to go for the split. She never said anything to me, but they claimed that they had her blessings. I never checked with her, which I should have done.'* So the split happened and the Congress (Tiwari), of which Sheila was a prominent member, was formed in 1995.

Sheila explains why some veteran Congressmen left the party. 'By that time, Rao had become very powerful as the prime minister. He was extremely successful but this large discontented group felt they were not getting their due. Two stalwarts, N.D. Tiwari and Arjun Singh, were on this side,' elaborates Sheila.* Throughout this period, she kept in touch with Sonia Gandhi. As for the split, Sheila feels that it was not difficult but it was not exciting either. 'When the Congress broke up in 1969, there was euphoria.

This time, though, it was only a message to the prime minster that all was not well. But Rao did not make any effort to make things better.'*

SHEILA LOSES THE ELECTIONS

The 1996 elections came and the Congress (T) candidates, including Sheila, contested. They all lost as the party didn't have a presence at the grassroot level and the faction was not able to garner support from the people. The party began to disintegrate slowly and merged with the Congress (I) when Sonia Gandhi came forward to lead the party in 1998.

SHEILA DIKSHIT'S FIRST TERM AS CM

In her first term, Sheila set the agenda for the party and the Delhi state government. The Congress Party was in the opposition in the Lok Sabha and Vajpayee was the prime minister. However, Sheila did not have much problem with the federal NDA government since she did not confront it over any issues. She also got along with Vajpayee and Advani, although the local BJP leaders were critical of her. In the 1999 Lok Sabha elections, the Congress faired poorly in Delhi. Pankaj Vohra points out that Sheila did not have any impact in Delhi politics after becoming the chief minister, as she could not secure a single Lok Sabha seat for her party.

As far as governance was concerned, Sheila launched some innovative schemes like Bhagidari, which focused on involving multiple stakeholders like NGOs, citizen groups and resident welfare associations in administration. She made an effort to improve the water situation in the city and also attempted, with mixed results, to provide uninterrupted power. Sheila also initiated an awareness drive which focussed on rain harvesting. She introduced a programme called Stree Shakti to empower women, particularly those from the weaker sections. All in all, her first five years in power were a mixed bag.

SHEILA'S SECOND TERM AS DELHI CM

The second milestone in Sheila's journey at the helm came when the Congress won in Delhi for a second time in 2003. Riding on the development wave—introduction of CNG-propelled buses and construction of new roads and flyovers—Dikshit led the Congress Party to a landslide victory. It got a two-thirds majority, demolishing the BJP and surprising everyone because the poll predictions were not so rosy for the Congress. This was the first time the party was re-elected in the National Capital Region. The Congress won more seats because the BJP was in disarray and did not have any outstanding leaders to counter the Congress. Learning the lessons from its 1998 Assembly debacle, the BJP went to the polls in 2003 on the plank of development and good governance, which did not click with the voters. The in-fighting among the BJP leaders led to their sabotaging each other's plans. Madan Lal Khurana was a notable leader but when the BJP lost, they sent him away to Rajasthan as governor so that he would not give any trouble to the Sheila Dikshit government. She continued to maintain good relations with Advani and Vajpayee.

Sheila managed to project herself as a "doer" and took credit for the electoral victory. Natwar Singh observes that her Delhi roots served her well and she was able to relate both to the rural and urban voters. He adds, 'It's not easy to remain the CM of Delhi. Look at the power centres that exist there. There is the PM, there is Sonia, and then there is the Parliament and the corporate world. She has been able to deal with all of them very gracefully.'*

The media gave full marks to Sheila for the spectacular win. Rediff.com described it as "the quiet magic" of Sheila Dikshit. It argued that according to opinion polls, a second term for her was a foregone conclusion and the party had her administrative acumen to thank for this. "Not only has her government converted Delhi from a city of doom to a city of boom by giving it a facelift and improving infrastructure like roads and overbridges, it has also ensured—though with more than a little prodding by the Supreme Court—that vehicular pollution is brought under control and polluting industrial units are relocated outside the city limits. These measures have changed Delhi's profile from that of a hopeless, ageing metropolis bursting at the seams (a population equivalent to that of Pondicherry is added to Delhi every year, according to one estimate) to a modern city catching up with its Western counterparts," the analysis added.[1]

Sheila claims that some of the concrete achievements during her first term as chief minister of Delhi from 1998 to 2003 include the introduction of the Metro, CNG-fuelled public transport to avoid pollution, numerous flyovers, cleaner environment, substantial increase in the green cover, reforms in the power sector, marked improvement in the standard and results of government schools, extended and quality public health infrastructure and various income generation schemes for the marginalised sections of the society. What also helped the capital city was the proactive participation of the people in the implementation of various civic services.

Of course, Dikshit's success in combating pollution, improving roads and streamlining traffic did not mean the city was in the pink of health. Power and water continued to be two areas of concern where successive governments failed to live up to the citizens' expectations. Neither the BJP nor the Congress could claim credit for having solved either of the two chronic problems, with shortages being the norm, especially in summer. The unchecked growth of slums and illegal, unauthorised colonies in the capital are also a cause for concern.

Sheila's supporters attribute her success to her political maturity in handling the faction-ridden party and her using the carrot and stick policy to deal with the bickering MLAs. Not only did the chief minister last her full five-year term without any real threat to her leadership, but also succeeded, despite various pulls and pressures, in securing the maximum number of election tickets for her supporters. Her critics, however, think otherwise. They feel Sheila's political management has always been weak. They complain that banking on her "special equation" with Sonia Gandhi, she gets things done. She is often said to have kept MLAs waiting for hours. Increasingly frustrated at being deprived of power, they became clamorous in dissent.

Notwithstanding those claims, Sheila has built up a credible public image. She was regarded as a performer even in her second term. Dissidents were under the impression that the party's popularity might increase with an anti-Sheila campaign but, according to a senior Delhi Congress leader, harbouring such a belief was just political *hara-kiri*. He further adds: 'To her credit, Sheila has managed to shift the political lexicon from the fixer-cum-politician to a more suave and articulate type which the city's middle class is more comfortable with. But in politics, a few hours can be decisive. Dikshit has stayed a step ahead of her rivals so far.'*

If Sheila expected that she would automatically get re-nominated as the chief minister for the second time, she was disappointed. Despite the spectacular victory, it took more than 15 days for Sonia Gandhi to give Dikshit another term. Sheila learnt some hard lessons when her detractors resisted her leadership. They appeared to challenge the widely held view that the victory in Delhi had more to do with her own reputation than with Sonia Gandhi's leadership or the party's organisational skills. In fact, Sheila's personal popularity became an albatross around her neck when her critics lost no time in filling Sonia Gandhi's ears, pointing out how Sheila was becoming a popular figure in her own right. In the Congress, it is not possible to claim that any one, other than Sonia Gandhi, could get votes based on popularity. The party rank and file know that anyone who grows bigger than the organisation or its president is in trouble.

Sonia Gandhi nominated her after marathon consultations with other Delhi leaders. She made it clear to Sheila that she should take everyone along with her and work as a team. The Congress high command also stressed that she could keep her job but should give a patient hearing to the MLAs and create a coordination committee to take decisions. But Sonia Gandhi proved that while some disgruntled elements sought to get rid of the "arrogant" chief minister, she would not easily comply with their wishes. Sheila Dikshit had not anticipated the cliffhanger prelude to her heading the Delhi government on December 12. The Congress MLAs harped on about her being an outsider. Sheila explains that she countered this argument by asking them, 'How am I an outsider? I was educated here and lived here. People do not think of me as an outsider.'* After announcing the decision, Sonia rang up Sheila and said, 'I am sorry it took so long. I cannot come for the swearing-in ceremony but best of luck.'*

About a year after the Delhi Assembly elections, the Congress' fortunes turned as the United Progressive Alliance (UPA), under the leadership of Sonia Gandhi, came to power at the Centre in 2004. Manmohan Singh was nominated as the prime minister. The BJP lost despite its "India Shining" campaign, which was meant to project the achievements of the NDA government. After the Congress government was formed, there was not much trouble in getting finances.

Sheila's troubles within the party, however, continued. Whoever became the state Congress chief, turned against her to gain political space. Arguably, this happens as the authority of a chief minister automatically reduces the role of the PCC chief. The Congress leadership also believes in keeping the chief minister under check by encouraging opposition from the Pradesh Congress Committee chief. This results in a lack of unity in the party, which leads to several other complications.

Sheila manages to fight her opponents in her own way. Natwar Singh points out, 'Just by her personality and low-key way of functioning, she has been able to succeed. She not only has a good understanding of Delhi, but also familiar with the administration, as her husband was an IAS officer. Bureaucrats cannot take her for granted. There are no rough edges and she is a well-rounded leader.'*

During her second stint, Sheila continued most of the schemes she had undertaken and also brought in some new ones. By the time she finished her second term, Delhi had acquired the status of a clean and green city. This was largely due to two reasons. One was Sheila's ability to implement environmental laws; secondly, the Supreme Court had ordered the Delhi government to bring down pollution levels, following which it had to improve fuel quality, phase out old vehicles, provide compressed natural gas (CNG) as an alternative to petrol, introduce mass emission norms for new vehicles and create public awareness about the dangers of pollution. Pankaj Vohra points out that none of these were her own innovations; she merely implemented the court orders.

A THIRD-TERM CHIEF MINISTER

Although she does not agree, Sheila's third term was almost a miracle. When the 2008 Assembly elections came, no one expected the Congress to win. The government had already been in power for two terms. Ten years is a long time for people to not get disenchanted.

A couple of factors made the 2008 Delhi Assembly election significant. The first was that it was a barometer of the political temperature for the Congress before the 2009 Lok Sabha polls. As the national capital, Delhi has its own importance. Secondly, the balance between the Congress, the BJP and the BSP was striking. The BSP did its best to cut the Congress votes. Although it won 11% of the votes, it was in no position to play a significant role. While Mayawati personally campaigned in Delhi, the BJP unleashed a battery of national leaders. Dikshit was the only star campaigner for the

Congress, although Congress president Sonia Gandhi and her son Rahul addressed two public meetings.

On November 26, terrorists made a bold and audacious attack in two of Mumbai's five-star hotels in which 166 people were killed, leaving the entire country stunned. The Delhi Assembly elections were held within three days of the Mumbai terror attack. Since the Congress was heading the UPA coalition at the Centre and also in Maharashtra, it was feared that the electorate might vent their anger against the party. Much to the surprise of everyone, including the Congressmen, the party won with an absolute majority (42 of the 80 seats). The minorities in Delhi, whether linguistic or religious, moved towards the Congress for safety.

The Statesman noted, "... after ten years of being in power, she (Sheila) has only grown stronger and taller as a leader as has been testified by the popular mandate the Congress got under her leadership and for her governance. Riding on the twin plank of governance and development, she proved futile all the attacks and criticism against her from within and outside Congress as she led the party to victory almost single-handedly."[2] Sheila was made the chief minister for the third time but the opposition within the party was much less this time because her detractors saw that Sheila had her share in the party's win.

The chief minister was appreciated for the developmental work she undertook during her ten years of rule. Delhi, along with India, grew tremendously in the past decade. But with growth came other problems like traffic congestion, pollution, insufficient electricity and water, coupled with inadequate public transportation, roads and housing. Added to that were the rising inflation and terror attacks. Yet Sheila managed to maintain a good pubic face and remained personally popular through her public relations and benefitted from the huge budget set aside for her publicity.

A telegram from the US embassy in New Delhi points out, "The votes assume greater significance because it occurred on November 29, during the Mumbai attacks. Bharatiya Janata Party's attempts to make terrorism an issue failed to resonate, with local issues such as water, roads and power foremost in voter's mind. Uttar Pradesh Chief Minister Mayawati's Bahujan Samaj Party (BSP) campaigned hard in Delhi and looked to possibly play spoiler or kingmaker but was unable to dent the Congress significantly.

The election remained a referendum on the performance of Chief Minister Dikshit. She passed with flying colors, but voters are still looking to apportion blame for security failures at the national level."[3]

Early in the campaign, the media and poll pundits predicted a large number of seats for the BJP, mainly due to the anti-incumbency factor. The city had grown in a haphazard fashion; the lack of water and power and the traffic congestion had made the voters keen for a change. But the BJP failed to capitalise on all these and focused more on terror. The party lacked a leader of stature at the state level and there was infighting among its ranks.

Sheila's supporters claimed that while it was probable for the Congress to win by a narrow margin before the Mumbai terror attack due to Sheila Dikshit's performance and the unimpressive campaign run by the BJP, this time, it was Sheila's victory. Unlike the two earlier times, her third-term election as the leader of the Congress Legislature Party was made in 90 minutes flat.

CONTROVERSIES ABOUND

Despite her positive image, Sheila was not able to remain free of controversies. In 2006, a huge dispute broke out over illegal construction of shops. Since 1962, shopkeepers, aided by corrupt civil servants in the Delhi Development Authority and Municipal Corporation of India, had ignored the Delhi Master Plan and had illegally constructed over 50,000 shops in residential areas. The corruption was so blatant and unchecked that it caused intense public outrage. Civil society, with the support of the media, and in conjunction with the courts, became outspoken and defiant. After some residents filed petitions, the Supreme Court ruled that these shops had violated the Master Plan and ordered them to be sealed. In response, the Confederation of All India Traders organised protests which turned violent. The Delhi government and the Centre caved in and went to the court for a stay order and also promised to provide relief to the traders. The BJP quickly took up the traders' cause and tabled a no-confidence motion against Sheila, which she barely survived. The Congress demonstrated that it was more interested in cultivating powerful vested interests than upholding the rule of law. This nexus between dishonest government officials and greedy businessmen was a classic example of how corruption holds sway even in the capital of the country.

COMMONWEALTH GAMES CONTROVERSY

A historic event held during her third term was the 2010 Commonwealth Games (CWG), which was mired in a huge controversy and attracted adverse international publicity. The media was not flattering towards the chief minister. Even before the Games began, there was negative publicity about the lack of preparedness and corruption among several organising agencies. Relations became strained between her and Lt. Governor Tejendra Khanna as each blamed the other for the delay. A *New York Times* report quoted *The Times of India*: "Delhi's lieutenant governor, Tejendra Khanna, had complained in a letter to Prime Minister Manmohan Singh that too much credit for the "turnaround miracle" in cleaning up the athletes' village was going to Delhi's chief minister, Sheila Dikshit."[4]

Sheila explained in several interviews that the multiplicity of agencies involved in the Games was one of the reasons for the confusion and delays in the preparations. She justified in an interview: "Perhaps one command would have made things easier. All these departments have their own fiefdoms. I am not sure how much it will help now, though.... The kind of coordination required has not been there... Across the world, a month or two before any major games, the situation is exactly the same as it is here in Delhi now. I was in Beijing two months before the Olympics and everything was in a mess—projects were incomplete, there was a dust haze over Beijing—and I thought they might not be able to meet the deadline. But they did."[5]

She also got into controversies because the reports of the Comptroller and Auditor General (CAG) and the Shunglu Committee set up by the prime minister blamed, among others, the Delhi government for the mess. The BJP demanded Sheila's resignation after the CAG indictment. She weathered the storm in Parliament and the Delhi Assembly with the support of the Congress leadership and the Central government.

Sheila claims that the Commonwealth Games had changed the face of Delhi, and according to a recent survey, Delhi is one of the affluent cities in the world. She notes, 'The problem is how long can we stretch it? As long as I am here, I will not allow the city to go horizontal. I feel terribly upset as an Indian because these Games were one of the best. India won 101 medals. We have replied to every point raised in the Shunglu Committee and the Comptroller and Auditor General reports—that too, paragraph by paragraph. My point is that a thousand things may have gone right, but when one thing goes wrong, one only look's at that. What kind of judgment is that?'*

Sheila found herself embroiled in yet another controversy pertaining to the Delhi Lokayukta's report. A BJP worker had complained to the Lokayukta in 2009 that Dikshit misused Rs. 3.5 crore received from the Central government under the Jawaharlal Nehru National Urban Renewal Mission. The Lokayukta later dropped these charges.

It was the chief minister's idea to trifurcate the corporation, as the BJP was controlling the Municipal Corporation of Delhi (MCD). She fought for it within the party and also with the Opposition, but her calculations went wrong. When elections were held, the Congress lost out completely, while the BJP won all three seats. The MCD elections were mostly fought on local issues such as water, power, drainage and parking. But Sheila Dikshit cleverly disassociated herself from the poll results and said she was not responsible for the poor show.

The year 2012 was a landmark year for the MCD for two reasons. One, this was the first time the civic body, with an annual budget of Rs. 7800 core, had been trifurcated into three separate bodies—one for North, South and East Delhi—to ensure better administration of the city. Two, this was also the first time that 50% of the seats in the municipal body had been reserved for women.

Pankaj Vohra claims that Sheila has been running the government more through officials; they are more powerful than the politicians. 'Sheila is a creation of the media. When the electronic media became more powerful, they were in search of articulate leaders whom they promoted. They found many in the BJP and also in the Congress. She will go down in history as the longest-serving chief minister of Delhi. As for exceptional leaders, the capital has produced only three—Chaudhary Brahm Prakash, H.K.L. Bhagat and Madan Lal Khurana.'*

Sheila ended the year with flak from the public when the gruesome gang rape of a 23-year-old medical student jolted the capital on December 16, 2012. She got her share of the blame, but tried to pass the buck on the police, which is under the Home Ministry and renewed her demand to hand over the department to the Delhi government. While she tried to sympathise with the angry flash crowds protesting against the incident, they booed her and damaged her son Sandeep's car, who is the Member of Parliament from Delhi. Under the watchful eye of hundreds of riot police, Sheila Dikshit's effigy was burnt by an irate mob of youth voters in Delhi. She tried to pacify them by announcing Rs. 1.5 million and a job as compensation to the gang rape victim's family. Sheila's job is going to be become even more difficult, as flash crowds gather whenever there are incidents that invoke public fury.

Has Sheila reached the end of her stint in Delhi? With just a few months to go for the next Assembly elections, Dikshit would not mind a place in the Union Cabinet since she has remained in Delhi for too long. It will be a Herculean task for her to win the state for the fourth time. Her friends feel that she should move on to another position, while her detractors are waiting to blame her if the party loses again.

Sheila Dikshit is an example of how personal popularity combined with hard work and a leader's patronage can make a woman leader successful. Unlike Mayawati, Mamata Banerjee or Mehbooba Mufti, her route to success was not through organisational abilities. She did not have significant party responsibilities, as administration was more her forte. She has made some bold decisions and stuck to them despite criticism from the public as well as the Opposition, like the trifurcation of the Municipal Corporation of Delhi. She has taken more credit than was due because of her ability to manipulate the media. For now, Sheila is waiting to make a bid for the chief ministership for the fourth time in 2013 and she would create a record if things go her way.

She claims that she is focused on whatever she does. "I am peculiar; I enjoy whatever I get. When I was a homemaker, I really enjoyed what I did. I am doing this job now, the day I feel I am bored with it or not enjoying it, I will just give it up. But to say, I wish I'd been this or that... Well, I wish I had been a painter or a writer," she told an interviewer.[6] Perhaps she is waiting to do just that when she retires from politics.

NOTES

1. Rediff .com, November 26, 2003.
2. "'Outsider' Dikshit unmatched in Delhi", *The Statesman* (India), 12 December, 2008; *Custom Online 150 Journals*, July 2, 2012.

3. http://wikileaks.org/cable/2008/12/08NEWDELHI3096.html.
4. Jim Yardley, "India Declares Commonwealth Games a Success", *New York Times*, October 14, 2010.
5. "This is not the time for blame-game. These are not the Congress's Games or the BJP's Games. They belong to the country", *The Indian Express*, 15 August, 2010; *Custom Online 150 Journals*, 2 July, 2012.
6. Priya Sahgal, "Past Tense, Future Perfect", *India Today*, 18 December, 2010.

Pratibha Patil

PRATIBHA DEVISINGH PATIL JOINED the elite club of 13 women leaders in the world when she became the president of India on July 25, 2007. Lady luck has always smiled upon her political career. Hers is a story of a simple ordinary woman who reached the height of her political career by becoming the first woman president of India.

With her oversized spectacles, head covered by the *pallu* of her broad-bordered silk saree and her full-sleeved blouse, Pratibha looked like a typical conservative woman when she showed the V sign for victory after getting elected. If anyone was looking for glamour in the new president, they would have been disappointed—she was a plain, ordinary-looking woman with the face of a next-door grandma.

Five years ago, she was propelled into the Rashtrapati Bhavan (Presidential Palace) almost by default. Her name surfaced just 12 hours before her nomination. Pratibha's career graph shows that positions of power came to her because of her connections with senior Congress leaders. When her candidacy was announced, most of the younger generation asked, "Pratibha who?" Even in political circles, she was seen as a politician on the verge of retirement who had been favoured with a governor's job for her past services to the Gandhi family.

TURNING POINT

The defining moment came almost at the end of Pratibha's political career when she was chosen to become the first woman president of India. On paper she had all the qualifications. The septuagenarian president has never lost an election in her long career spanning more than five decades. She had held various positions in the Maharashtra Assembly as an MLA, junior minister, Cabinet minister, Leader of the Opposition and later she became the deputy chairman of the Rajya Sabha. At the party level, she was the Maharashtra Pradesh Congress president in 1980 when the Congress party came to power, but narrowly missed becoming the chief minister. Although Pratibha was disappointed since the Pradesh Congress Committee (PCC) president normally gets the claim to become the chief minister, she did now show it. Due to other considerations, the party leadership chose Abdul Rehman Antulay, but he ruled briefly. Antulay quit when he got embroiled in the cement scandal. The shrewd Patil knew that keeping a low profile helps, and it certainly helped her reach the Rashtrapati Bhavan.

Governor Patil was visiting Mount Abu in Southern Rajasthan when the news broke out. She was surprised and delighted to receive a phone call from Congress president Sonia Gandhi: 'I could not believe it when she called me while I was returning from Mount Abu and told me I have been chosen as the United Progressive Alliance (UPA) candidate to contest the presidential poll.'* She immediately left for Delhi the next day to meet Sonia Gandhi and Prime Minister Manmohan Singh. She was not among the front-runners and was nowhere in the reckoning. It was through sheer luck that her name cropped up as a presidential candidate. It was indeed a big jump for the modest-looking Pratibha.

She had withdrawn from active politics after she completed her Lok Sabha term in 1996 and chose to lead a quiet life, dedicating her time to her family and her institutions. She would rarely visit Delhi, the seat of power. Her luck turned unexpectedly when the Congress leadership took note of her after the UPA government came to power in 2004. It was the then Home Minister Shivraj Patil who suggested her name to Sonia, and recognising her loyalty, Gandhi made her governor of Rajasthan on November 8, 2004. Pratibha hardly imagined that she would at a later date become Shivraj Patil's rival in the 2007 presidential race. Incidentally, she was the first woman governor of Rajasthan, which is known for its social and economic backwardness. So it was a double promotion for the 72-year-old Pratibha to become the tenant of the 350-acre Rashtrapati Bhavan campus.

Prior to her nomination, hectic political activities took place in the capital. There was no consensus on any name, although a dozen leaders, including the then External Affairs Minister Pranab Mukherjee, former Union Minister Karan Singh, Home Minister Shivraj Patil, amongst others, were in the fray. Mukherjee was the first to lose out; when the Left leaders proposed his name, Sonia Gandhi shot it down, demanding, "Who will run the government?" This was attributed to her mistrust of Pranab Mukherjee, although later in 2012 she made it clear that she had no misgivings by nominating him as the UPA presidential candidate. Sonia Gandhi's first choice was former Speaker Shivraj Patil. She had both encouraged and trusted him—a gentleman to the core—as her deputy when she was the Leader of the Opposition in the Lok Sabha. He became a central minister and Speaker of the Lok Sabha, and was known for his loyalty towards the Nehru-Gandhi family.

It was the Left parties that prevented Shivraj Patil's candidature. They had a say in the choice, as they had a big bloc of 60-plus MPs—the maximum representation the Left had ever had. They pointed out Shivraj's devotion to the spiritual leader Sathya Sai Baba and objected to the life-size photograph of the god-man in his drawing room. Although he was not the only prominent political figure to go to Sathya Saibaba's abode in Puttaparthi, the Left sabotaged his chances. Other UPA allies like Rashtriya Janata Dal chief Lalu Prasad Yadav, Dravida Munnetra Kazhagam chief M. Karunanidhi and Lok Jan Shakti chief Ram Vilas Paswan did not warm up to his nomination.

The Left also turned down the names of Karan Singh and Sushil Kumar Shinde. Singh, the erstwhile Maharaja of Jammu and Kashmir, had aspired to occupy the Rashtrapati Bhavan for several years, and Shinde was regarded as a fit choice because he is a Dalit and had been a successful chief minister of Maharashtra, and later governor of Andhra Pradesh. As the Congress and the Left groped in the dark to find a suitable candidate, Communist Party of India leader Ardhendu Bhushan Bardhan suggested, 'Why not a woman?'* Every one immediately accepted the idea. The prime minister, who had done his homework, formed a panel which included Patil. Bardhan immediately exclaimed: 'I know her from my Nagpur days! She is a good candidate.'* Her four-decade long political resume was impressive. And being the governor of Rajasthan was another plus point. Like Vice-President Bhairon Singh Shekhawat, she too was Shekhawat Rajput; he was contesting as an independent candidate with the support of the National Democratic Alliance and it was speculated that he might garner all the Rajput votes. So politically, it was seen as a masterstroke to field Pratibha, besides getting kudos for choosing a woman. Thus, Sonia switched her choice from one Patil to another, to the surprise of her aides! Other contenders did not protest since Pratibha was neutral.

However, she was by no means a unanimous candidate. There was a bitter no-holds barred contest and ample confusion among the opposition parties too. Some regional parties wanted a Dalit candidate, others a member of another low caste, and the third front suggested a continuation of President A.P.J. Abdul Kalam for a second term. Bahujan Samaj Party (BSP) chief Mayawati, who had come back into national prominence with a massive majority in the 2007 UP elections, also had her say in the selection. Finally, the picture became clear when the Left and the BSP came on board to support Pratibha. It was a shot in the arm when the Shiv Sena, a nationalist party and a constituent of the National Democratic Alliance (NDA), announced its support based on her Maharashtrian roots.

Interestingly though, she was not the first choice even among the women candidates. The inner group first considered Delhi Chief Minister Sheila Dikshit, who had successfully served two-terms. She hailed from a well-known Congress political family from Uttar Pradesh (UP) who had been close to the Gandhis for generations. However, her name did not enthuse some of the senior Congress leaders; therefore it was dropped. Sheila won Delhi for the third time in 2008. Former Union Minister Margaret Alva and Acharya Vinoba Bhave's close associate Nirmala Deshpande too did not find favour.

BJP DIGS OUT DIRT ON PRATIBHA

When Sonia sprung the surprise of producing a woman candidate, the BJP was taken aback; it did not know how to oppose a woman because doing so would mean losing women's votes. At the same time, it also had to protect the interests of Vice-President Shekhawat. So the BJP-led Opposition made all efforts to malign Pratibha with wild allegations and slander. The saffron party led the vilification campaign, claiming that she was a most unsuitable candidate to occupy Raisina Hill, the area where important government buildings and the Rashtrapati Bhavan are located. The BJP further revealed that both Patil's husband and brother were under investigation in connection with the unrelated deaths of a teacher and party worker in Jalgaon. She was accused of financial irregularities in her institutions and shielding her brother from murder charges. It was left to the Congress to protect her from this onslaught. The bitterness was apparent all around, but Pratibha chose to remain quiet.

Adding fuel to the fire were her spiritual episodes with the Brahma Kumari's guru. Soon after her nomination, Pratibha revealed in front of the media that she had conversed with the Brahma Kumari's spiritual guru, the late Dada Lekhraj, who had advised her on what course to follow. Even the Congress managers were stunned on how to deal with these freely-expressed superstitious beliefs. Then she offended the Muslims by saying that Indian women first covered their heads to protect themselves during the 16th century Muslim invasion. If that was not enough, her critics dug up comments she was said to have made when she was the health minister of Maharashtra in 1975—that people with hereditary diseases should be sterilised. This was during the time of the Emergency when the Congress earned a bad name due to forced sterilisations.

The Times (UK) wrote, "It was supposed to be a formality: a low-profile regional politician, chosen by the ruling Congress party, would become India's first woman president. In a country where women are routinely treated as second-class beings, the election of Pratibha Patil as the "first citizen" of India should have been a dream ticket, pairing her with Sonia Gandhi, the Congress party leader regarded widely as the real head of state. Yet far from showing how far India has modernised, the bumpy ride of Mrs. Patil from the governor's residence in Rajasthan to the presidential palace in Delhi has illustrated how historic party divisions run deep in a system still dogged by the old spectre of corruption."[1]

Pratibha filed her nomination, with Pranab Mukherjee and Sonia Gandhi proposing and seconding her name on the afternoon of June 23, 2007. A confident Sonia escorted her to Parliament where she filed her papers before the returning officer. On July 2, after scrutiny, it was clear that the contest was essentially Shekhawat versus Shekhawat.

A DIFFICULT CAMPAIGN

Pratibha's campaign, however, was not an easy one, as there was strong speculation that Vice-President Shekhawat, along with his friends across parties, might swing votes in his favour. Senior Congress leader Priya Ranjan

Dasmunshi became her campaign manager and took her across the country to mobilise support. To make things easier for both the groups, the UPA argued that Patil should be the unanimous choice and the NDA-backed Bhairon Singh Shekhawat would be given a second term as vice-president. But the NDA rejected this proposal and the contest was inevitable.

There was tremendous excitement on July 19, the day of polling, and the huge turnout of voters showed the mobilisation power of the UPA and NDA: almost 88.5% of MPs and 91% of legislators exercised their franchise.

Tamil Nadu chief minister and All India Anna Dravida Munnetra Kazhagam (AIADMK) chief Jayalalithaa, who was part of the newly-formed UNPA, upset the front's plans and asked her party legislators to vote for the NDA-backed Shekhawat. The United National Progressive Alliance (UNPA) was a group of eight political parties who were neither part of the UPA nor the NDA nor the Left wing. This alliance had approached President Kalam to contest the presidential elections and Rasheed Masood was their vice-presidential candidate. It was a short-lived love affair which disintegrated after the 2007 presidential elections. Though the Samajwadi Party supported the UNPA for President Kalam's candidacy, it later joined the UPA and supported it in the trust vote. When Jayalalithaa broke the unity of the front, it was rumoured that the BJP had struck a deal with her to help her in her future bid to return to power in Tamil Nadu.

Breaking away from its long-time ally, the BJP, the Shiv Sena announced on June 25 that it would support Patil, a fellow Maharashtrian, in her bid for presidency. This sent tremors through the 21-year-old partnership between the Shiv Sena and the BJP. Shiv Sena supremo Bal Thackeray called it a choice between a Hindu and a Maharashtrian. For him, having a president from Maharashtra carried more weight. The BJP leaders appealed to Thackeray to reconsider his decision but he refused.

Describing the presidential elections, a US embassy telegram from New Delhi noted: "After courting controversy and enduring a Bharatiya Janata Party (BJP)-led assault on her alleged corruption, Pratibha Devisingh Patil swept the Indian Presidential election on July 19, becoming the first woman president to hold the mostly ceremonial but prestigious office... The newly formed United National Progressive Alliance (UNPA)'s leader, Jayalalithaa, unexpectedly broke ranks from others in the UNPA to encourage her AIADMK party members to vote, not abstain, revealing early cracks in the alliance. While the NDA/BJP is left to lick its wounds, Congress is sitting pretty, having regained confidence and strength after ensuring a solid win thanks to its coalition and Left allies. In Patil, Congress now has a loyalist who will help their cause after the 2009 national election."[2]

When the results were declared, Pratibha had won more than half of the total number of votes. Obviously, some NDA members too had voted for her on the basis of caste. His hopes dashed, Bhairon Singh Shekhawat went home a disappointed man.

Although the BJP leaked all manner of dirt they could dig up on Patil, attacking her character because of the corrupt dealings of her relatives, legislators ignored the appeals to their conscience. The Left demonstrated unwavering support to the Congress and remained a true ally. The US embassy telegram pointed out, "Additionally, Gandhi has a strong Congress loyalist in the President's office, which could prove useful in the very realistic likelihood that no one party or coalition will win a clear majority in the 2009 national elections."[3]

The president is the formal head of the executive, legislature and judiciary of India and is also the commander-in-chief of the Indian armed forces. After the general elections he/she appoints the prime minister, who is most likely the person to command the support of the majority in the Lok Sabha, usually the leader of the main party or the coalition. So he/she has an important role to play when there is a hung Parliament. The president then appoints the other members of the Council of Ministers, distributing portfolios to them on the advice of the prime minister. The ministers remain in power in keeping with the president's wishes, but in practice they must retain the support of the Lok Sabha. The Council of Ministers cannot be dismissed as long as it commands the majority of the Lok Sabha.

The US telegram further observed that although the Congress lauded the event as a landmark for women, even women's organisations did not see her as an ally to achieve legislative advances for women. "Patil's selection solely for her pliability has raised the eyebrows of the average Indian citizen enough that many are questioning the current process for electing a president."[4]

The first woman president took the oath of office on July 25, 2007, in the historic Central Hall of Parliament. She was escorted in a procession from her temporary South Avenue residence to Rashtrapati Bhavan. The presidential procession went through a line of about 1,000 armed guards, drawn from the three services, who gave the customary 21-gun salute to the president and the president-elect sitting in a black limousine. The Central Hall of Parliament was packed with chief ministers, MPs, Supreme Court judges and other dignitaries. Chief Justice of India K.G. Balakrishnan administered the oath of office and secrecy to Pratibha Patil amidst cheers from the gathering. After her brief speech, the new president changed places with the outgoing president. After the usual guard of honour, Pratibha accompanied Kalam to his residential quarters to bid him farewell. Thus began the five-year term of the 12th president of India and its first woman president.

PRATIBHA AS DEPUTY CHAIRMAN

If ascending to the presidency was her moment of glory, Pratibha was also surprised and elated two decades earlier, when Prime Minister Rajiv Gandhi called to inform her that she had been chosen as the Rajya Sabha deputy chairman since Najma Heptullah had to be replaced. This was another watershed in Pratibha's life, as it introduced her to national politics. A demure-looking Patil, with her head covered, ruled the House with an iron hand. She had entered the Rajya Sabha barely a year ago and was little known in Parliament. Again it was her loyalty to the late Indira Gandhi which seemed to have won her the post.

It was in 1970 that Indira Gandhi, during a visit to Maharashtra when Jalgoan was engulfed in riots, declared in front of a large audience that she was depending on Pratibha *tai* (elder sister) to take care of the people. She told them that she entrusted the task of bringing back normalcy to Pratibha, who was then a deputy minister. The time to test her loyalty came when Indira Gandhi was thrown out of power in 1977. After the Emergency and the new Janata Party government taking over, there was a split in the Congress party. Several senior leaders joined the Congress led by Devraj Urs. When Sharad Pawar formed the coalition government in Maharashtra, Pratibha stood by Indira Gandhi. When Indira was arrested on December 19, 1977, by the Janata Party government, Pratibha also went to jail in Maharashtra and came out after ten days once Indira Gandhi was released. "Thus was forged a lasting bond between the Gandhi family and Pratibha Patil, who served them in many ways in times of difficulty and even managed the kitchen in Indira Gandhi's house after Sanjay Gandhi's death."[5] She became the Leader of the Opposition in Maharashtra and Indira Gandhi promoted her political career. Rajiv Gandhi remembered this loyalty later and made her the deputy chairman of the Rajya Sabha.

Running the House of Elders was no easy task, as there were several veteran opposition leaders in it. Politically it was a tumultuous time for Rajiv Gandhi and the Congress. Every day there was a new controversy. The government was moving from crisis to crisis. Looking back, she claims, 'Every position I held was challenging. When I was the deputy chairman I had a very trying time. There were many issues like Bofors and Sumitomo which happened at the time.'* The Opposition held that there was a kickback of Rs. 64 crore to secure the Bofors gun deal, which was given to the Gandhi's family friend, Italian businessman Ottavio Quattrocchi. Rajiv denied this in Parliament, stating that neither he nor anyone in his family was involved in the kickbacks but the Opposition was belligerent and would not allow both Houses of Parliament to function. It demanded a joint parliamentary probe and when it was announced, boycotted it. The Opposition resigned en masse, forcing Rajiv to call for elections a few months ahead of schedule. Ultimately, it was the Bofors controversy which was responsible for Rajiv Gandhi losing the 1989 Lok Sabha polls. It was tough going for Pratibha as well; for a few weeks from July to September 1987 she had to act as chairman when Vice-President R. Venkataraman was elevated to president. 'I had to hold both the chairman and deputy chairman's posts until a new vice-president was elected. I had a difficult time controlling the House. There were stalwarts like Advani, Vajpayee, Gurudas Dasgupta and Basudeb Acharya present,' Pratibha admits.*

Her brief tenure as deputy chairman had its share of pain as well as exuberance. During the debates on Bofors, naturally the Congress expected her to be soft, while the Opposition was keeping an eagle eye on her, looking out for any bias. She had to do a balancing act to be seen as fair. But the Opposition felt that she was leaning towards the Congress in her rulings.

EARLY LIFE

Before going further one should understand Pratibha's personality. Born into an orthodox family from a small town in Jalgaon, Maharashtra, her life has been a fairy tale of how an ordinary woman can rise to become the president of India. As a child, Pratibha wanted to study medicine but her father Nanasaheb, a government prosecutor, vetoed it on the grounds that there were no medical colleges near Jalgaon. He advised her to choose the humanities stream, so she opted for political science.

It was Anna Patil, a friend of Pratibha's father, who first sowed the seeds of political ambition in the young girl's mind. One day Anna told Nanasaheb that he has a proposal and needs his blessings. Pratibha had just completed her Master's in economics and political science and was being trained as a teacher. Anna Saheb suggested that she should enter politics. Her father wondered how it would be possible since Pratibha had been brought up sheltered and cosseted. He came up with objections including her marriage and how no girl from the family had joined politics earlier. Anna rejected all of them and managed to get his consent. He convinced Nana *sahib* that the state's chief minister, Yashwantrao Chavan, was keen to enlist young and educated women into politics. When Nanasaheb asked his daughter for her opinion, her first instinct was to reject the proposal. "Politics is not my forte. I have studied political science but putting it into practice is different. Please don't coerce me into joining active politics. I am witness to the intricacies of the election process... I abhor the idea of soliciting votes."[6] These were the firm words of the young girl who later became president of the country, not losing a single election to the Assembly or the Lok Sabha.

GETTING A TICKET TO CONTEST

Pratibha's initial brush with a politician was with Chief Minister Y.B. Chavan. Taking his call to invite young girls to join politics seriously, she arrived at his bungalow one day. Her first meeting impressed the leader enough to recommend her for an Assembly ticket in 1962; she contested and won.

Her father advised her to remain simple and unassuming so that people would find it easy to interact with her; he wanted her to be real. And she adhered to his advice, wearing simple clothes and covering her head with her saree's *pallu*. Once, when she was a junior minister, she was on a panel of six in a meeting in Pune. One of the speakers scornfully watched Pratibha adjusting her *pallu*. During her speech the lady commented, "What women's emancipation are we talking about? Women are not free at all; they're neither educated nor have come out of their mould of yesteryears. It is sad that even those who are educated are regressive in their appearance and outlook. Where is the progress?" When the time came for Pratibha to speak, she was blunt: 'Let us first define what women's liberation is. In the past they used to pull the *pallu* over their face, which made even breathing difficult. But if somebody is observing our tradition willingly and, if it is not obstructing the path to progress, then what is the harm in doing so? If the level and degree of advancement is to be decided by the type of clothes one wears, then discarding the saree and wearing a frock would be more appropriate.'* "During one of her visits to the US, where she stayed for three months, American women had many queries about her typical Indian way of dressing, her *mangalsutra* (a symbol of married women), her vermillion and her bangles, which emerged as excellent ice-breakers."[7]

AS MAHARASHTRA'S DEPUTY MINISTER

Contesting a seat during the 1962 Assembly elections was a major turning point in Pratibha's life. At the age of 27, she was the youngest member of the Assembly, where she performed well while also finding the time to complete her law degree. In 1967, when the next elections came, she could not decide whether to contest or not. In the meantime, she married Devi Singh and had her first child, who was just six months old. But her seniors persuaded her and she contested from Edlabad, a new constituency. Impressed by her performance, Chief Minister Vasantrao Naik made her deputy minister during her second term.

A BALANCING ACT

During this period, she fought a battle to maintain harmony in her family and political life. One day, fed up with a quarrel with her husband, she handed in her resignation to the chief minister. However, Chief Minister Vasantrao Naik called both husband and wife and mediated a compromise. And so, she took back her resignation. Pratibha admits, 'Many times I thought of giving up politics. It was difficult. Public life is a full-time job. I found some time for my family but it is much more difficult for a woman to carry on with both roles. But the workers had faith in me and they held me back.'*

THE INDIRA GANDHI CONNECTION

It was her relations with Prime Minister Indira Gandhi which brought her closer to the Gandhi family. She had a long and enduring relationship with Mrs. Gandhi and their bond survived the Congress party split of 1978. As mentioned earlier, after Indira Gandhi's arrest in 1977, Pratibha defied police orders and went to jail. She continued to be a staunch supporter throughout and soon got recognition for it. In 1978, when Sharad Pawar formed the Progressive Democratic Alliance government, she was made the Leader of the Opposition. Stalwarts like Vasantdada Patil worked under her leadership.

Although she led the party to power in 1980, Pratibha's claim to the chief ministership was not accepted and the leadership chose A.R. Antulay, a Muslim, for political reasons. Even when Antulay resigned over the cement scandal, she did not get the top post. She remained a Cabinet minister until 1985. Though disappointed, she kept on working for the party.

MOVING TO THE NATIONAL SCENE

The next year, she was chosen as a Rajya Sabha member. Many thought that she may find it difficult to adjust to national exposure and Delhi politics but she proved them wrong, taking an active part in the business of the House. The result was that when Rajiv Gandhi was looking for someone to replace Najma Heptullah, he zeroed in on Patil. The belligerent Opposition initially thought that they could take advantage of her but soon found that she was tough and knew the procedures.

AS GOVERNOR OF RAJASTHAN

After 1988, Pratibha was sent back to Maharashtra as the PCC president—an important post in the party. She led the Congress in the 1989 elections but Rajiv Gandhi lost and V.P. Singh became the prime minister. With successive changes of governments in two years, when the party went in for polls in 1991, Pratibha contested the Lok Sabha elections and won. During this phase, even though she remained a Congress member and participated in the debates of the House, there was a lull in her political engagement. After 1996, she went into political wilderness and remained that way until Home Minister Shivraj Patil resurrected her career by recommending her name as the governor of Rajasthan. BJP Chief Minister Vasundhara Raje Scindia was ruling the state, and the Congress needed a tactful governor. She did not have many altercations with the chief minister and spent a quiet, low-key life, touring the state and addressing meetings.

Although she was the first woman governor of Rajasthan, Pratibha did not do anything spectacular during her term. It had been a lonely time as governor for three years. Unlike her predecessors, she did not throw parties, hold *durbars* to meet people or take part in cultural evenings. "As governor, Pratibha chose a very simple life, incurring very little expenditure on herself, so much so that sometimes the budget even lapsed."[8] She did not add furniture, crockery or anything else to the Raj Bhavan and followed a simple vegetarian diet.

At times, she showed an independent streak. She stirred up a controversy when she returned the Rajasthan Religious Freedom Bill 2006 unsigned. "The Rajasthan government had introduced the bill alleging that some 'religious and other institutions, bodies and individuals are involved in unlawful conversion from one religion to another by fraudulent means or forcibly.' She refused to sign it because she found some of its provisions infringed upon the fundamental rights of freedom of speech, freedom to practice and propagate religion."[9] When the chief minister re-sent the bill, Pratibha referred it to President Abdul Kalam, little knowing that she may have to settle the issue later when she succeeded him. Later in 2007, when violence erupted in Rajasthan due to Gujjar protestors demanding scheduled tribe status, instead of their current higher OBC (Other Backward Class) status, she played a crucial role in dealing with the situation by briefing the Centre on how to handle the rioters. She also reined in Vasundhara Raje, admonishing her for ineffectively handling the issue. It was during this period that she became closer to Sonia Gandhi. Some attribute her refusal to sign the anti-conversion bill to her independent streak. The army was called in to control the situation when Gujjar supporters blocked vehicular traffic even on the highways. This was one of the reasons why the BJP lost the state in the Assembly elections next year.

CONTROVERSIES ABOUND

Pratibha had to face a flood of controversies once she was nominated president. The opposition parties collected unsavoury details about her past and the BJP led a maligning campaign. Booklets were prepared by BJP leader Arun Shourie titled "Does this tainted person deserve to become the president of India?" They were distributed all over, embarrassing both the Congress and the Patils. It was further alleged that a cooperative bank, floated by her in 1973 called Pratibha Mahila Sahakari Bank, had its license revoked by the Reserve Bank of India due to alleged financial irregularities. At the time, she was not only the director but also the chairman of the bank. The counter-argument was that she was chairman for just a month. Shortly afterwards, another controversy surfaced: a cooperative sugar factory, of which she was a founding member, defaulted on a bank loan worth Rs. 17.5 crore. She was not only its chairman but also a director until she became the governor of Rajasthan. The factory was sealed in January 2007, a few months before she was appointed governor.

The Congress, was supported by Nationalist Congress Party (NCP) chief Sharad Pawar, a fellow Maharashtrian, who came to her rescue and spoke against the maligning campaign. But that was not the end; even after she became the president, controversies dogged her. On one of her trips to South America, her son Rajendra Shekhawat left the presidential delegation to visit Florida, which reflected poorly on his mother's office.

AS PRESIDENT OF INDIA

Pratibha's role as president was lacklustre. She could do nothing spectacular during her five-year term. Nor were there any opportunities to do so; she had no challenges unlike other presidents who took historic decisions. The one time when a president has a role to play is during the installation of a new government. In her case, the results of the 2009 elections were so clear that there was no role for the president; the UPA had won an absolute majority. Secondly, the Congress and the UPA had already decided that Manmohan Singh would be the prime minister. There was no drama like in 2004 when Congress president Sonia Gandhi declined the prime minister's post and named Singh as her nominee. Throughout Patil's term, there were no other constitutional matters which needed her attention. She had the distinction of masterly inactivity. She played her ceremonial role, hosting presidents and prime ministers at the Rashtrapati Bhavan, interacting with world leaders, including those from Russia, US, China, France and the United Kingdom, who are the five permanent members of the United Nations Security Council. She rubbed shoulders with statesmen, visited several countries and represented India in various world fora. The only bright side was that she made no faux pas during her talks with these world leaders. She fondly recalls how Russian President Medvedev congratulated her after she flew a Sukhoi. Women are not allowed to fly the fighter jet, just as they are banned from nuclear submarines, but, as the supreme commander of the armed forces, Pratibha was adventurous enough to wear the heavy helmet and special uniform. 'US President Obama was very frank and discussed issues with me very freely. Michelle Obama was also very articulate. We had excellent meetings with Russian Prime Minister Putin, French President Sarkozy, and others,' Patil recalls.* Queen Elizabeth II of England hosted her in 2009. Pratibha also visited Tajikistan and Spain, where no Indian President had ever gone before, as well as Laos and Cambodia—the first Indian presidential visit after 50 years. She claims that these foreign trips had fostered cultural, economic and political ties.

Patil also had a harmonious relationship with Prime Minister Manmohan Singh. Most of her predecessors, from the first president Rajendra Prasad onwards, have faced some friction at times between the Rashtrapati Bhavan and the South Block, where the prime minister's office is located. The differences between Rajendra Prasad and Nehru were revealed in their exchange of letters during their terms. Sanjiva Reddy and Indira Gandhi did not get along, as the former did not forget how she supported V.V. Giri during the presidential elections instead of him. Rajiv Gandhi had a troubled innings with Giani Zail Singh, although the latter, without any hesitation, agreed to Rajiv's swearing-in after Indira Gandhi's assassination. Prime Minister P.V. Narasimha Rao had some differences with Shankar Dayal Sharma. With such a history behind the office, Pratibha managed to enjoy a peaceful time at Rashtrapati Bhavan. She met Manmohan Singh at least once a month on average and also tried to have good relations with UPA Chairperson Sonia Gandhi, to whom she owed her position.

Her one action which raised eyebrows was the large-scale presidential pardons. Some newspapers called her an "angel of mercy". Article 72 of the Indian Constitution empowers the president to pardon, grant reprieve, suspend, remit or commute sentences of persons convicted of any crime. Her predecessor Kalam had 25 mercy petitions on his desk; out of these, he rejected Dhananjoy Chatterjee's plea and commuted another to a life sentence, while rejecting the others. His predecessor K.R. Narayanan sat on ten mercy petitions and disposed of only one.

Before demitting office, Patil scored a new record. While rejecting three mercy pleas, she commuted the death sentence of as many as 35 prisoners to life—including those convicted for mass murder, kidnapping, rape and killing of children. Just before completing her term, she pardoned four more prisoners on June 12, 2012. This was surprising, considering India has not abolished capital punishment. Since 1981, more than 90 convicts have pleaded for mercy. Patil's critics feel that she had shown haste in making these decisions since the convicts pardoned had committed heinous crimes. However, Patil has not shown the same mercy towards political assassins like the killers of Punjab Chief Minister Beant Singh or Rajiv Gandhi. She had also not taken any decision on Afzal Guru, who was sentenced to death for attacking the Indian Parliament. It was President Pranab Mukherjee who later rejected his mercy plea, leading to Afzal's execution.

Her term ended just as it began. She got embroiled in a controversy over her post-retirement house in Pune, which she is entitled to as the ex-president of India. Pratibha is truly an example of how an ordinary, conservative, low-profile woman can reach the heights of power in politics without a mentor, family name, riches or a caste card. There are very few politicians who could be comparable to her. As she herself admits, her long journey in politics has sometimes been smooth, sometimes rough, but she has faced all problems over the last fifty years of her political life with composure.

Her critics sum up that Patil did not leave an impressive legacy as president. Rashtrapati Bhavan will have gained nothing except for her portrait adorning the walls along with those of her predecessors, they claim. But she neither had the opportunity nor took any bold or imaginative initiative to leave her mark. So when she completed her term, she left unsung and unwept as a lacklustre president.

NOTES

1. Ashling O'Connor, "First woman president gets a bumpy ride", *The Times (UK)*, 20 July, 2007; *Custom Online 150 Journals*, July 3, 2012.
2. http://wikileaks.org/cable/2007/07/07NEWDELHI3336.html.
3. Ibid.

4. Ibid.
5. Ritu Singh, *President Pratibha Patil: India's First Woman President*, p. 54, Rajpal and Sons, August 2007.
6. Rasika Chaube, Dr. Chhaya Mahajan, *An Inspirational Journey: Pratibha Devisingh Patil*, p. 8, S. Chand Publishing, 2010.
7. Ibid., pp. 125–126.
8. Ritu Singh, *President Pratibha Patil: India's First Woman President*, pp. 8, 11.
9. Ibid.

Sushma Swaraj

SUSHMA SWARAJ IS A prime minister in waiting. What she would need though is a streak of good luck. A lot depends on whether the Bharatiya Janata Party's parent body, the Rashtriya Swayamsewak Sangh (RSS), and her rivals within the party, will let her reach the top. In a male-dominated BJP, she has made it as the Leader of the Opposition in the Lok Sabha—the first woman to do so in the party. She has fashioned herself as the quintessential traditional Hindu *nari* (woman), with the large *bindi* on her forehead and *sindoor* in the parting of her hair.

A DEFINING MOMENT

Sushma is a veteran of many electoral battles and has contested ten direct elections. She has been a Member of Parliament (MP) six times and a Member of the Legislative Assembly (MLA) thrice. She has fought elections from Haryana, Delhi, Madhya Pradesh and Karnataka. She was the youngest MLA and the youngest minister at the age of 25 in Haryana in the 1970s. Her defining moment came when the BJP chose her to contest against Congress President Sonia Gandhi in 1999. In those elections, she projected the image of a *swadeshi beti* (home-grown daughter) as a contrast against the Italian-born Sonia Gandhi. Their contest was called a fight between the *swadeshi beti* (country's daughter) and the *videshi bahu* (foreign daughter-in-law).

The national and international media watched their fascinating campaigns with great interest. Sushma made it to international newspapers like *The*

New York Times and *The Washington Post*. *The New York Times* headlined, "In India's Power Struggle, Two Women Collided Head-On."[1] Sushma was perhaps chosen for her ability to take on rivals. Besides, she is the most articulate and impressive woman leader of the BJP.

The 1999 Lok Sabha polls came after Prime Minister Atal Bihari Vajpayee lost the vote of confidence by one vote. His 13-month old government was pulled down by three women—Congress leader Sonia Gandhi, All India Anna Dravida Munnetra Kazhagam (AIADMK) chief and Tamil Nadu Chief Minister Jayalalithaa, who was a partner in the National Democratic Alliance (NDA) coalition led by Vajpayee, and Bahujan Samaj Party (BSP) leader Mayawati, who abandoned Vajpayee at the last minute. Despite this setback, the NDA was in high spirits at the time after winning the Kargil War against Pakistan.

Sonia Gandhi, who took over the Congress Party in March 1998, was successful in arresting the erosion in its rank and file, and united the party. Although she was reconciled to the Congress sitting in the Opposition, when the NDA came to power, she grew impatient after some months. So when she sensed that the AIADMK chief was getting ready to pull the Vajpayee government down because of differences with the BJP, she ganged up with Jayalalithaa. She tried to muster support in Parliament. Sonia thought once the government goes, she being the head of the largest party, would have a chance to rule. However, this did not materialise as she could not mobilise the magic numbers and elections were announced.

Sonia was not an MP when she took over the reins of the Congress in 1998. She decided to contest for the first time in the 1999 Lok Sabha polls. Wanting to prove herself as a leader acceptable to both the North and the South, and after discussions with her inner coterie and her children, Sonia chose to contest from two seats: Amethi, the family pocket borough represented earlier by her husband Rajiv Gandhi, and from Bellary, a safe Congress seat in Karnataka, where the *"Indiramma* magic" still worked.

The BJP, after spending a large sum of money on the campaign, was in high spirits and was confident about putting up a good fight. The party thought it judicious to field a formidable woman candidate against Sonia Gandhi. At this point, Sushma was keeping a low profile after losing the Delhi Assembly elections although due to no fault of hers. She entered the contest just three months before the elections at a time when the BJP government in Delhi was very unpopular. The anti-incumbency factor as well as the price rise and scarcity of onions resulted in the BJP's defeat. It was then that the party high command thought of fielding her against Sonia Gandhi.

Sonia had adopted a cloak and dagger approach to her entry into politics and kept her choice of constituency a secret. The BJP had no clue where Sonia would be contesting from, apart from Amethi. There was a rumour that she might choose Cuddapah in Andhra Pradesh, another staunch Congress stronghold.

Interestingly, neither Sushma nor Sonia had any links with Bellary; both were more comfortable in the North. Sushma recalls how the decision was conveyed to her by party president Venkaiah Naidu over the telephone at 2.30 am. She had just returned from a rally in Ambala and was getting ready to retire. Naidu told her, 'They are keeping it a secret from where Sonia Gandhi is going to fight. We had earlier discussed who should be fielded against her and thought of Thippanna of the Lok Janshakti (a regional party in Karnataka), but then we reconsidered this choice and spoke to Hegde (president of Lok Janshakti). He asked us whom we had in mind. We suggested Rajasekhara Murthy (a former minister), to which Hegde responded, "If you want to contest that seat, ask Sushma Swaraj to take on Sonia Gandhi. She is the only one who can give her a good fight."'*

BJP leader L.K. Advani, who had spotted Sushma's talent and promoted her, says that she was chosen because the party was sure she was a good choice. 'We knew Sonia Gandhi may win but we wanted the fight to be tough. I also found that Sushma was not only a good orator but could understand and speak different languages. This was her exceptional trait and that was the reason we chose her for Bellary.'*

Sushma, who had been sidelined after her defeat in Delhi, asked Naidu, 'Is that an order or a suggestion?' And he said, 'We have already discussed all this. I have spoken to senior leaders like Kushabhau Thakre, Advaniji and others, and I will talk to the prime minister tomorrow, as he is sleeping now. There is no time to wait for him and then come back to you. I am asking you to contest.'* Naidu wanted her to board a 6 am flight to Bangalore that morning; he had his secretary Satya hand over the tickets to her in the early hours. Sushma was to reach Bangalore by 8.30 and was told, 'There will be a helicopter to take you to Bellary immediately for filing your nomination.'* But there was an unforeseen problem: she needed a voters' list for filing her nomination, as she needed the address proof of her residence. Jagmohan, another BJP candidate and a former minister who was contesting from South Delhi, had a list. Sushma called him up, asking for the list. She told Jagmohan, 'I am your voter and my name must be on your list.'* Jagmohan promptly sent his aide to open his office from where Sushma's assistant Satish Gupta got the document.

Sushma instructed her staff to pack two suit cases—one for three days and the other, a larger one, for a longer stay. She instructed them that if she had to spend more time in Bellary she would send for the larger suitcase. She did not know whether Sonia was contesting from Bellary or Cuddapah. If it was the latter, Telugu superstar Vijayashanti was to contest against her. 'All this happened on August 18 and the elections were on September 5. I managed to board the plane, reached Bangalore and gave the voters' list to the advocates who met me at the airport. As we did not know Sonia's plans, we asked Civil Aviation Minister Ananth Kumar to track it down from the airport authorities.'*

When Sushma reached Bellary, Sonia Gandhi had already landed there unannounced with a lone Special Protection Group bodyguard from Hyderabad. A lot of enthusiastic Congressmen, however, accompanied her to file her nomination papers that afternoon. 'Within a few minutes I also filed mine,' recalls Sushma.* She felt encouraged when she saw an enthusiastic crowd cheering her as she looked out from the first floor balcony of the magistrate's office. She stayed on in Bellary for the next three days to see if Sonia withdrew her nomination. Sonia, however, decided to contest both the seats. Sushma's campaign thus began with much fanfare and over the next 15 days, she undertook a whirlwind tour of the area, covering a vast distance.

I had gone to Bellary to cover the 1999 election and one day, I found Sushma addressing a large crowd at a crossroads. It was a five-minute speech and the crowds cheered her for speaking in their mother tongue. How did Sushma learn Kannada in such a short time? She explains, 'See, Pannaji, who was from the Lok Janshakti, was given the ticket earlier. He was very happy to see me contest. He became my Kannada guru; I made him sit with me in the car wherever I went. His Kannada was very good and he also knew English and Hindi well. Moreover, Kannada has many Sanskrit words. I wanted to relate to the people in their own language and my hunch worked.

I felt otherwise I would not have been able to strike an equation with the electorate.'* As they toured the constituency, they found that people of this rural area still remembered Indira Gandhi and some were not even aware of her assassination! It was clear that Sonia had to do nothing but remind the voters of *Indiramma*.

The Independent, a British newspaper, describes the contest: "Mrs. Gandhi now finds herself against this tiny, vivid Hindu nationalist dynamo, an ex-minister in the BJP government and one of the party's few political celebrities. A 'nattering *nari*' (woman), as she has been called, who can take the legs off a dining table."[2]

Meanwhile, this *swadeshi beti* versus *videshi bahu* contest acquired a high profile with almost the entire national and international media landing up at the small constituency, which was unable to handle the crowds. Deputy Prime Minister Advani launched the campaign and Prime Minister Vajpayee visited later. The media mobbed Sushma wherever she went.

While Sushma concentrated on Sonia's foreign origin, the latter decided to not even mention her name in her campaign. She relied on the "*Indiramma* magic" and sought votes reminding the local electorate how Karnataka had come to her mother-in-law's rescue two decades ago when Indira Gandhi had lost the elections in almost the entire country after the Emergency, and the voters in the state had stood by her. Sonia brought her daughter Priyanka Vadra along. Priyanka, who resembles Indira Gandhi, was a great asset for Sonia. The focus on invoking the Gandhi family legacy helped her win.

Sushma justifies her loss: 'The problem was we did not have any party structure in that small place. In fact, this was the only district where we had no party structure. Moreover, we had got into an alliance with J.H. Patel (chief minister of Karnataka from the Janata Dal (United)), which was also harmful for my campaign as all the anti-establishment votes went to Sonia Gandhi. On top of all this, the Assembly elections were also held simultaneously with the Lok Sabha polls.'*

Sonia Gandhi won both in Bellary and Amethi. Sushma, who lost by only 56,000 votes, was satisfied with her performance, as it was achieved in 15 days and, that too, in a constituency which was totally unfamiliar to her. 'This was in contrast to the Amethi seat where Sonia Gandhi won by 3. 70

lakh votes. I got one lakh votes more than my MLAs and Mrs. Gandhi got one lakh less than her MLA. So Bellary was a wonderful experience and experiment', admits Sushma.'*

OPPOSITION TO SONIA AS PRIME MINISTER

After the 2004 elections, came the drama of choosing the Congress prime minister since the party was leading the United Progressive Alliance (UPA) coalition. Everyone expected Sonia Gandhi to head the government; something that was anathema to the BJP. In a heavily publicised and emotionally-charged crusade, Sushma threatened to shave her head, don a white saree, eat only grams and sleep on the floor if the Italian-born Sonia became the prime minister. 'It was my conviction. Even in Bellary, I said only two things. As Indira Gandhi's daughter-in-law, she was entitled to our love and affection. As Rajiv Gandhi's wife, she was entitled to our respect. But if she wants to become the prime minister of this country, I will say no, no and no, three times. We got our independence only 60 years ago. So many people died amidst so much bloodshed. We can't put the crown on a *firangi* (foreigner). When I opposed this possibility, I was speaking on behalf of the sensibilities of all Indians. Even today, I feel the same way. This is not a question of just Sonia Gandhi, I am talking about all foreigners. Has *Bharat Mata* (Mother India) not produced a single Indian who could be the prime minister?' she asks.*

Another BJP leader, Uma Bharti, supported her. The RSS also jumped into the fray. It was an all-out attempt to prevent a foreign-born woman to head the country. Sonia saw through all the vitriol and ultimately, "listening to her inner voice", decided to appoint Manmohan Singh as the prime minister. The Congress leaders were disappointed, as were those who had voted for her party. Sushma reiterated in a TV interview much later that "... today if she (Sonia) claimed that post, I will do the same thing. This is my duty towards democracy."[3]

HER EARLY DAYS

Sushma Swaraj feels that the turning point in her life was her participation in the Jayaprakash Narayan movement in the mid-seventies. Affectionately called JP, the socialist leader had fought against Indira Gandhi's authoritarian regime. It was under his leadership that Indira was voted out for imposing the Emergency on India. Sushma recalls how she jumped into the political cauldron after completing her law degree, when she was just 22 years old. During the 1977 Lok Sabha elections, when the Janata Party was formed, she was sent to campaign for the candidates because she was an inspiring orator. Sushma was from the Akhil Bharatiya Vidyarthi Parishad (ABVP), the student wing of the Jan Sangh, one of the political parties that was a constituent of the Janata Party in 1977.

After the Emergency and Indira Gandhi's ouster, the Janata Party, consisting of parties of several hues, swept the polls. A shocked Indira realised her mistake but could do nothing except bide time. The Janata Party government, led by Morarji Desai, had senior Jan Sangh leaders like Atal Bihari Vajpayee and Lal Krishna Advani as ministers. The new government went about foisting cases against Indira Gandhi and also set up the Shah Commission to investigate into the omissions and commissions of her government.

SUSHMA'S ENTRY INTO THE HARYANA LEGISLATURE

Six months after the Janata government came to power, all State Assemblies were dissolved, as they had exceeded their terms. Elections to the Haryana Assembly was also announced. By now, Sushma had turned 25—the permissible age for contesting elections. It was Jayaprakash Narayan himself who suggested that she should contest elections. He told the party, 'Sushma is an impressive orator and such a good campaigner. I want her to contest.'*

Meanwhile, Sushma fell in love and married Swaraj Kaushal, whom she had met in the law department of the Punjab University in Chandigarh. The two had participated in inter-collegiate debates as a team; Sushma in the Hindi contests, Swaraj in the English ones. So when the Emergency was declared on June 26, 1975, Swaraj proposed that the two tour the country to rally support against it. Sushma's parents suggested that they should get married before the campaign. So, within 18 days of the Emergency, they were married.

After JP's suggestion that Sushma should contest the elections, she consulted her husband, who said, "Why not". He pointed out that one of them could be in politics, while the other would practice law. Sushma contested and won the seat, becoming the youngest member of the Assembly. JP then wished that Sushma be made a minister and so she was, in her first term itself in 1977; this made her the youngest minister ever. 'From then on, there was no looking back,' recalls Sushma.*

AS THE YOUNGEST MINISTER

Her first term as the labour minister was not all that smooth due to her ideological differences with Chief Minister Devi Lal. During a meeting with state industrialists, one of them told Devi Lal, "Your minister has reopened all our agreements with trade unions." Sushma was in favour of tripartite solutions to labour issues. Devi Lal, right there in the meeting, retorted that he would change her portfolio, which hurt the young pragmatic minister, and she immediately resigned. But within 21 days, she was reinstated because of the pressure from national leaders like Morarji Desai and Janata Party president Chandra Shekhar, who insisted that Devi Lal take her back. This episode served to cast her in the image of a firebrand. Once back, Sushma was given eight portfolios, all of which she enjoyed handling.

Soon, there was a churning on the national political scene. The Morarji Desai government fell in March 1979, and Charan Singh took over for a brief period with the support of the Congress. But he resigned shortly thereafter without even facing Parliament because the Congress withdrew its support. The Janata Party broke up when the Jan Sangh pulled out of the alliance and formed a political wing called the BJP. Elections were forced on the country in 1980, in which Indira Gandhi made a triumphant comeback.

While these momentous events could have affected Sushma's fortunes, insiders say that Janata Party president Chandra Shekhar prevented her from contesting the Lok Sabha elections and wanted her to be confined to Haryana. When she succeeded in the state, he engineered dissidence against her. She wanted to contest the Bhiwadi Lok Sabha seat, considered favourable for her, but she was asked to contest from Karnal, which was a difficult seat. After these setbacks, Sushma remained out of action and did not contest the 1982 Assembly polls. She also resigned from her state presidentship and reconciled to being an ordinary party member for some time.

THE BJP BECKONS

Sushma remained in the Janata Party for the next four years. The party had lost its sheen and was disintegrating after its defeat in 1980. In 1984, Syed Shahabuddin, a former Indian Foreign Service officer and an active member of the party, raised the question of banning the RSS. Sushma opposed it and the RSS mouthpiece *Panchjanya* called it a "voice of reason". The BJP too was looking for able politicians; its president L.K. Advani contacted Sushma, asking whether she would like to join his party. He recalls that although she was not in the BJP, her father was a member of the RSS, so she had that connection. He pointed this out to her and reiterated that the BJP would be a natural choice for her. Sushma consulted her husband once again and decided to join the BJP.

The date for Sushma's formal entry into the BJP was fixed for October 31, 1984. A press conference was to be held for the occasion at the BJP headquarters on Ashoka Road in New Delhi. When she reached there, Advani informed her that Prime Minister Indira Gandhi had been assassinated by her Sikh security guards at ten o'clock in the morning. The press conference had to be cancelled; Advani told her she had four or five more days to think about joining the party. 'I assured him that there was nothing to think about and that I would join after a few days. That was how I entered the BJP,' recalls Sushma.*

The political atmosphere had quickly turned volatile when Indira Gandhi was assassinated. India had been jolted by this assassination. When Rajiv Gandhi succeeded her, he announced elections within a month in December. Sushma also contested the Lok Sabha polls from Karnal in Haryana. Like most non-Congress candidates, she too lost the elections. The BJP got only two seats in the whole country. The Congress, under Rajiv Gandhi, won a massive mandate and got 405 out of 542 seats. The sympathy wave swept away everything in its path.

PICKING UP THE PIECES

The BJP had to be rebuilt right from scratch. Sushma was given substantial responsibilities towards that task. The period between 1984 to 1998 was the most difficult for the party. Sushma was first made the national secretary of the BJP in 1984 and after two years, the all-India secretary. Then she became the national spokesperson of the party. In those days, parties had only one spokesperson and she handled the job well. She acquainted herself with every reporter who covered the party and developed a one-on-one equation with them. The year 1998 was special for the BJP because it forged various alliances with other parties and was poised to come to power. The Congress's influence was waning and the BJP could project itself as a viable alternative. It had a dynamic leader in the person of Vajpayee. In 1988, Sushma was made the party's general secretary along with three other high profile leaders—Pramod Mahajan, Kushabhau Thakre (who became the president later) and Govindacharya (who was thrown out of the party later). Creating another record, she became the first woman in the BJP to reach the level of general secretary. The same year she also became a member of the BJP's top decision-making body, its Parliamentary Board, where she continues to be a member. As an insider points out, several attempts had been made to make her lead several frontal organisations—she was once offered the national presidency of the youth wing of the BJP—but she never wanted to be seen as working for a section and always saw herself as a mainstream politician. Besides, she had always wanted to be recognised as a mature leader and not just as a youth leader. While Sushma strives for the inclusion of more women at the time of ticket distribution, she has always shied away from becoming a factional leader. In the party, she is a loner and does not want to belong to any group.

BJP PROMOTES SUSHMA

Sushma rose up the ranks in the BJP because the party did not initially have many women leaders. Rajmata Vijayaraje Scindia of Gwalior was an important woman leader in the party but she had acquired that stature because of her roots. She was a crowd puller and could swing the vote in favour of the BJP in at least 11 Lok Sabha constituencies—all part of the erstwhile Gwalior state in Madhya Pradesh. She was indeed an asset to the party, but she had not risen through the ranks. Her daughters, Vasundhara and Yashodhara, were not yet in politics. Advani explains that Vasundhara later became a popular leader in her own right when she became the first woman chief minister of Rajasthan. According to him, 'Her position in Rajasthan politics is unique.'* There were other women members like Sumitra Mahajan and Mridula Sinha, but they did not have the same potential as Sushma, who had an immense appeal among the middle classes without any pedigree or mentor. The BJP, smarting from the humiliation of a defeat in the polls, wanted to project an image of a fighter, and Sushma was right there for the taking. So while she was indeed a strength for the party, the conditions prevailing within the BJP were a great opportunity for Sushma.

Her rise has all the same not been very smooth due to jealousies and internal manipulations by her rivals. She has had her share of problems all along and has had to contend with those who have worked against her, defamed her or put her down. She has faced problems that are the wont of women in India, as it is a patriarchal society that does not accept the domination of women. However, once a woman leader has established herself, it's a different matter. Part of this complex social equation is also the mother concept. So while at one level a woman gets respect, at another, she has to prove that she is more than a man. According to a close friend, Sushma has an extraordinary memory. If, for instance, she reads four or five pages, all of them will get engraved in her mind. She can repeat the contents page for page without a mistake. She also has a sound knowledge of Sanskrit.

Sushma had to contest from Ambala in Haryana much against her will in 1987 because the party wanted her to. She became the education minister in the state and tried to reform the department which was notorious for perpetually transferring teachers. She formulated a consistent policy on the issue, which satisfied a lot of people. But Sushma's heart was in national politics.

ENTRY ON THE NATIONAL STAGE

Swaraj Kaushal was posted as the governor of Mizoram in 1990. Sushma found it difficult to shuttle between Mizoram, Delhi and Ambala. So in 1990, when a vacancy arose, she requested Advani to nominate her for a Rajya Sabha seat. Sushma then moved to Delhi but continued to travel often to Mizoram. At that time Advani was the BJP president and Sushma, along with Govindacharya, Pramod Mahajan, Venkaiah Naidu and Kushabhau Thakre, became part of a formidable team. Talking about her performance in Parliament, Advani says that Sushma was an outstanding parliamentarian and if she has become the Leader of the Opposition now, it is because of her merit.

After Rajiv Gandhi's assassination in 1991, P.V. Narasimha Rao became the prime minister. He headed a minority government and a BJP member became the deputy speaker of the Lok Sabha. The year 1992 saw the demolition of the Babri Masjid in Ayodhya, which was a rude shock for Rao, who felt betrayed by the BJP since it had promised peace in the temple town. Sushma was in Mizoram on the day of the demolition, although she did accompany Advani on the *rath yatra* (chariot ride) he had undertaken. The atmosphere in the country had become charged with communal tension. Piqued by the betrayal of the BJP, the Centre dismissed the governments in the BJP-ruled states and imposed President's rule there. Swaraj was also asked to resign and come back to Delhi.

By 1996, Sushma was all set to fight the Lok Sabha elections. She contested from the elitist South Delhi constituency and won. The BJP emerged as the second largest party with 136 seats. When the Congress decided to sit in the Opposition with 146 seats, the BJP staked its claim and was asked to form the government. The BJP government, however, lasted for only 13 days as no other party was willing to support it. In that 13-day government led by Vajpayee, Sushma was the first and only woman minister of the BJP; she was given the portfolio of Information and Broadcasting. Advani recalls that she was the only woman who was outstanding and deserved to be a minister. During those 13 days, she took a decision to telecast the Lok Sabha proceedings. The no-confidence motion proceedings were thus telecast live for the first time. The Congress propped up the Deve Gowda, and then the I.K. Gujral, government for the next two years. When the Gujral government fell because of the Congress's withdrawal of support, elections were announced in 1998. Once again Sushma contested from South Delhi and won the seat.

FIRST WOMAN CHIEF MINISTER OF DELHI

In October 1998, there was a concerted move to get Sushma out of the NDA government through deception. One day Prime Minister Vajpayee called her to his residence and told her that he wanted her to be the chief minister of Delhi; the capital was going to the polls in a few days. There were three other BJP leaders—Advani, Kushabhau Thakre and Pramod Mahajan—sitting with the prime minister when she met him. Sushma was surprised by her selection for the post. She was holding two Cabinet portfolios then—Communications and Information and Broadcasting. Sushma resisted, saying that Delhi BJP strongman Madan Lal Khurana should be chosen instead. Vajpayee explained that the incumbent chief minister Sahib Singh Verma was opposing it and was agreeable to Sushma leading the party in Delhi.

Sushma found herself in a very difficult situation. She knew that the results would not be in favour of the party, as the BJP government in Delhi had become unpopular with the people. She knew her hands would be tied and she would not be in a position to take any decision as the model code of conduct was already in place. She asked for some time to consider the decision but Vajpayee refused and insisted on her taking charge immediately. 'I said okay, went out and sat in the car. That is how I became the chief minister of Delhi,' recalls Sushma.*

As expected, the BJP was humiliated, while the Congress won a landslide victory in Delhi. Sheila Dikshit became the chief minister. Sushma had the option of retaining the Rajya Sabha nomination or her newly-won MLA seat, as she was an MP when she contested. When she wanted to get back to national politics, her detractors in the party worked against her yet again, and Vajpayee insisted that she needed to stay in the Assembly, wondering how she could run away when she had led the party to the polls. She saw through the design and resigned her Assembly seat. Sushma was dejected; she sat at home brooding for some months and did not want to contest the 1999 elections. Her rivals almost managed to finish her then.

Sushma's star was back on the ascendant when the BJP bosses thought of fielding her against Sonia Gandhi in Bellary. From then on her luck turned and she became an international figure for taking on the Gandhi *bahu* (daughter-in-law), a contest in which she gave a good fight and lost by a small margin. The pressure was now on the party to rehabilitate her.

RANKLING GENERAL MUSHARRAF

In 1999 and 2000, Sushma kept herself occupied with party work and was neither a minister nor an MP. Prime Minister Vajpayee was forced to bring her back, make her a Rajya Sabha MP and also a minister again in 2000. In September, Sushma was once again given the Information and Broadcasting portfolio.

When Vajpayee resumed the peace process with Pakistan and President General Pervez Musharraf came for a summit to Agra on 15 July 2001,

Sushma briefed the media. Some detractors put the blame on Sushma for derailing the Agra peace talks. 'While the talks were going on, Ashok Tandon, the media adviser to the prime minister, came and told me that General Musharraf had said that Kashmir was the core issue. On our behalf, we had to clarify that we were not only talking about Kashmir but also other issues like Siachen, Sir Creek and other related matters. That is all I said at the briefing. I was not a part of the talks but General Musharraf took offense. I did not jump the gun or speak out of turn.'* There are many who think that Sushma purposely sabotaged the Agra summit.

MENDING FENCES WITH SONIA GANDHI

Sushma also became the health minister and later the parliamentary affairs minister in January 2003. During this period, Sonia Gandhi was the Leader of the Opposition. Since she had to run the House and needed the cooperation of the Opposition, Sushma called on her. The two leaders, who had contested against each other, met in a cordial atmosphere at Sonia Gandhi's residence. Sushma sought her cooperation for passing the Women's Reservation Bill, which has been languishing for years. Sonia was responsive and said she would ask Shivraj Patil, who was the deputy leader of the Congress Parliamentary Party, to keep in touch with her. The bitter memories of trading charges and counter-charges during the poll campaign didn't seem to be on either's mind. The thawing of the relationship began then and it has since blossomed into a friendship. Today the roles have been reversed: Sushma is the Leader of the Opposition and Sonia Gandhi the "super prime minister". Sushma recalls that, as the Leader of the Opposition, Sonia was not particularly active and spoke in the House only once or twice. Patil represented the Congress in most of the sessions and it was through him that she got her work done.

DEPUTY LEADER IN THE RAJ SABHA

The NDA lost the Lok Sabha elections in 2004 and sat in the Opposition. Soon, Vajpayee fell ill and Advani became the Leader of the Opposition in Parliament. Sushma was re-elected to the Rajya Sabha and became the deputy leader of the BJP. When Advani was forced to resign as the president of the party in 2005 by the RSS, which wanted a younger leader at the post, Sushma was mentioned as one of the prospects to succeed him. It was, however, Rajnath Singh who was chosen ultimately. Sushma had to confine her activities to the Rajya Sabha.

Over the years, Sushma's friendship with Sonia Gandhi has grown. It has evolved from being on nodding terms to one where they are often seen smiling, joking and whispering to each other. 'I think this is the beauty of democracy. I am the Leader of the Opposition and she is the chairperson of the ruling UPA. We are not enemies. We are only ideologically opposed to each other and there is disagreement on policies,' explains Sushma.* Sonia Gandhi has also changed over the years. According to Sushma, 'Earlier, she was very quiet. She never used to speak, very rarely smiled and did not interact with others. Now she interacts and has opened up.'* Her detractors have noticed this blooming friendship and often criticise her for taking a soft line on the Congress.

AS THE LEADER OF THE OPPOSITION

In the 2009 Lok Sabha elections, Advani was projected as the NDA's prime ministerial candidate. Sushma contested from Vidisha in Madhya Pradesh and won a record victory, with the highest margin of 4.1 lakh votes. Subsequently, she became the deputy leader of the BJP Parliamentary Party in the House for a few months. Due to the poll debacle, murmurs had begun that Advani should make way for younger leaders. There was stiff competition for the post of the Leader of the Opposition from senior leaders like Murli Manohar Joshi, Jaswant Singh and Rajnath Singh, but Advani supported Sushma. She became the Leader of the Opposition, replacing him in December 2009. 'When the time came to choose, Sushma was the natural choice,' admits Advani.*

Advani was also keen on her becoming the BJP president. "... Sushma Swaraj was offered the post of party president... [but] said she had turned down the offer as she preferred to remain in her parliamentary post as deputy to Leader of Opposition L.K. Advani."[4] The party had initially considered Arun Jaitley, Venkaiah Naidu, Gujarat Chief Minister Narendra Modi, as well as Sushma Swaraj, for the party chief's post. Nitin Gadkari's name came up only after a month and a half. On reconsideration it was felt that Sushma and Jaitley should retain their parliamentary positions. Modi's name was dropped because there was no alternative in Gujarat and Venkaiah Naidu lost out because he had already been the party chief once. Nitin Gadkari became the BJP chief with the blessings of the RSS. Sushma became the Leader of the Opposition soon. Thus the baton was passed on to the next generation, while Advani continued to be the mentor.

SUSHMA'S TROUBLES IN THE PARTY

Controversies, particularly on her Karnataka connections, have often dogged Sushma. Her critics once claimed that she was protecting the Reddy brothers—local mining barons of Bellary—whose wealth grew in a short time thanks to political patronage. The brothers are now languishing in jail but the issue had taken centre stage for some time. Sushma denies any wrongdoing. "... I have no hand in the political making of Bellary brothers. I had nothing to do in making them ministers or in building up their stature as political leaders. When the Bellary brothers were made ministers, Jaitleyji was the *prabhari* (in-charge), and Yediyurappa was the chief minister, Venkaiahji and Ananth Kumar were there as senior leaders. Whatever discussion happened, happened between these people," claims Sushma.[5]

Unlike her male rivals, Sushma does not believe in using the media to fight her battles. She believes in sorting out differences away from the public glare. She's also aware that rivals within the party and outside it use the media liberally to damage her reputation, but she has emerged stronger after every battle and continues to do so. She knows the real strength of a politician comes from the people and that is why after every setback, she has gone back to the people for their support. Fortunately for her, the RSS has not actively opposed her in the selections for senior positions in the BJP. One reason is that she has the image of a conservative Indian woman. If she had had a more western appearance and demeanour, the RSS would not have allowed her to grow. Although, the RSS is a dyed-in-the-wool patriarchal organisation, and it is difficult for its leaders to relate to a woman, on no occasion have they tried to hinder her progress. But whether its high command will support her as the prime minister is a question mark, as an obvious glass ceiling exists.

Senior columnist T.V.R. Shenoy doubts that the RSS will support her. 'The Sangh Parivar is very whimsical. Today BJP chief Nitin Gadkari is the blue-eyed boy. The Parivar is willing to amend the BJP constitution to give him a second term. Sushma cannot run a party by herself and she could only be a good number two. As of now, I do not consider her becoming the

BJP's PM candidate. In India, greatest acceptability is not the factor; least acceptability is the factor. So in that event, she might have a chance. Men run the Parivar and there is no woman there. Men trust only men. An RSS backing would be key for her.'*

Although Sushma claims she has no mentor, it was Advani who promoted her and other second-generation leaders like Arun Jaitley, Venkaiah Naidu, Pramod Mahajan and Ananth Kumar. He has actively supported their growth within the party and groomed them to take up challenges, although he has not been able to stop their internal squabbles. He considers Sushma's oratory skills equal to that of Vajpayee's. 'She creates the same complex in me as Vajpayee did,' he admits.*

The coast is clear for Sushma to reach the top post in the party and her eyes are set on prime ministership. Gujarat Chief Minister Narendra Modi's impressive victory for a third term in Gujarat has resulted in the party workers demanding his selection as the prime ministerial candidate. Modi has become an icon for *Hindutva* and the poster boy of the BJP. His bugbear are allies like the Janata Dal (U) and whether they would accept his leadership in view of his polarising image, which would alienate Muslim voters. Sushma had proved once again in 2013, when Advani insisted on proposing her name for the post of the party president, that she has the support of her seniors but the RSS stuck to Nitin Gadkari getting a second term. Advani opposed Gadkari until the last minute but had to ultimately yield to the pressure by the RSS bosses. Sushma was also not keen on taking the party post, as she thinks that she could do better as the Leader of the Opposition.

Sushma has many hurdles to overcome before she can become the prime minister. The first is the glass ceiling, which she has already reached in the BJP. The second is the uncertainty on the RSS backing her, a woman, instead of Modi. The third is the number of seats the BJP will get in the 2014 Lok Sabha polls. So, even as the *swadeshi beti* tackles the many ifs and buts that lie strewn on her path to political glory, she will have to contend with the proverbial slip between the cup and the lip.

NOTES

1. Barry Bearak, *New York Times*, August 20, 1999; *Custom 150 Online Journals*, July 2, 2012.

2. Peter Popham, "Nehru dynasty wilts in the heat of general election", *The Independent* (UK), September 4, 1999.
3. Interview with Shekhar Gupta from *The Indian Express* on "Walk the Talk", aired on NDTV, January 11, 2011.
4. Mohua Chatterjee, "Sushma Swaraj turned down BJP top job", *The Times of India*, November 20, 2009.
5. "No Hand in Political Making of Reddy Brothers: Swaraj", *Outlook* magazine, May 27, 2011.

Mehbooba Mufti

THE PEOPLE'S DEMOCRATIC PARTY (PDP) president Mehbooba Mufti occupies a special place in Indian politics because she hails from the riot-torn Jammu and Kashmir and has emerged as a force in a male-dominated Kashmiri Muslim society. Appearances are indeed deceptive in Mehbooba's case. She looks conservative with her head covered and the traditional Kashmiri *abaya* (loose black robe) covering her body, but at heart she is quite modern. Until she joined politics in 1996, she wore jeans and T-shirts and behaved like any other modern Indian girl.

Mehbooba represents dynastic politics in the Indian context. Coming from a political family, it was easy for her to find a place in Kashmiri politics. Since childhood she has heard politics being discussed at the dining table, as her father, Mufti Mohammad Sayeed, was an important Congress leader of the state. 'My father always talked politics, breathed politics and lived politics,' she points out.* But Mehbooba never wanted to enter the rough-and-tumble arena of politics. 'I never imagined I would become an MP or an MLA. I led a normal life and did not want to take up any profession. I just wanted to take it easy,' claims Mehbooba.*

Mufti Mohammad Sayeed wanted Mehbooba to become a doctor like her other two sisters. Though a good student, she did not fare well in her tenth and twelfth board exams. This disappointed her father. Since she could not get admission into medical school, she studied English literature and then law. She was working in a bank when she got married; it was an arranged alliance. She had two children but soon realised that the marriage was not working out. As a result, Mehbooba opted for a divorce and returned to her parents' house. She busied herself with raising her children: sending them to school and picking them up, playing with them, tying their shoe laces, teaching them—everything a mother does.

THE TURNING POINT

Her defining moment came in 1996. Jammu and Kashmir was going through the height of militancy at that time. The turbulence, which started in 1989, was at its peak. Mufti Mohammad was observing the scenario and, being the shrewd politician that he is, thought this was perhaps a good time to anoint his political heir. He was disappointed in his son who went away to Canada to make films. He thought that Mehbooba had the political instincts and could be groomed. So just before the 1996 elections, he asked his daughter whether she would contest the Assembly elections. Mehbooba thought for a minute and replied "yes". She decided to go along with her father's wishes. After all, since she could not fulfil his wish of her becoming a doctor, she felt she could at least please him by becoming a politician. 'I came into politics when no woman wanted to. It was during the height of militancy in the state and when my father asked me to contest, I thought, why not?' recalls Mehbooba.*

Many wondered why Mufti Mohammad chose Mehbooba and not her sisters or brother. Mr. Bahn, a senior Supreme Court advocate and friend of the family, points out that since Mufti Mohammad did not have an heir apparent, he might have thought of Mehbooba. 'He nurtured her, as she was available. She had suffered emotional trauma and so had he. Therefore, in order to alleviate it and make her happy, he brought her in. He also might have recognised that she had political instincts.'*

Ghulam Hassan Mir, another family friend and a minister in the present Omar Abdullah government, confirms this and points out that politics was a rough field but she 'was able to pick it up very quickly and soon got recognition.'*

Kashmir had been facing turbulent times since 1989, when militancy first began to raise its head. Over the years the situation deteriorated further. Governor's rule was the only option for a few years. When elections were held in 1996, people were not willing to come out to vote for fear of the militants and it was left to the Central forces to help them reach polling booths.

It was in this atmosphere that Mehbooba started her political career. She contested from Bijbehara Assembly constituency. Her campaign was quite interesting. 'I used to go around the constituency holding a mike in my hands but no one would come near me. Even women used to stand far away and look at me with suspicion,' Mehbooba reminisces.* Soon she found things were changing as she persisted in her campaign. One evening when she was in her car in the interiors some militants attacked her. A few children who were climbing up a nearby tree to pick walnut saw what was happening. Mehbooba's security guards caught hold of them to interrogate them about the attackers. Meanwhile she saw a group of women coming towards her shouting and screaming. She soon realised that they were asking for their children to be released. Mehbooba directed her guards to set them free but they refused. So she declared that she too would not move until the children were freed. 'This incident changed the situation and people started looking at me with trust,' Mehbooba remembers.*

Syed Altaf Bukhari, a business magnate and PDP leader, observes that soon Mehbooba was able to connect with the women without much effort. She would just sit in her car and go to any place where she thought her presence was needed. Peerzada Mansoor, a PDP MLA who has seen her growth, adds, 'She went to every nook and corner of the state. Whenever someone was killed by the army or militants, she would go to his family and mourn with them. If there was an atrocity she would visit the victims. She soon became a household name.'*

But not everyone agrees with her supporters. Dr. Hameeda Khan, a professor in Srinagar University and a human rights activist, has a different view of Mehbooba's election. 'Mehbooba came to power because she was her father's daughter and not because there was a demand for her. Nobody even knew about her.'* Criticising the 1996 polls, she claims that those elections were boycotted and there was gross violation of human rights. "There was no sanctity in those elections. Some people were brought by the army at gunpoint to vote. She won precisely because nobody was willing to contest. The Central government wanted to tell the world that we have had elections and the people are with us.'*

LEADER OF THE CONGRESS LEGISLATURE PARTY

The long and short of it was that Mehbooba won the elections by a 3000 vote margin. There were only half a dozen Congress MLAs and she was the only one from the Valley. Soon the party high command decided to make her the leader of the Congress Legislature Party. It was indeed a big honour for the youngest MLA who was just making her debut. Mufti Mohammad also had a hand in the decision; but Mehbooba did not disappoint her leaders and functioned effectively and fearlessly, opposing the then chief minister, Dr. Farooq Abdullah. The ruling National Conference had a brute majority in the House but her voice was not muffled. Mansoor argues that Mehbooba had come to power on her own. 'I don't think Mehbooba rose up only because of Mufti. She entered politics because of Mufti but she rose on her own merit.'*

But Hurriyat leader Sajjad Lone is critical of her. He claims, 'Mehbooba sat at home and they made her win. She did not have to go anywhere. The 1996 elections were a sham.'* Agreeing with this, Hameeda says there were no takers for contesting the polls. 'We had already lost 60,000 people. Mehbooba does talk about human rights but she does it for the sake of saying it. She has no deep commitment and takes it up just to embarrass the government. Who will come to politics when there is so much political uncertainty?' she asks. *

Soon Mehbooba started working at the ground level. She often visited the houses of those who were killed or injured in the crossfire. People were suffering due to both the militants as well as the Central forces. So she took up the cause of several young men who were wounded or killed, or whom the forces harassed. She became a regular visitor to the army headquarters, pleading on behalf of a civilian or a militant who had given himself up. 'I often used to go to the commandant's office to get the innocent released. I also took up the cause of terrorists who surrendered.'* While she got kudos from the sufferers, her opponents alleged that she was soft on militants.

TAKING UP THE PEOPLE'S CAUSES

Syed Altaf Bukhari admits that it is difficult for a woman politician to rise up the ladder in Kashmir. It is predominantly a Muslim society, and that too, a conservative male-dominated one. Mehbooba turned this challenge into an opportunity. 'She knew her people suffered because of the long-standing turmoil and was able to convince the masses that she was one of them. She would argue with the security forces and soon people believed that she was echoing their voice.'* Mehbooba realised that at that time security was a priority and not developmental issues. The safety of young boys was important, as every 400 feet they were stopped and checked. She addressed two critical issues—security and liberty. Altaf claims that this was the basis of the "healing touch" policy which Mufti Mohammad adopted when he came to power in 2002. Mehbooba played a vital role in shaping this policy.

The Congress, headed by P.V. Narasimha Rao, lost the 1996 elections. The BJP led a 13-day government after which the Congress decided to support the successive H.D. Deve Gowda and I.K. Gujral governments from outside until 1998. The Congress party held Rao responsible for losing the elections. He also got embroiled in court cases. The party was now rudderless as the new Congress president Sitaram Kesri was unable to lead them. Sonia Gandhi had not yet decided to take over the leadership. Several Congress leaders like Mamata Banerjee, Mani Shankar Aiyar, Aslam Sher Khan, Dilip Singh Bhuria and others started deserting the party. Mamata even floated her own regional outfit—the Trinamool Congress. Meanwhile, the BJP became aggressive and lured as many Congressmen as possible. It was in this atmosphere that the 1998 Lok Sabha elections were held. Seeing the writing on the wall—that the BJP could not form the government on its own—the BJP forged alliances with several regional parties and formed the National Democratic Alliance (NDA), which turned out to be effective arithmetic. Coming under pressure from her party men, Sonia Gandhi came out to campaign and soon took over as Congress president, removing Kesri. She had still not decided to enter Parliament; hence she made Sharad Pawar the Leader of the Opposition, while holding the reins of the party.

MILITANCY IN JAMMU AND KASHMIR

It is important to understand the Kashmiri psyche at this point. The beautiful state had been suffering due to militancy for almost two decades. Among the separatists there were three diverse opinions—accede to Pakistan, or opt for *azadi* (independence) or demand the plebiscite promised by the late Jawaharlal Nehru. Among the two main separatist groups, one was willing to enter into a dialogue with New Delhi while the other opposed it. The mainstream parties were also equally divided. The ruling National

Conference (NC) advocated autonomy, the PDP wanted self-rule and the Congress opted for status quo. The common factor among them was that they accepted the accession to India. The leaders in New Delhi believed in dialogue while the separatists want tripartite talks between Pakistan, Kashmir and New Delhi. And so the same situation continues.

MUFTI MOHAMMAD FORMS THE PDP

After the 1996 elections Dr. Farooq Abdullah and his National Conference became too big for Mufti Mohammad. With his party's brute majority he became too powerful even for the Congress. Bahn observes that keeping in mind the sentiment of separation in the social milieu of Kashmir, which was predominantly Muslim now after the forcible exit of the Pandits (the Hindu minorities), Mufti decided to create a space within this society but it was an uphill task for him and his daughter. Mainstream Muslim politics was dominated by the NC, whereas mainstream national politics was controlled by the Congress. The BJP had a presence in some pockets, while the rest were irrelevant.

Within three or four years, Mufti Mohammad Sayeed felt suffocated in the Congress and began looking for other options. With a leadership crisis in Delhi, the Congress men were confused and the party started disintegrating. Mufti was fed up of the Congress, as one often had to humour the party's high command and the pygmies around it; he felt it was like a woman having several husbands. Mufti wanted to use the anti-Delhi sentiment of the Kashmiris to his advantage.

Ghulam Hassan Mir, a PDP founder, declares that by 1998 they had formed a separate group within the Congress and Mehbooba became their representative. 'She carved out a role for herself. She said let us adopt a pro-people role. At that time, guns were heard all around and militancy was prevalent. The people had no voice; the only voice was that of the separatists who talked of cessation or mainstream national parties which talked of India. Mehbooba became our voice,' observes Hassan Mir.* However, Mir was disappointed when Mehbooba soon chose sides—that of the separatists. 'She should not have done that. Her role was no longer that straightforward, positive or realistic,' Mir criticises.* This is what many other critics of Mehbooba have to say. They claim that she built her political clout by meeting the separatists at least half-way.

Meanwhile Mehbooba learnt the tricks of politics under her father's tutelage. She quickly discovered what would get her the support of the people and started voicing what is called "Kashmiri grievances or hurt". Bahn notes, 'Whatever aggression she showed in articulating the grievances of the people, she translated that same aggression into the lawmaking forum of the state. She spoke exceedingly well in the House also and this was an asset for her.'*

According to Mir, Mehbooba's instant popularity was due to the separatists. 'In the state, the BJP had no leader, Janata Dal had no leader. The other parties had no voice. The NC was the only big party. She voiced the people's problem and got recognition for that; she became the only face of the Opposition,' compliments Mir.* However a top retired government of India official who has dealt with Kashmir claims that Mehbooba 'was bordering on side of the mainstream as well as separatists. There was a thin dividing line. She had the separatists' sympathy and this was where she drew her strength from. If Mehbooba had become a prominent figure in the state's politics, it was because of the separatists.'* He adds that there were stories that she was involved with the Hizbul Mujahideen boys; even Mufti had some reservations and felt Mehbooba was moving too fast. Being a former home minister and someone familiar with Delhi, Mufti probably felt that if you move too fast you might land up on the wrong side of the power centre in Delhi.

When Prime Minister Atal Bihari Vajpayee formed the NDA government in 1998, Mufti Mohammad wondered, why not start a regional party as an alternative to the National Conference, which was led by the Abdullahs? The father-daughter duo and a few other leaders supporting them felt that Delhi did not understand ground realities. They were not able to convince the Congress leadership about some of the steps they wanted to implement. Local needs were not development but security. The people of Kashmir had to feel that they were secure. So in January 1999, the four wise ones—Mufti Mohammad, Mehbooba, Hassan Mir and Muzaffar Hussain Beig—decided to launch their own outfit.

In the interim, important developments had taken place at the Centre. In 1999, barely 13 months after the NDA government came into power, Tamil Nadu chief minister and the AIADMK chief Jayalalithaa—a partner in the NDA government—plotted with the Congress and pulled the Vajpayee government down. He lost by a single vote. The

Congress tried to form an alternate government but did not have the numbers. Then came the Kargil War, and ultimately elections were held in 1999.

MEHBOOBA MUFTI LAUNCHES NEW PARTY

Mehbooba resigned from the legislature and by July they floated the new regional party. The elections in 1999 were also one of the reasons which hastened the People's Democratic Party's formation, according to Mir. Mufti Mohammad was able to lure some former NC members and several others from the Congress thanks to his long association.

Pushp Saraf, a senior journalist who watches developments in Kashmir, points out that Delhi also wanted Mufti to launch a party to counter the NC. But Mehbooba denies this, saying it is propaganda against the PDP. 'On the one hand they maintain that PDP is pro-Pakistan and pro-separatist and on the other hand they claim Vajpayee wanted it. Make up your mind. You can't have both things,' she argues.*

Explaining her party's formation, Mehbooba puts in perspective the necessity of doing so. 'Things started getting awfully difficult for us in the Congress. I also arrived and started creating my own space. So things became even more complicated.'*

PDP MLA Mansoor explains that the political system in Kashmir is a little different. The Congress could not win more than two or three seats in the Valley. Many people fought Sheikh Abdullah but they could not succeed because of his stature. 'When the PDP was formed, the timing was right because people were fed up of militancy as well as the politics of Delhi. They were given a choice when the PDP came,' he asserts.*

Sensing the mood of the people, Mufti Mohammad and the PDP's co-founders quickly promised that they would end the army raj if their party came to power. The PDP was also against the Prevention of Terrorism Act (POTA)—a draconian law enacted by the NDA government—as the impression was that it allowed the police to harass many innocent people, instead of protecting them. Mehbooba was in the forefront, articulating these promises, which touched a chord in the people. As a result, the PDP slowly clicked.

However, Hurriyat leader Sajjad Lone points out that prior to the launch of the party, Mufti Mohammad had never won an election. In 1977 and 1983 he lost, and he used to lose by a wide margin. He describes the PDP as 'an alliance of some individuals, with the strongest leading it. It does not have a vote; individuals have a vote and when they join the PDP, the party wins.'*

Bahn is of the opinion that Mehbooba was popular because she was seen as somebody who could articulate the people's cause in a bold, courageous and aggressive way. 'It was the first time that someone became the people's voice in the Valley. In the process, Kashmiris were sandwiched between two gun cultures—that of the militants and the security forces. There was hardly any succour for them. Mehbooba played a crucial role in providing some respite.'*

She contested from the Srinagar parliamentary constituency in 1999 but lost to National Conference leader Omar Abdullah. When the PDP drew a blank in the 1999 Lok Sabha polls, Mehbooba, Mufti Mohammad and their friends were not disappointed. Every one who contested, including Mehbooba, lost. 'We were not dejected because we did not expect to win. We had just founded a new party. Everything was new. There were many who wondered why the party was formed in the first place; the cadres were not there; and the Congress was a huge party. But the elections gave us a chance to reach out to every nook and corner,' says Mehbooba.*

Though the PDP did not gain a single seat, it won some vote percentage. 'We were able to cut into everybody's vote. We got a very big chunk of the Congress's votes because it was mostly the Congress which dominated the south. We got votes, which were not committed to anyone. We were also able to get the NC's votes,' claims Mehbooba.*

BUILDING UP THE PARTY

Mehbooba worked at the ground level for the next two or three years after resigning from her Assembly seat. Militancy was at its height but she continued to tour rural areas. Once there was a blast near her car in the Marmat-Doda constituency and she had a narrow escape. 'There were attacks on me earlier as well. My Sumo was torn into pieces once. There was a grenade blast near Dras but I escaped all of these attacks,' she says.* Mansoor points out that even when the security forces had stopped her, she would courageously visit places which were hit by militancy. 'I thought she would sit at home after those attacks but she did not.'*

HER NEW BRAND OF POLITICS

Mehbooba played a new kind of politics. A top Indian intelligence official stresses the fact that the separatists with whom he was dealing with pointed out: "You are trying to ask us to show some restraint but how can we when Mehbooba is provoking us?" Being in the mainstream and airing her views openly has won her a lot of popularity. 'Mehbooba is with the Hizbul Mujahideen; Mufti with the Jamaat-e-Islami—that's the father-daughter combination,' he claims.*

Mansoor gives all credit to Mehbooba for building up the party from scratch since Mufti Mohammad was seen as a Congressman. 'Winning the 2002 elections was because of her crusade,' he asserts.*

The NDA government came back to power in 1999 after the elections. In February 1999, prodded by the US to launch confidence-building measures between India and Pakistan, Vajpayee launched a bus service between Lahore and Amritsar and the then Prime Minister Nawaz Sharif received him with much fanfare in Lahore. The inaugural bus service carried several celebrities including Dev Anand, Javed Akhtar, Kuldip Nayar, Satish Gujral and Kapil Dev, among others. Both governments proclaimed the Lahore Declaration was a symbol of friendship between the two nations. However, it did not last long since the Kargil War followed quickly on the heels of this peace initiative. The war ended when US President Bill Clinton put pressure on Nawaz Sharif, but Indo-Pak relations continued to be strained. Things were changing fast in Pakistan; a military coup led to the removal of Nawaz Sharif and General Pervez Musharraf, who had ordered the Kargil attack, took over the reins. India was willing to do business with General Musharraf. Soon Indo-US ties were also improving, which had soured after India went nuclear. The Americans were trying to build bridges between the two neighbours. There was great bonhomie, with US President Bill Clinton visiting India and Pakistan in 2000. India's growing economic clout and large middle class made the US sit up and take note of New Delhi. The right wing BJP-led government also played along. Then the Parliament attack by Pakistan-based terrorists took place in 2001 and the bus service was stopped; it was resumed in 2003, two years later.

PDP COMES TO POWER

Meanwhile Mehbooba worked hard, reaching out to remotes areas of the state. With Mufti Mohammad's political skills and Mehbooba's hard work on the ground level, they formed a formidable duo. By the time the 2002 elections to the Kashmir Assembly took place the atmosphere in the Valley had improved significantly. The elections received international attention and the Vajpayee government made much of the peaceful polls. *The* New York Times observed, "Ms. Mufti promised an unconditional dialogue with militants, saying they need to be given a way to put down their arms with "honor and dignity". She openly discussed the accusations of human rights abuses by Indian and state governments, promising to dismantle a reviled state police force accused of atrocities."[1] There was a hung assembly with no party getting a majority, resulting in the political parties trying various permutations and combinations.

Mehbooba, along with her father, led the party in the 2002 polls and propelled it to form a coalition government with the Congress. She contested from the Pahalgam Assembly constituency and won. The Congress was not willing to go along with the NC and was trying to form the government with the PDP. The two parties arrived at a formula of power sharing, with each party ruling for three years. Mufti bargained to rule for the first three years. 'We also wanted a Common Minimum Programme,' recalls Mehbooba.* This arrangement was arrived at after Mehbooba, on the advice of her friends, called up Congress President Sonia Gandhi one morning and persuaded her to agree to these conditions. It was this phone call that clinched the deal. 'We knew that the first three years would be difficult. Only a person with the stature of my father could have convinced the Congress leadership or Vajpayee to agree to the "healing touch" policy.'* So Manmohan Singh, Mehbooba and her party leaders sat down to draft the Common Minimum Programme (CMP) in Delhi.

THE POWER BEHIND THE THRONE

The PDP had a free hand for the first three years. Mehbooba had her own role to play in the Mufti Mohammad government. This became easier when she was made the president of the PDP in 2003. She was the first woman president of the party and became its face in the state as well as the Centre. She was integral in implementing the "healing touch" policy, which was shaped by her, and her father was happy to give her all the credit. Both Vajpayee and Sonia Gandhi also supported this policy.

When Mufti Mohammad met Prime Minister Vajpayee after taking over the reins, he received ample support from him and Home Minister L.K. Advani. The NDA government wanted to take credit for the successful elections in the state and the fact that peace efforts had been taken forward. Vajpayee promised the Centre would work hand in hand with the state government to give it a new direction. Mehbooba remained in the background throughout, watching these developments closely.

She gives full credit to the Centre for allowing the Mufti government to implement the "healing touch" policy. The people had lost confidence in politicians, who were seen as power hungry. Mehbooba claims, 'We sent a message that we will let you do what you want but you let us do what we want. For the first time people felt that Delhi was sitting by the side of the state government.'*

Meanwhile Mehbooba carved out her role in the state politics. Her father also shrewdly kept her in the background although he gave her all the respect and referred to her "Mehboobaji", consulting her on many issues. He also used her to build a bridge with Sonia Gandhi. But her critics look at her role differently. Hassan Mir alleges that Mehbooba was actually the one who called the shots. 'She used to call ministers and order them and had more power from behind the scenes than anyone else. She became arrogant.'* Hameeda Khan dismisses Mehbooba: 'What could she do except making noises here and there. She had become the president of the PDP because of her father and not on her own merit.'* Denying that she was arrogant, Mehbooba explains, 'My role was very interesting. I was doing what I am doing now. Inside the Assembly and outside the Assembly I was more or less playing the role of the Opposition. If there was any violation, I was the first to raise it. When I was in Parliament also I used to speak about these things.'*

There are many who feel that Mufti Mohammad had done a good job while he was the chief minister, but there are also critics who find certain flaws. Abdul Ghani Bhat, a Hurriyat leader, points out: 'When it comes to roads and buildings he has done a lot. But you have to seek answers to some basic elements that constitute the dispute of Kashmir. You can silence the sentiments for a day, for a month or for a year but not always.'* Bhat goes on to explain the sentiment, which is that Kashmir belongs to the people of Kashmir. 'They do not accept hegemony from any government, be it Delhi or Islamabad. I am not talking about the accession to India or Pakistan but what we need to do is to find an acceptable and honourable solution for the people of India, Pakistan and Kashmir.'*

Mehbooba contested the 2004 Lok Sabha polls and won from Anantnag. She was the PDP leader in Parliament and excelled as an orator, raising concerns pertaining to Jammu and Kashmir and atrocities on women. She had constant access to Sonia Gandhi.

MUFTI STEPS DOWN AND AZAD TAKES OVER

Mufti Mohammad's three-year reign slowly brought some normalcy to the state. It was a fine balancing act and he successfully managed to contain violence. This proved to be a turning point. Gradually, the resentment towards Delhi gave way to resentment towards the militants. Mufti Mohammad would have liked to continue after completing three years but the Congress took over. The transfer of power happened at a time when things were becoming normal.

There were several editorials which suggested that Mufti should continue in power in order to supervise earthquake relief and facilitate Delhi-Srinagar dialogue. Many think tanks also felt that Mufti had done much to calm the situation in the Valley. He had acted as a circuit breaker of sorts to protect the Centre from the Kashmiri's ire towards the government. However, after much humming and hawing Sonia Gandhi decided to oust Mufti and bring in her own man—senior Congress leader Ghulam Nabi Azad, who hails from Jammu. The then US Ambassador to India, David Mulford, assessed the scenario in a telegram to Washington: "Sonia knuckled under to intense pressure from power-hungry Congress MLAs who were outraged at the possibility that, for reasons of national interest and due to the earthquake, Sonia might allow Mufti to continue in power."[2]

Another US Embassy telegram from New Delhi predicted that Azad had "a tough job ahead of him, including quashing terror, managing popular expectations in J&K, sustaining Kashmir's march toward normalcy, and avoiding the impression he is Sonia Gandhi and the Delhi government's errand boy."[3] The restless Congressmen even threatened to defect to the

PDP if they did not come to power. Azad had taken over in the aftermath of the worst natural disaster. He had to demonstrate that his government would effectively provide succour to the earthquake victims.

The telegram pointed out that while Mehbooba seemed gracious on the outside, she was seething from within, furious that her father had been fooled around with. For weeks they knew the coup de grâce they had expected was nearing, but they had been led to believe it might be delayed. The terrorists viewed the democratic transfer as a bit of a sneeze. Some felt it was an internal matter, while hardliner Geelani said it would make no difference; others felt Mufti was not a sacred cow and his departure did not affect them.

In his comment, the ambassador noted: "Sonia's decision also suggested that the UPA really is feeling vulnerable in managing its coalition and could not afford the additional dissent that a decision not to pursue the Chief Ministership likely would have provoked among the Congress rank and file. While the Hurriyat have carefully remained out of this PDP-Congress power drama, the National Conference of Farooq and Omar Abdullah are delighted that their PDP nemeses are out of power."[4]

AMARNATH YATRA ROW

Although Azad promised to continue the "healing touch" policy of the Muftis, he used his own methods of increasing the Congress's popularity. While initially the PDP and the Congress got along together, soon there was friction between them. Having got used to power, the PDP was unable to play second fiddle to Azad. Two years passed with both sides sniping at each other but things came to a head over the Amarnath Yatra row in 2008. Meanwhile Ghulam Nabi was trying to woo the NC to his side. When Azad allocated a large chunk of land for the use of the Amarnath *yatris*, the PDP opposed it vehemently. There was opposition from other quarters as well. Azad was in the midst of this row, as the PDP wanted the order to be cancelled. Even though the PDP was part of the Cabinet decision to allot land, it adopted a different stance publicly. Mufti and Mehbooba viewed this as the Congress's expansion plans in the Jammu area. They argued that, being aware of the consequences, Mufti Mohammad had rejected the proposal when he was chief minister. So why should Azad go ahead with it? They felt it could lead to various other sections blowing it up into a controversy. And that was exactly what happened; the PDP jumping into the fray. Mehbooba criticised Azad for playing a double game. 'In the Valley he said it was the PDP's decision and in Jammu he said the PDP was opposing it. So people turned against us. Congressmen close to Azad made provocative statements. He might have given the land thinking it could result in some advantage to his party in the Jammu region but why did he do so just six months before the elections. Why not in 2007 or 2008?' asks Mehbooba.*

The Amarnath Yatra controversy led to violence all over the state. Things were getting out of control; tensions were high on all sides. Mehbooba, who was returning from London in July that year, was stopped on her way home and advised not to take that route, as the people were extremely angry. She defied the advice. On returning home she called all the PDP ministers over and told them that it was not possible to continue in the Cabinet in this manner—they had to resign. She felt it was imperative to do so because the people had put a lot of faith in the PDP and it was time to make a sacrifice. She wanted to send a message that the PDP was not clinging to power. Soon the party pulled out, resulting in a minority government. 'Ghulam Nabi knew he had to reverse the decision. Within 24 hours he withdrew the order,' adds Mehbooba.* She is of the opinion that Azad was hoping to get the support of the NC but Dr. Farooq was in London and Omar was not taking his calls. Ultimately Governor's rule was imposed to bring a semblance of normalcy. Thus ended the saga of the PDP–Congress alliance.

PDP ISOLATED

Another US embassy telegram from New Delhi touched upon the churning in the mainstream political parties of the state, pointing out that the PDP found itself secluded. "Mehbooba, whose PDP party increasingly finds itself isolated as Congress and the National Conference look to each other to forge a coalition in 2008, is feeling isolated and vulnerable. She said the central government is terrifying people in PDP areas, acting more arrogantly than usual, and seeking to intimidate PDP supporters from voting on April 24."[5] It pointed out that "Mehbooba has a right to feel jilted. Her ostensible Congress coalition partner is openly courting the National Conference and she feels trapped. When we dined with Omar and Farooq Abdullah of National Conference, they seemed as content as could be, lending credence to reports of a budding Congress/NC alliance. Omar's NC has also decided not to contest the election that Chief Minister Ghulam Nabi Azad will seek in Doda, a decision *Greater Kashmir* newspaper termed akin to giving the Chief Minister a 'cakewalk'. We checked with Tarigami (from the Communist Party of India (Marxist)), however, who said he had seen no evidence of the activities Mehbooba reported."[6]

The telegram was also critical of the lifestyle of some Kashmiri leaders: "A recurring theme throughout all of our interactions with Kashmiris is how Indian and Pakistani money has made all Kashmiri political actors dependent on handouts. Omar and Farooq Abdullah, descendants of the Sheik who first figured out Delhi's money game, live in fabulous houses in Srinagar and Delhi, wear matching Panerai watches, serve Blue Label to the guests, and travel all over the world first class courtesy of the Indian government. Mirwaiz is alleged to have real estate in Dubai courtesy of Pakistan. The state administration gets rivers of money for development but the streets in J&K are appalling, even by Indian standards. Army officials, we have heard, allegedly bribe their superiors for postings to J&K to get their hands on the logistics contacts and 'hearts and minds' money. Sajjad lamented that conflict remained lucrative to many, and he is right."[7]

NATIONAL CONFERENCE TAKES OVER

The bitterness between the Congress and the PDP continued. The Congress was annoyed with the PDP for curtailing its term. The politics of tit for tat began; when the elections were nearing it formed the government with the NC, allowing Omar Abdullah to rule for the next six years. The PDP did comparatively well by getting 21 seats but had to sit in the Opposition. Mehbooba, who contested the Assembly seat, became the Leader of the Opposition.

She continues her fight with Delhi as well as the state government by exposing its misdeeds. Her aim is to function effectively as the Leader of the Opposition, fight for economic improvement and prepare her party for the 2014 Lok Sabha elections and then the Assembly elections. While expressing her vision for the state, Mehbooba points out that it is the economy which can take Kashmir forward. 'That is why we say open the trade routes between the two Kashmirs. We can do business with Central and South Asia through the Silk Route so that Kashmir can once again become the gateway. Only Kashmir connects Central Asia through the land route as it was way back in 1947. So if we think of opening up all routes and make Kashmir an economic free zone with no taxes, it will make the state affluent.'* She admits that for this to happen you need peace but 'you can't wait for the last gun to fall silent. You have to take these small steps.'*

Mehbooba and the PDP are also talking of self-rule. Questioning the concept of self-rule, a top government official elaborates, 'When the PDP talks of self-rule, again it is Mehbooba's touch. Nobody has been able to define it and it is just a different name for autonomy. But she is able to turn it to her advantage. For her, self-rule means power. They (Mehbooba and the PDP leaders) cannot be dictated by Delhi and they cannot have the army always.'* But Mehbooba has her own description of self-rule. According to her, 'If they are able to go to Pakistan and Central Asia you can understand what kind of satisfaction it can give to the people of Kashmir. Open up new routes, deal with the water resources treaty. If we can save money on security then we can use that money for more development in the state. So much money is spent on organising conferences. Representatives from both sides could meet twice a year in Srinagar and PAK (Pakistan administered Kashmir). Our point is that as a sort of permanent solution we should have a permanent joint advisory council which can discuss things like tourism, disaster management or how to get a pipeline from PAK. This need not be constitutional or legal. It will give a chance to both sides of Kashmir to get together. If we can have conferences in the US, Bangkok or Delhi, then why not this mechanism? People in Delhi will have to come out of their old mindset, as we are in a different age now.'* However, Sajjad Lone disagrees with her. He claims that Mehbooba does not even know what she is talking about. 'I have my document on self-rule; ask her to discuss it. General Musharraf had proposed self-rule. She has hijacked it saying we want self-rule. There are two words which are catchy: autonomy and self-rule. Autonomy has been hijacked by the National Conference and self-rule by Mehbooba. You should understand how they restrict space by stealing ideas.'*

Mehbooba does not agree that ultimately the fight is between the Abdullahs and the Muftis, although others in the state think so. Mehbooba explains, 'Look at Sheikh Abdullah's family. Everything has been handed down to them. My father is a simple man. We have to fight hard to get where we are. So I don't think dynasty counts at all for me. It is not a fight between two dynasties.'*

Although she does not admit it, Mehbooba is waiting to become the chief minister. Some say that Mufti Mohammad will be the next CM, while there are others who think it could be Mehbooba's turn. She herself says, 'Every father would like to put their children in a good place, especially if they have contributed in some way. I still feel that J&K needs a mature politician like my father, who would be able to manage things in a better manner. If my father does not want to be the CM, there are many others who would like to. So it is not my birthright.'* But Mehbooba believes in destiny. The government official thinks that Mufti Mohammad is still looking for a second innings. Now the question arises, what happens after Mufti? It may be difficult for the party to survive. There are a lot of people in the PDP who have reservations about Mehbooba. The senior leaders feel that they should be number two or number three. There are also reservations about her tilt towards the separatists. That impression has not gone away; it may go away when she becomes the chief minister. Power sobers you down. At the same time, Mehbooba is respected in the party and has a role to play. Her role is to address "Kashmiri grievances or hurt", or whatever you call it. She has highlighted these and that was why Mufti called it the "healing touch" policy.'*

Over the past four and a half years, as the Leader of the Opposition in the State Assembly, Mehbooba has raised issues such as human rights, corruption, withdrawal of the Armed Forces Special Powers Act (AFSPA) and Afzal Guru's hanging. Her father has left it to his daughter to handle all these issues and does not interfere.

The recent Presidential rejection of the mercy petition of Parliament attack convict Afzal Guru has become a contentious issue in the state. Afzal Guru hails from Jammu and Kashmir. In this Muslim dominated state, his execution is a sensitive point. After long deliberations, the Supreme Court gave him the death sentence. His mercy plea had been lying with the president for some years and it was only in February that the new President Pranab Mukherjee decided to reject it. Mehbooba blamed the Centre and the state government for this decision. "The Government of India has jumped the queue on hanging Afzal Guru. The decision about the killers of former Prime Minister Rajiv Gandhi and former Chief Minister Beant Singh is still pending. They have not taken a decision on them. But they jumped the queue and hanged Afzal Guru. Why did New Delhi jump the queue? It was the question of justice. They have done it in a shameful manner."[8]

Mehbooba led the attack on the state government in the Assembly and staged a walk-out over Guru's sentence, leaving the floor to the BJP; it had now developed into a Jammu versus Kashmir issue. The PDP had its own angle: playing to the galleries, it had made an appeal to the President of India in 2011 to grant clemency to Guru and commute his death sentence to life imprisonment. Clarifying the PDP's stand, Mehbooba said, "We feel that at a time when there is a need to step up measures to reduce the trust deficit between the state and rest of the country, the execution of Afzal Guru could produce results to the contrary. Our party is generally in favour of scrapping death penalty from the statute book and we reiterate that position once again."[9]

However, Mehbooba's critics, like senior journalist Iftikhar Gilani, who has followed her career, is of the opinion that she is whimsical and emotional when it comes to tackling issues. He also believes that she is willing to wound but afraid to strike. She does not cross the threshold in her attack on the Omar Abdullah government beyond a point, fearing it might annoy Delhi. The PDP thinks that it could not come to power in 2008 because it annoyed the Centre by breaking the Congress alliance on the Amarnath Yatra row. The Muftis hope that the PDP might win the state in the next elections and would like to be on the right side of Delhi. Of course, this also depends on who comes to power after the 2014 Lok Sabha polls, but no matter who does, the PDP will keep its options open. This has been its policy right from the beginning. Mehbooba is only biding time until the next elections, as she is confident of anti-incumbency working against Chief Minister Omar Abdullah.

On the whole, Mehbooba's political fight shows how a woman can build up a party by projecting herself as the voice of the people. It is her organisational capacity which has aided her phenomenal rise in Kashmiri politics. She is working within the confines of an orthodox Muslim society to make a name for herself and so far she has succeeded. However, many people express doubts about the post-Mufti era and whether she will be able to keep the flock together. Only time will tell.

NOTES

1. Amy Waldman, "A New Face Signals Political Change in Embattled Kashmir", *New York Times*, October, 12, 2012.

2. http://wikileaks.org/cable/2005/11/05NEWDELHI8510.html.
3. Ibid.
4. Ibid.
5. http://wikileaks.org/cable/2006/04/06NEWDELHI2365.html.
6. Ibid.
7. Ibid.
8. "Omar, Mehbooba slam Centre over Afzal hanging, fear long-term fallout of his execution", *Mail Today*, February 10, 2013.
9. "Afzal Guru: Mehbooba Mufti calls execution disappointing, Kashmir valley placed under indefinite curfew", *The Times of India*, February 9, 2013.

PB
32962